American Education, Democracy, and the Second World War

American Education, Democracy, and the Second World War

Charles Dorn

AMERICAN EDUCATION, DEMOCRACY, AND THE SECOND WORLD WAR
Copyright © Charles Dorn, 2007.

All rights reserved. No part of this book may be used or reproduced in any manner whatsoever without written permission except in the case of brief quotations embodied in critical articles or reviews.

First published in 2007 by
PALGRAVE MACMILLAN™
175 Fifth Avenue, New York, N.Y. 10010 and
Houndmills, Basingstoke, Hampshire, England RG21 6XS.
Companies and representatives throughout the world.

PALGRAVE MACMILLAN is the global academic imprint of the Palgrave Macmillan division of St. Martin's Press, LLC and of Palgrave Macmillan Ltd. Macmillan® is a registered trademark in the United States, United Kingdom and other countries. Palgrave is a registered trademark in the European Union and other countries.

ISBN 978-1-349-53969-7   ISBN 978-0-230-60888-7 (eBook)
DOI 10.1057/9780230608887

Library of Congress Cataloging-in-Publication Data is available from the Library of Congress.

A catalogue record of the book is available from the British Library.

Design by Scribe Inc.

First edition: October 2007

10 9 8 7 6 5 4 3 2 1

Transferred to Digital Printing 2011

For Mary Ann Dorn and Katherine Bulkley Philips, veterans of the World War II homefront, and for LeRoy Edmund Dorn and Charles Earl Philips, veterans of the World War II battlefront.

Contents

List of Illustrations		ix
Acknowledgments		xi
1	Introduction: Democracy's Citadel	1
2	Promoting the "Public Welfare" at Stanford University	25
3	Palo Alto Schools at War	61
4	"An Avalanche Hits Richmond"	95
5	Wartime Nursery Schools in Richmond	127
6	Education in a Time of War	163
Notes		179
Selected Bibliography		227
Index		251

List of Illustrations

Figure 2.1	Stanford University enrollment, 1940/45	29
Figure 2.2	Uniformed students—Members of the Army Specialized Training Program on the history corner steps during World War II	41
Table 3.1	Number of class periods offered per week, Palo Alto High School, 1939/45	69
Figure 3.1	Palo Alto VEND expenditures, 1940/45	80
Figure 3.2	Palo Alto average daily attendance, 1939/45	81
Figure 5.1	USMC nursery school, c. 1943	149
Figure 5.2	Two-year-old student art	150
Figure 5.3	Four-year-old student art	151

Acknowledgments

This book would never have been completed had it not been for the advice, encouragement, and enthusiasm of a great many colleagues, mentors, friends, and family members. I acknowledge their contributions here and thank them, wholeheartedly, for their continuing support and assistance.

This book began as a dissertation and, as such, I owe an overwhelming debt of gratitude to my dissertation committee members. Through their patience and dedication they guided my scholarly development while also modeling excellence in teaching and research. My advisor, Daniel Perlstein, regularly opened his door to me. Reading more than his fair share of my writing, Dan consistently took time from his own important work to edit and comment on mine. Paula Fass, an intellectual mentor with whom I am extremely grateful to have had the opportunity to work, provided encouragement and helpful criticism at important moments in my graduate career. Judith Warren-Little, who took an interest in this project at an early stage in its development, was very kind to offer me a home in her research group at UC Berkeley. David Tyack has been a friend and mentor for over a decade. I am grateful for the many walks and talks we have shared. This book is a far better work of history because of him.

I am quite fortunate to have found a group of considerate and remarkably talented colleagues at Bowdoin College. Education Department members Doris Santoro Gómez, Nancy Jennings, and Penny Martin have consistently supported my work as a researcher. History Department members Matt Klingle and Connie Chiang have generously provided advice and encouragement. Lynn Brettler and Tasha Graff have been invaluable in assisting in the completion of this project. As an institution, Bowdoin College has been very supportive in providing the time and resources necessary to bring this book to fruition. In particular, a Faculty Leave Fellowship during the 2006–07 academic year provided a well-timed sabbatical.

The History of Education Society has been a wonderful scholarly organization through which to learn the historian's craft. I am thankful both for the intellectual community it fosters and for the opportunity it has provided to receive valuable feedback on earlier versions of the case studies comprising this project. I am especially grateful to Barbara Beatty, Jack Dougherty, Linda Eisenmann, David Gamson, Judith Kafka, Heather Lewis, Bill Reese, Bethany Rogers, Wayne Urban, Kathleen Weiler, and Jon Zimmerman.

I am also obliged to the many librarians and archivists who assisted in locating the sources necessary for my research. The staff members at Stanford University's Cubberley Library were extremely generous in welcoming a Berkeley student into their midst. Kelly Roll, in particular, deserves many thanks for continued trips to the basement. Equally gracious were Maggie Kimball and the staff of the Stanford University archives. Staff members at UC Berkeley's Ed/Psych Library, the Palo Alto City Library, the Richmond Museum of History, and the Richmond City Library also offered crucial assistance, especially Lynnea Kleinschmidt. I am particularly appreciative of Bowdoin College research librarian Ginny Hopcroft for consistently helping to identify and locate excruciatingly obscure sources, more than once.

I am grateful to Amanda Johnson Moon at Palgrave Macmillan for taking an interest in this project.

Portions of Chapter 2 were originally published as "Promoting the 'Public Welfare' in Wartime: Stanford University During World War II," *American Journal of Education* 112, no. 1 (2005): 103–28 (Copyright 2005 by the University of Chicago. Reprinted by permission.) Portions of Chapter 4 were originally published as "'I Had All Kinds of Kids in My Classes, and It Was Fine': Public Schooling in Richmond, California, During World War II," *History of Education Quarterly* 45, no. 4 (2005): 538–64 (Copyright 2005 by Blackwell Publishers. Reprinted by permission.) I offer my thanks to these publishers for permitting the use of these materials.

Finally, friends and family members share in the successful completion of this project precisely because they were so much a part of it. Kent Koth and Ling Yeh are pillars of support and good friends.

Alec Morrison has consistently provided emergency revisions. As is typical, my brother Richard provided affirmation at just the right moments during the writing of this book. My wife, Susie, has tolerated my obsession with wartime schooling for far too long. I am very thankful for her patience and support. Our son, Niles, was born the year I began this project. Now seven, he consistently reminds me of what is most important. My mother-in-law, Kay Philips, has been extremely helpful in connecting me with oral history subjects while also reading and editing numerous drafts of my work. My father-in-law, Charlie Philips, served as a host for several relaxing trips to the mountains, where he also shared parts of his life's story with me—his wartime experiences are related in Chapter 2. My parents, Mary Ann and LeRoy Dorn, insisted over the course of many years that I study hard and do well in school. I am forever thankful for their loving support.

My parents and my in-laws are the sources of inspiration for this study. My mother and Kay are veterans of the World War II homefront; my father and Charlie, veterans of the battlefront. In many ways, the story told in this book is their story—and so it is dedicated to them.

1

Introduction: Democracy's Citadel

In August 1939, Columbia University's Teachers College hosted a unique conference on education's role in fostering citizenship in democratic nations. Unlike many conventional academic gatherings, the "Congress on Education for Democracy" involved educators from the United States and Great Britain as well as representatives from such influential national organizations as the U.S. Chamber of Commerce, the National Association for the Advancement of Colored People, the American Bar Association, the National League of Women Voters, and the American Federation of Labor. Over the course of three days, former prime minister of Great Britain Stanley Baldwin, economic historian Charles A. Beard, and U.S. Commissioner of Education John Studebaker, among others, addressed Congress participants as they engaged in a discussion of education's historic and contemporary civic functions, beginning their deliberations with the assertion, "No more important problem faces civilization than the defense and advance of democracy; no more important problem faces America than the education of the citizen."[1] Involving a formal dinner at the Waldorf Astoria and a mass closing session held at Carnegie Hall (for which more than 3,000 people were turned away due to lack of seating), the Congress was exceptional both because of its remarkably high profile—the *New York Times* called it "probably the most significant conference of its kind ever held by an educational institution"—and because participants incorporated all levels of public and private educational provision into their conversations, including nursery schools, elementary and secondary schools, and colleges and universities.[2]

Anticipating the importance of the gathering, President Franklin Delano Roosevelt posted a letter of congratulations to Teachers College Dean and Congress Chairman William F. Russell, writing, "I share the general feeling of gratification that a Congress on Education for Democracy is being held under the auspices of Teachers College of Columbia University. Everyone knows that democracy can not long stand unless its foundation is kept constantly reinforced through the process of education." Roosevelt continued, "What goes on in the schools every hour of the day, on the playground and in the classrooms, whether reflecting methods of control by the teacher, or opportunities for self-expression by the pupils, must be checked against the fact that the children are growing up to live in a democracy. That the schools make worthy citizens is the most important responsibility placed upon them."[3]

Although history had established schooling's importance in developing civic competence in the United States, the heightened significance that Roosevelt and Congress participants assigned education was undoubtedly inspired by the times. By the summer of 1939, totalitarian dictatorships had already become firmly established in Europe and Asia, resulting in the Japanese invasion of China, Italy's conquest of Ethiopia, and Germany's annexation of Austria. Indeed, just weeks following the Congress on Education for Democracy, Hitler's Wehrmacht stormed across the border into Poland, igniting World War II. A little more than two years later, on December 7, 1941, the Japanese attack on Pearl Harbor destroyed the United States' stronghold in the Pacific. Democracy, it seemed, was in full retreat. Rather than withdrawing, however, America began a massive mobilization effort. "The political benefits resulting from Japan's attack were great," historian William O'Neill wrote, "for it silenced isolationists and united Americans. Polls showed that a large majority supported the fullest possible effort, including a national service plan similar to that of Great Britain—a level of mobilization beyond what even the government wanted."[4]

In response to the United States' declaration of war, the "Educational Policies Commission," appointed by the National Education

Association and the American Association of School Administrators (which included among its members such educational luminaries as George Counts and James Bryant Conant) issued "A War Policy for American Schools." Calling for "Quick Decisions; Instant Action," the commission declared, "When the schools closed on Friday, December 5, they had many purposes and they followed many roads to achieve those purposes. When the schools opened on Monday, December 8, they had but one dominant purpose—complete, intelligent, and enthusiastic cooperation in the war effort. The very existence of free schools anywhere in the world depends upon the achievement of that purpose."[5] Over the next four years, many Americans called for educational institutions to serve as *weapons* in the nation's *arsenal* of democracy rather than *citadels* in promoting democratic citizenship, as President Roosevelt and the Congress on Education for Democracy had urged.[6]

This book investigates the ways that education responded to the exigencies of war while maintaining an historic commitment to fostering democratic citizenship in the United States. Historian David M. Kennedy observed that World War II "had shaken the American people loose and shaken them up, freed them from a decade of economic and social paralysis and flung them around the country into new regions and new ways of life."[7] Placing the personal and professional lives of wartime Americans, including children, adolescents, and adults, in the foreground of this study, I compare and contrast the ways that the war experience changed institutions at all three levels of educational provision—higher education, public elementary and secondary schooling, and early childhood education. In contrast to studies representing educational institutions as rigid in their bureaucratic operation or faddish in adopting popular reforms, it is my contention that these institutions were conservationist in their responses to defense mobilization between 1940 and 1945; that is, although wartime pressures in the United States affected nursery schools, public elementary and secondary schools, and universities to varying degrees, these institutions resisted efforts to be placed solely in service to the nation's war machine and instead maintained a sturdy commitment to fostering civic mindedness in a society characterized by rapid technological advance and the perception of an ever-increasing threat to national security.[8] Frequently condemned as foot-dragging in times of peace and stability, such conservationism was a virtue in wartime.

Education's Civic Function

President Roosevelt's claim, "That the school makes worthy citizens is the most important responsibility placed upon them," reflected a conception of American education dating back to the founding of the republic.[9] As a number of historians have shown, American statesmen such as Thomas Jefferson, John Adams, Benjamin Rush, and Noah Webster, knowledgeable as they were of history's failed attempts at democratic government, frequently expressed anxiety over their new nation's civic health and looked to a state-supported, comprehensive system of schooling to educate American citizens for self-governance.[10] Representative of this axiom was Jefferson's proposal to establish an educational system, including elementary schools, regional grammar schools, and a university, at public expense in his home state of Virginia. First introduced into the Virginia legislature during the American Revolution, Jefferson's "Bill for the More General Diffusion of Knowledge" articulated a common theme of the Founding Fathers, that the "most effectual means" of guarding the new nation against "degeneracy" and "tyranny" was to "illuminate, as far as practicable, the minds of the people at large."[11] John Adams similarly urged the active involvement of the state in educating American citizens, especially the poor, whom he saw as a potential threat to the long-term stability of the new nation. "Children should be educated and instructed in the principles of freedom," Adams wrote in 1778. "The instruction of the people, in every kind of knowledge that can be of use to them in the practice of their moral duties, as men, as citizens, and Christians, and of their political and civil duties, as members of society and freemen, ought to be the care of the public, and of all who have any share in the conduct of its affairs, in a manner that never yet has been practised in any age or nation."[12]

Although Jefferson, Adams, and other proponents of citizenship training failed to convince state legislatures to finance the development of comprehensive school systems in their homes states, they nevertheless provided a central rationale on which reformers eventually built the foundations of public education.¹³ During the antebellum period, "common school crusaders" such as Horace Mann frequently reiterated the importance of an educated citizenry to the future of the republic. Proclaiming the schools' role as citadels of democracy, Mann wrote in 1841, "Forts, arsenals, garrisons, armies, navies, are means of security and defense, which were invented in half-civilized times and in feudal or despotic countries, but schoolhouses are the Republican line of fortifications, and if they are dismantled and dilapidated, ignorance and vice will pour their legions through every breach."¹⁴

The rapid rise of immigration and industrialization during the antebellum period altered both social relations and the political economy of the United States, providing a compelling justification for Mann's proposals and those of his fellow crusaders. Reflecting on the characteristics of the reformers' program, historian William J. Reese wrote, "Among the keywords that dominated educational discourse in the antebellum period, none was so ubiquitous as republicanism. Hardly a local school report, stump speech, or appeal for a graded school, nicer building, or better textbooks escaped the embrace of this hallowed word. It underpinned the civic purposes of the common school."¹⁵ Indeed, as historian Carl Kaestle has suggested, citizenship education "elicited broad support as an important and almost self-evident purpose of common schooling."¹⁶ By the beginning of the Civil War, then, it was not unusual for school officials such as the Illinois superintendent of public instruction to pointedly claim, "The chief end [of education] is to make GOOD CITIZENS. Not to make precocious scholars . . . not to impart the secret of acquired wealth . . . not to qualify directly for professional success . . . but simply to make good citizens."¹⁷ Yet, according to scholar David Labaree, at almost the same moment that the goal of "democratic equality" and its core element of citizenship training achieved the status of conventional wisdom, a "shift away" from educating for democratic citizenship began, supplanted by the goals of "social efficiency" and "social mobility."¹⁸

Labaree describes social efficiency as representing the "educational perspective" of the taxpayer, who believes American education should take as its primary concern the training of a skilled workforce to efficiently meet the demands of the labor market, which will result in a prosperous economy from which all Americans benefit.[19] Social mobility, on the other hand, represents the educational perspective of the consumer, who holds that education is a private good existing for the central purpose of fostering personal advancement.[20] According to Labaree, Americans have held all three "competing visions" concurrently throughout the history of the United States. From the new national period through Reconstruction, however, democratic equality was the "dominant goal" of education, while social efficiency and mobility were "visible but muted."[21] In the latter part of the 1800s, Labaree asserts, social efficiency and social mobility began their rise to prominence, "radically narrowing the significance of citizenship training."[22] As Americans' conception of education's role in citizen formation became further eclipsed throughout the first half of the twentieth century, according to Labaree, social efficiency and social mobility commanded even greater attention, either because of national concerns that educational institutions were not effectively providing the workers necessary to produce a robust economy or because of Americans' desires for schools, colleges, and universities to provide access to occupational achievement, or both.

Labaree's work reveals the exceedingly high and frequently conflicting expectations that Americans have held for educational institutions over time. A useful contribution to understanding the historical trajectory of educational goals in the United States, his framework nevertheless tends to ignore periods of upheaval in American society—moments, frequently initiated by national crises, when citizens are inspired to challenge the prevailing direction of their nation's central political, economic, and social institutions, including those dedicated to educating America's citizenry. As scholar David Tyack has written of the history of public schooling in the United States, "During periods of sharp demographic change, or war, or ethno-religious conflict, or economic challenge . . . foundational principles of civic education came into sharper relief because they were less taken for granted."[23]

World War II provided such a crisis. Although Labaree may be right in asserting that Americans greatly valued social efficiency and social mobility as educational goals by the middle of the twentieth century, the proceedings of the Congress on Education for Democracy reveal that Americans also continued to prize education's civic function, especially as democratic nations came under threat around the world. Indeed, as the Educational Policies Commission's War Policy for American Schools illustrates, Americans again called for the reorientation of education's goals following the attack on Pearl Harbor—this time away from democratic equality, social efficiency, *and* social mobility and towards national survival. Throughout the war era, then, as tensions between those who wanted educational institutions to serve as arsenals and those who wanted them to serve as citadels escalated, nursery schools, elementary and secondary schools, and colleges and universities were compelled to negotiate Americans' conflicting demands in ways that honored their historic civic function while satisfying the needs of a nation at war.

World War II in American Life

A total war requiring the active engagement of civilians on the homefront and armed forces on the battlefront, World War II had a tremendous impact on American life. More than a year before Pearl Harbor, young men between the ages of 21 and 36 began registering for the first peacetime draft in U.S. history. In 1942, the draft age was lowered to 18. By the end of the war more than 31 million men had registered with the Selective Service, with half that number serving in the armed forces.[24] Combined with the need for workers resulting from defense mobilization, the draft created the most severe labor shortage in the history of the United States. Between 1940 and 1944, the unemployment rate in the United States dropped from 10 to less than 2 percent, the lowest rate ever recorded. In response, the federal government formed the War Manpower Commission to meet military and industrial labor demands. By 1943, however, as the "manpower" pool began to run dry, defense industries began actively recruiting women into the labor market.[25] Single women, wives, and mothers enthusiastically responded to the call, so much so that between 1940 and 1944 women increased their presence in the manufacturing workforce from 22 to 33 percent.[26]

Although significant, this rise does not reveal the transformative impact the war had on women's work. The entrance of more than 3 million women into the manufacturing workforce during the war years reflected a 141 percent increase over the figure for 1940.[27] More striking was the 460 percent increase in the number of women employed in "male-dominated basic industries" mobilized for war production.[28] By war's end, 49 percent of the women working in factories and shipyards were new to the nation's labor pool, while 27 percent had left behind lower-paying occupations.[29] Moreover, although not drafted and technically not permitted in combat, almost a quarter of a million women served in the armed forces between 1941 and 1945.[30]

Female employment during the war years frequently caused friction on and off the factory floor. Although desperate for workers, many employers resisted modifying historically defined gender roles. Their initial reluctance to hire women, which developed into only a grudging acceptance for some, made it difficult for women to secure employment in traditionally male-oriented workplaces. Moreover, even when women obtained paid positions in defense factories and shipyards, many found it challenging to successfully fulfill the disparate roles of worker and wife.[31] Mothers of young children, in particular, struggled to meet family obligations while holding down full-time jobs. Whether moving into and out of the job market or consistently working, mothers' acceptance of paid employment throughout the war era exposed them to criticisms of child neglect and abandonment.[32]

For many Americans, male and female, the possibility of finding well-paying work was worth uprooting families and moving across the country, as had many during the Great Depression. Emigrants flowed into defense areas, with western cities—such as Los Angeles, San Diego, and Richmond, California; Portland, Oregon; and Vancouver, Washington—drawing staggering numbers of newcomers.[33] As reported by Sibyl Lewis, who journeyed to California to secure defense work at the beginning of World War II, "'Go West,' that was the theme. 'Everything is great in California, all doors are open, no prejudice, good jobs, plenty of money.'"[34] More than 15 million people, not including those who left home to join the military, changed their place of residence by the end of the war, a demographic shift rivaling European immigration to the United States at the turn of the twentieth century.[35]

Blacks, in particular, used defense work opportunities to escape racial oppression. As historian Gretchen Lemke-Santangelo has shown, the percentage of blacks living in the southern United States decreased from 77 to 68 percent between 1940 and 1950, while their percentage as urban dwellers increased during the same period from 49 to 62 percent. For black women especially, the war offered previously unavailable financial opportunities. Between 1940 and 1944, black women's presence in industry increased from 6 to 18 percent of the female workforce, while the rate at which they engaged in domestic work declined from 60 to 45 percent. During World War II, more than half of the blacks who took jobs in defense industries were women.[36]

Throughout the United States, however, both newly arriving adults and their children were often made to feel like unwelcome outsiders.[37] As historian Richard R. Lingeman has noted, "If the newcomers had different skin color or if they came from another part of the country and spoke with different accents and looked like 'low life,' the conservative towns-folk tended to turn up their noses and erect a screen of rationalizations on the worthlessness of the newcomers."[38] Indeed, America's fight for democracy overseas clearly contradicted its practice of racial, ethnic, and cultural discrimination at home. Historian Ronald Takaki has illustrated how minority groups called for a "Double Victory" against oppression both in the United States and abroad during World War II, with racial segregation providing the most explicit example of America's failure to fulfill the promise of democracy.[39] In the midst of the twentieth century's greatest military conflict, President Roosevelt refused to integrate the nation's armed forces, while defense industries, crucial to the successful prosecution of the war, frequently relegated minorities to positions as janitors and cafeteria workers regardless of their skills and prior training.[40] Moreover, racial riots such as those against Mexican-American "zoot-suiters" in Los Angeles in 1943 led many minorities to wonder whether they had more to fear from Jim Crow than Adolf Hitler.[41] By the end of the war, however, it was the internment of Japanese-Americans that provided the clearest indication of the United States' willingness to sacrifice civil liberties at home while simultaneously claiming to liberate others from oppression abroad.[42]

For many who lived during this period, memories of the war years are remarkably vivid. Charles Philips entered high school in Phoenix, Arizona, in 1940. His father, who for a short time had studied engineering sciences but became a sewing machine salesman instead, encouraged Philips to become an engineer. After the United States declared war, Philips saw his opportunity. Introduced by a military recruiter to the Army Specialized Training Program (ASTP), he graduated early from high school and enlisted. In February 1945, Philips was called up and sent to Stanford University for engineering training as part of the ASTP. His time at Stanford was brief, however, for the Army soon sent Philips to Naples, Italy, to support Allied operations at the end of the war in Europe.[43]

Henry Martin graduated from Palo Alto High School in northern California in 1931. Attending Stanford University, Martin received a degree in chemistry in 1935 and moved to Nevada, where he worked as a high school science teacher. Hoping to return to the San Francisco Bay Area, Martin applied for jobs nearer his hometown, and in 1940 his alma mater hired him to teach high school chemistry and physics. Although Martin initially enjoyed teaching in the same rooms in which he had previously learned as a student, the school soon assigned him responsibility for instructing students in aviation and Morse Code, wartime obligations for which he had little or no training.[44]

Peter Edmondson was a student in Henry Martin's science class. Edmondson and his future wife Sally Allen attended Palo Alto High School between 1942 and 1946 and were both actively involved in war-related extracurricular projects sponsored by the school. Picked up by a school bus at 5:00 a.m. and taken to nearby agricultural fields, Edmondson frequently volunteered to harvest crops that might otherwise have rotted on the vine due to the wartime labor shortage. Allen also picked fruit but preferred to demonstrate her patriotism through buying and selling war stamps and rolling bandages for the school's Junior Red Cross. Contributing to the war effort fostered a sense of responsibility in Edmondson and Allen. As much as the war influenced their extracurricular activities, however, that influence never seemed to cross over into their academic classes. Although Edmondson spent several weeks in his woodshop class making small models of enemy airplanes as part of a civil defense project, neither he nor Allen experienced significant war-related changes in their core courses.⁴⁵

When the United States declared war in 1941, Evelyn Haag was enrolled as a junior at the University of California, Berkeley. Like most colleges and universities during the war years, UC Berkeley offered an accelerated program of studies. Eager to complete their undergraduate degrees, Haag and her fiancé took classes through the summer of 1942 and graduated in February 1943. Soon after marrying, Haag returned to Berkeley, obtained an elementary/junior high school teaching credential, and began student-teaching in nearby Albany, California. She soon received a job offer for a second-grade teaching position at Nystrom Elementary School in the Richmond City School District, not far from Berkeley. Having grown from a small, prewar city with a population of approximately 23,000 into a war "boomtown" of more than 90,000 residents only three years later, the city of Richmond was irreversibly transformed by World War II. Unaware of the profound effects that mobilization was having on Richmond's public schools, Haag came to realize the challenges that awaited her when, on the first day of school, more than 100 students met her in a classroom designed to seat fewer than 40.⁴⁶

Mary Hall Prout was born in San Francisco and attended San Jose State University from 1939 to 1943. After graduating with degrees in Psychology and Education, Prout learned of a large childcare program in Richmond established to serve the young children of mothers working in the local shipyards and defense plants. Prout applied and she was hired to teach at the Maritime Nursery School. Although her career in Richmond eventually spanned 41 years, with half of those spent as director of the city's nursery schools, Prout's professional arrangement initially confused her. Employed by the Richmond City School District, she taught in a building constructed by the U.S. Maritime Commission and was compensated through a combination of parent fees and federal subsidies. Her confusion dissipated, however, as Prout came to enjoy working in Richmond's innovative experiment in early childhood education.⁴⁷

Philips, Martin, Edmondson, Allen, Haag, Prout, and many of the other individuals featured in this book shared a common experience between 1940 and 1945—wartime imperatives changed the schools, colleges, and universities in which they taught and learned. In higher education, the expansion of the draft led to a dramatic decline in the number of civilian male students attending the nation's colleges and universities. Between 1943 and 1945, average enrollment in these institutions declined to 54 percent of what it had been in 1940, and at some men's colleges enrollment plummeted to only 10 percent of the prewar total.[48] At the secondary level, vocational education surged during World War II, with the federal government providing approximately $375 million for the creation of vocational training programs in schools throughout the nation.[49] During the same period, high school graduation rates plunged. Following a period of significant expansion during the Great Depression, public secondary school attendance stood at an all-time high. Nationally, 6,714,000 students were enrolled in grades 9 through 12 during the 1940/41 academic year. By 1943/44, this number had dropped to 5,560,000.[50] Simultaneously, the number of employed 14- to 17-year-olds rose from 1.7 million to 4.6 million.[51] In the field of early childhood education, the wartime crisis justified the development of an entire additional layer of educational provision. The federal government allocated more than $50 million for the construction, operation, and maintenance of more than 3,000 nursery schools nationally during World War II. At their height, these nurseries enrolled 130,000 children throughout the United States, serving an estimated 600,000 children over the course of their existence.[52]

Considering the war's disruption of American education profound, *Time* magazine declared in 1942 that "no 'revolutionary' movement in U.S. education ever held a candle to this one."[53] Three years after the war's end, philosopher of education I.L. Kandel concurred with the *Time* assessment in the only published work to examine the Second World War's influence on all levels of U.S. educational provision. In *The Impact of the War Upon American Education*, Kandel wrote that during the war years "every aspect of American education was subjected to scrutiny.... Suggestions for the reconstruction of education poured forth in a body of literature larger even than in a corresponding number of peace years. How soon the fruits of these discussions and suggestions will appear depends on a large number of forces. One point is clear—the blueprint for the next advances in American education has been drafted."[54]

Both *Time* and Kandel, however, drew their conclusions regarding the war's consequences too close in time to the crisis to accurately assess its impact on American education. This study, then, investigates to what degree and in what ways the forces of homefront mobilization altered educational institutions in the United States. It is framed by the following set of questions: Was World War II a turning point in the history of nursery schools, elementary and secondary schools, and colleges and universities, or were many of the prewar trends in American education simply accelerated as a result of the crisis? Which institutions were the most susceptible to change, and what adjustments did they make? How did educational leaders perceive the benefits and costs of adapting their institutions to wartime demands? How did the educators responsible for teaching America's children, youth, and young adults respond to these demands? How did students react? How were public perceptions of education altered, if at all, as a result of increasing threats to national security? And how do these events, considered cumulatively, illuminate our understanding of the role of education in fostering civic-mindedness in a democratic republic?

World War II in Educational History

During the 1970s and 1980s, historians published a number of important works investigating the significance of World War II for America's social, political, and economic life. These studies, which included Richard Lingeman's *Don't You Know There's A War On?*, Geoffrey Perrett's *Days of Sadness, Years of Triumph*, John Morton Blum's *V Was For Victory*, Karen Anderson's *Wartime Women*, and Studs Terkel's widely praised *The Good War*, established the foundation for a burst of historical inquiry into the war experience surrounding the fiftieth anniversary of the conflict.[55] In 1994, Doris Kearns Goodwin published her Pulitzer Prize-winning *No Ordinary Time: Franklin and Eleanor Roosevelt, The Homefront in World War II*, while David M. Kennedy won his Pulitzer in 1999 for *Freedom From Fear: The American People in Depression and War, 1929–1945*.[56] William O'Neill's *A Democracy at War: America's Fight at Home and*

Abroad in World War II and William Tuttle's *Daddy's Gone to War: The Second World War in the Lives of America's Children*, both published in 1993, are also noteworthy contributions to our understanding of the impact of World War II on American society.[57]

Although differing in their investigative frameworks, many of these scholars take as their central concern the question of whether or not World War II was a watershed moment in the political, economic, and social history of the United States. Drawing conflicting conclusions, they nevertheless agree that, as a national crisis, the war had serious ramifications for the United States. Why, then, have educational historians generally neglected the war era as a critical period of scholarly analysis? Distinguished curricular historian O. L. Davis has observed that "the nation's wartime curriculum, even as a curiosity, has received more attention in American social histories than in histories of education. The obscurity of the American wartime curriculum illustrates the larger neglect of the war's impact on schools by educational historians and other educators."[58] As Davis indicates, histories of public schooling tend to use World War II as a chronological marker indicating a study's beginning or end (such as Diane Ravitch's *The Troubled Crusade: American Education, 1945–1980*) or else they ignore the war entirely (Henry Perkinson, Joel Spring, and Lawrence Cremin have all published well-respected school histories without considering the war's importance).[59] Remarking on this surprising lack of attention, Ronald Cohen has also observed how educational historians "have concentrated on the early decades of the century, and rightfully so, but in the process have generally ignored the last fifty years. The World War II years, in particular, have been glossed over."[60] Similarly, Alan Garrett has noted, "Reactions of the American educational community to the events and conditions precipitated by World War II remain largely unexplored."[61] Moreover, the relatively few historians examining American education during the war years have typically conducted circumscribed analyses of single levels of educational provision. Within those levels, however, these scholars have generally offered useful insights into the ways that the crisis of war shaped educational institutions in the United States.

At the level of higher education, historians have usually directed investigations of wartime colleges and universities towards either the genesis of the Cold War's military-industrial-academic complex or higher education's embrace of vocational and military training programs. Roger Geiger, Stuart Leslie, and Rebecca Lowen suggest that university administrators demonstrated an increasing interest in government and industry contract-driven research during World War II in an effort to both secure additional sources of revenue and bolster their institutions' national reputations. [62] Such lucrative agreements, they conclude, provided administrators with a valuable lesson regarding the benefits of government and industry patronage while also shifting their institutions' prewar research agendas. Modifying research agendas, however, was only one consequence of higher education's adaptation to the forces of mobilization. Many colleges and universities also became directly involved in the vocational education and training of defense war workers and military recruits during the war years. As Louis Keefer and V.R. Cardozier have shown in their respective works, higher education administrators eagerly sought contracts with military and government officials to make use of their facilities and personnel to teach engineering, science, foreign language, and management courses.[63] According to Keefer and Cardozier, the resulting "enrollment" of tens of thousands of uniformed recruits militarized many campuses' previously collegiate atmosphere.

As beneficial as these studies are in contributing to our understanding of higher education's wartime experiences, few investigate the war's influence on colleges' and universities' historic commitment to promoting civic mindedness among students. As John Thelin has shown, institutions of higher education have traditionally defined their missions to include advancing the "common" or "public" good.[64] How these commitments translated into curricular and extracurricular programming over time, however, is generally unknown. "The role of education—especially higher education—in demarcating the bounds of twentieth century citizenship has been largely overlooked in the literature," Christopher Loss has recently observed.[65] Loss's claim holds especially true for the war era. Between 1940 and 1945, debates erupted in the United States over colleges' and universities' proper role in educating for democracy. "Here was no obscure quarrel between academics," Geoffrey Perrett writes of the controversy, "the entire country was drawn into the fight."[66] Instead of examining the essence and resolution of this quarrel, however, historians have traditionally focused their attention on wartime training programs and the postwar evolution of the modern research university.

As with their belief that colleges and universities should make a significant contribution to national defense, many Americans during World War II called for dramatic changes to elementary and secondary school programs. According to Gerard Giordano, political conservatives "revolutionized" schools during the war years in an effort to foster among students "altruism, patriotism, knowledge of the war, and national unity."[67] "The volume, breadth, intensity, and rapidity of the changes they made were staggering," Giordano writes. "The reformers themselves were intelligent, zealous, foresightful, organized, and attentive to detail. However, so were most of the other crusaders who had failed in their attempts to change the schools. Those who had not been successful complained about the redoubtable barriers that the educational establishment had thrown before them. The World War II conservatives breached these defenses, assumed command of the schools, and achieved an epic victory."[68]

Were Giordano's analyses accurate, the war era would stand as a unique moment in the history of America's public schools. However, Giordano frequently mistakes conservatives' wartime rhetoric for genuine reform. To be sure, the war affected elementary and secondary schools across the nation. To what extent the crisis changed schools' curricular and extracurricular programming, however, and whether those modifications altered schools' previous commitments to educating for democratic citizenship continues to be a matter of dispute. By comparing schools in the United States and Australia, for instance, historian Andrew Spaull has uncovered substantive changes in wartime secondary school social studies curricula. "The War brought immediate changes to the content and scope of social studies," Spaull writes. "First, the War accelerated geography and international relations. Second, the War revitalized the secondary school's interest in national history and politics."[69] Claiming that a focus on national history became a fairly common trend in American high schools during World War II, Spaull suggests that the "ideological nature of the War" presented opportunities to "restate national ideals and achievements" and that a fear of military attack and invasion "reinforced those demands."[70] O.L. Davis's investigations, however, although allowing for modifications such as those Spaull describes, reveal the extreme to which Giordano overstates claims of "revolutionary" change. Davis indicates that wartime proposals to transform elementary and secondary school academic programs often failed to actualize in the classroom. "Without question," Davis writes, "prewar curriculum emphases, organizations, assumptions, and legitimations continued as part of wartime curriculum structures."[71]

On the other hand, World War II undoubtedly had a profound impact on early childhood education. As historians Sonya Michel, Barbara Beatty, and Elizabeth Rose have all shown, wartime labor shortages provided the federal government with the justification necessary to subsidize nursery schooling for the children of working mothers. These scholars differ, however, regarding the consequences of this development for early childhood education in the United States. In *Children's Interests/Mothers' Rights*, Michel suggests that highlighting the educational aspects of federally subsidized nursery schools for the young children of working mothers during World War II undermined women's campaign for the right to childcare.[72] Beatty, through a comparison of three preschool advocacy organizations, concludes that merging early childhood education with childcare during the war years resulted in advances for both.[73] Tacking in a slightly different interpretive direction, historian Elizabeth Rose has observed that World War II provided a "sort of watershed in *attitudes* toward day care and women's paid labor."[74] Claiming that wartime nurseries furthered a shift in Americans' conceptions of nursery schools begun during the Great Depression, Rose argues that during World War II many Americans came to view preschools as federally supported, educationally enriching programs for young children rather than welfare measures provided for the destitute.

Although all three of these excellent studies refer to nursery school teachers' instructional efforts during the war years, it is Emily Stoltzfus's work, *Citizen, Mother, Worker*, that most clearly demonstrates how early childhood education practitioners and advocates perceived nursery schools as places where children were first exposed to the principles of democracy. Following the war, according to Stoltzfus, activists in California framed their advocacy of government-supported preschool education by arguing that the state had a vested interest in nursery schools' role in teaching young students "productive citizenship."[75] For the most part, however, Stoltzfus's study examines postwar developments and therefore investigates neither the unique organizational and funding structures nor the pedagogical approaches that wartime teachers actually used with their students—approaches that led postwar observers to conclude that wartime nurseries were designed "to develop socially healthy, well-adjusted junior citizens."[76]

Building on these bodies of literature, this book also differs from them in important ways. By drawing on a number of historiographies, including urban history, labor history, women's history, children's history, the history of education, and the history of the American West, I conceive of the war as a crucible and apply this conceptualization to a systemic examination of American education—its students, educators, and institutions, from preschool through graduate school—allowing for a comparison and contrast of these individuals' and institutions' experiences and permitting a more substantive interpretation of the consequences of World War II for American education. Through this approach, I bring the fields of social and cultural history into conversation with educational history while contributing to a more informed understanding of education's role in responding to and molding American society.

The San Francisco Bay Area

This book, which examines educational institutions in the San Francisco Bay Area, constitutes a regional history with national significance. Although World War II created an American homefront characterized by a sense of national unity as well as social distress, the forces of mobilization affected certain areas of the country more directly than others. California was one such area. It received more defense contracts between 1940 and 1946 than any other state in the nation (totaling $35 billion of the $360 billion in federal defense outlays) and received 12 percent of all war orders, primarily for the production of ships, aircraft, and steel.[77] These three industries were largely responsible for the dramatic increase in the value of the state's manufactures during the war years, from $2,798,000 in 1939 to $10,141,000 in 1945.[78]

Given the wartime economic boom, it is hardly surprising that Americans seeking defense work moved to California in greater numbers than anywhere else. Between 1939 and 1947, the number of production workers in California rose from 271,290 to 530,283.[79] By the end of World War II, more than 1.5 million people had moved into the state, with the San Francisco Bay Area second only to San Diego as their final destination.[80] For the most part, these new arrivals shared the characteristics of their Depression-era counterparts. They were, on average, under 30 years of age and urban in origin, arriving to the state primarily in automobiles. Unlike during the previous, largely white migration, however, they were strikingly diverse in their racial, ethnic, and cultural make-up.[81]

As scholars such as Gerald B. Nash and Roger W. Lotchin have demonstrated, California's response to this sudden economic and social expansion served as a bellwether for the nation as well as a progressive standard against which many other states judged their efforts to mobilize. Community studies by Marilyn Johnson and Shirley Ann Wilson Moore have also identified important parallels between the Bay Area's wartime experience and that of other major metropolitan areas. Moreover, the National Park Service's selection of the city of Richmond, in northern California, as the site for its "Rosie the Riveter/World War II Home Front National Historical Park" underscores the significance of the Bay Area to national wartime history.

Within the Bay Area, I have deliberately chosen one stable and one unstable wartime community to serve as sites of investigation for this study. Like an earthquake with an epicenter near enough to rattle the windows but distant enough to prevent severe damage, the effects of mobilization were felt in Palo Alto even if it was not a site of direct impact. Now thought of as unique in its connection to the high finance of Silicon Valley, Palo Alto typified an emerging middle-class suburb prior to the war. Circling in the orbit of San Francisco, Palo Alto had 16,774 residents in 1940 and was relatively homogenous in its demographic composition. Home mostly to whites, the city also claimed a small number of other racial and ethnic groups as residents, including Asian Americans, African Americans, and Chicanos.[82] Palo Alto's proximity to Stanford University fostered a rich intellectual and cultural environment and provided an economic base not reliant upon industry.

In contrast to Palo Alto's experience, the forces of mobilization occasionally converged on epicenters that were profoundly transformed by the war. In northern California, no city endured more severe tests during World War II than Richmond. Prior to the conflict, as Marilynn S. Johnson has noted, Richmond was a "relatively small, pastoral community" of approximately 24,000 residents located in the East Bay of the San Francisco Bay Area.[83] When Henry Kaiser announced plans to build a shipyard along the town's waterfront, however, he put forces in motion that eventually earned the town the dubious distinction of "Purple Heart City."[84] Located only several miles north of the deepwater ports of Oakland and situated near the terminus of the Santa Fe and Southern Pacific railroads, Richmond was a prime site for wartime industrial development. "More wartime contracts descended upon the city than it could absorb," historian Gerald Nash has written of Richmond, with a resulting population increase to more than 90,000 in less than three years.[85] Along with Kaiser's four shipyards, Richmond's establishment of more than 50 other war industries pushed the city's civic capacity to the limit.

Palo Alto and Richmond serve as excellent examples of the effects of World War II on communities throughout the United States. Intentionally juxtaposing them, I attempt to reveal the cities' strikingly different wartime experiences as well as their educational institutions' varied and occasionally conflicting responses to defense mobilization. I make no claim, however, that Palo Alto and Richmond are representative of the American homefront. Rather, they are intended to be illustrative only. Where appropriate, therefore, I place the Bay Area in a broader comparative perspective by examining data from centers of defense production throughout the United States, including those in and around Detroit, Pittsburgh, Chicago, Vancouver, and Seattle. Yet as thoughtfully chosen and well-constructed case studies in the history of American education should, this examination of a compelling period of national crisis illuminates tremendously important questions about the meaning and purpose of education in a democratic society.

The Plan of This Book

Chapter 2 investigates Stanford University's divergent responses to homefront mobilization. A respected center of higher learning in the western United States, by 1941 Stanford stood at an institutional crossroads. Prior to the war, university administrators had begun to improve their contacts with industry in the hopes of reaping the financial benefits associated with contracted research. World War II catalyzed those efforts, leading Stanford to negotiate defense research contracts with industries and the federal government as well as to secure lucrative agreements with the armed forces to train military personnel. Out of these arrangements evolved the privileging of academic disciplines contributing directly to wartime technical training and research. This development did not go unchallenged, however. Running counter to perceived trends in higher education, Stanford established a School of Humanities in 1941. Demonstrating the importance it assigned the liberal arts, the university publicly reaffirmed its historic obligation to foster civic mindedness among students, even in the midst of national crisis.

Chapter 3 examines how, following America's declaration of war, Palo Alto district administrators responded to proposals for public elementary and secondary schools to be placed in service to the war effort. School officials, for instance, militarized physical education to prepare students to serve on the battlefield and instituted aviation instruction at Palo Alto High School. Extracurricular programs, too, were dramatically refashioned to meet war needs, with the buying and selling of war stamps and bonds, collecting scrap, and tending to Victory Gardens becoming popular activities for many students. Palo Alto also received federal funding through the Vocational Education for National Defense program to establish the district's first daytime vocational school, the Peninsula Defense Training Center. School officials clearly reoriented programs peripheral to students' core courses to allow them to make direct contributions to the war effort. Curricular consistency in the academic classroom, however, undermined administrators' claims that they would "meet any needs dictated by the war," revealing the schools' continuing commitment to educating students for democratic citizenship.

Chapter 4 examines the impact of boomtown developments on Richmond's elementary and secondary schools. If their prewar educational systems were similar, the contrast between Palo Alto's and Richmond's wartime experience could not have been more dramatic. School enrollments provide one striking example, with Palo Alto's student population remaining fairly steady during the war years while Richmond's skyrocketed from 6,417 to more than 21,000 by 1944. As student-teacher ratios consistently rose, Richmond school administrators desperately sought physical space for students, eventually implementing "double sessions," which cut the length of each school day in half. A teacher shortage, moreover, worsened conditions in the city's classrooms, leading School Superintendent Walter Helms to both recall retired teachers to service and recruit others from throughout the nation. Even more remarkable was the demographic transformation of Richmond's student enrollment. Emigrant families came from across the United States to obtain employment in Richmond's defense plants and shipyards, including many blacks, who increased their presence in Richmond by more than 5,000 percent during the war era. In response, city officials and industry executives implemented discriminatory policies in Richmond's defense industries and public housing. Public school teachers and administrators, however, considered it their duty to educate "all" students for democracy, revealing the "civic-professionalism" that infused their approach to public schooling during World War II.

Chapter 5 examines Richmond's wartime nursery schools. Established to serve the young children of mothers working in defense industries, the nurseries were initially intended as custodial programs. Richmond's nursery school teachers, however, developed and implemented pedagogy and curricula emphasizing creative expression and democratic citizenship. Two of these nurseries represented a unique nexus in early childhood education in the United States. Impatient with the pace of nursery school provision for the children of mothers working in his Richmond shipyards, Henry Kaiser helped found the Maritime and Pullman nursery schools in 1943. Catalyzed by private industry, constructed and subsidized by the federal government, administered by the Richmond public school district, and supported through parent fees, Maritime and Pullman were nationally acknowledged as examples of excellence in nursery school provision.

The wartime nursery schools, however, although grudgingly accepted as a necessary preventative for child neglect by 1945, never developed a strong national constituency. As a result, the federal government eliminated its financial support following the war. In California, however, the state government assumed fiscal responsibility for the schools, permitting many to continue operations well into the postwar era.

Historian William Reese writes, "History provides some valuable perspective, but not answers, to grave matters of public policy in the contemporary world."[86] As I write this book, the United States is once again experiencing the instability resulting from a national crisis. Although the characteristics of the so-called "war on terror" only slightly resemble those of the twentieth century's total wars, military engagements in Afghanistan and Iraq, as well as potential conflicts with Iran and North Korea, are significantly influencing America's central political, social, and economic institutions. As a critical event in the history of the United States, World War II provides a meaningful period of analysis through which to glean important insights into these grave contemporary developments. In Chapter 6, I conclude by reflecting on the ways that wartime mobilization influenced education in the United States, offering perspective on the role that Americans have attributed to institutions of higher education, elementary and secondary schools, and centers of early childhood education in advancing a democratic society over time.

2

Promoting the "Public Welfare" at Stanford University

> The liberal arts, we are told, are luxuries. At best you should fit them into your leisure time. They are mere decorations upon the sterner pattern of life. . . . Men and women [however] who are devoting their lives to such studies should not be made to feel inferior or apologetic in the face of a PT boat commander or the driver of a tank. They and all their fellow citizens should know that the preservation of our cultural heritage is not superfluous in a modern civilization. . . . It is what we are fighting for.[1]
> —U.S. Presidential Candidate Wendell Willkie, 1943

Stanford University celebrated its Golden Anniversary in 1941, beginning with a 21 to 13 win over the University of Nebraska at the Rose Bowl in Pasadena. The victory was an auspicious beginning to a notable year, one marked by numerous galas, a Commemorative Symposium themed "The University and the Future of America," and the dedication of a 285-foot-tall tower as part of the university's Hoover Library on War, Revolution and Peace.[2] As entertaining as the festivities reportedly were, however, war news from Europe and Asia provided a constant reminder of the possible challenges facing the university community in the years ahead. Inaugurated during World War I, Stanford University President Ray Lyman Wilbur was fully aware of the disruptions the university might confront if the United States was again drawn into a European conflict.[3] Donald B. Tresidder, president of the university's Board of Trustees and a Stanford undergraduate during World War I, was also concerned for the university's future. Tresidder's worries, however, stemmed less from America's involvement in the war than from a belief that Stanford had lost touch with the institutional realities confronting most colleges and universities in the United States, particularly those increasingly involved in research.

Two decades earlier, Stanford had begun charging tuition for the first time in its history, permitting a significant expansion of the institution's physical plant.[4] Student fees, however, narrowed Stanford's appeal to applicants of primarily middle- and upper-class origins.[5] As a consequence, the university acquired a reputation as a "country club" institution, with *Time* magazine identifying it as a "rich man's college."[6] Administrators' heavy reliance on tuition dollars also undermined Stanford's fiscal stability and admission standards during the Great Depression. After enrollments declined from 4,674 students in 1928 to 3,855 students in 1933, for instance, the university's Academic Council, desperate to keep students registered, agreed to end student dismissal on the grounds of poor academic performance.[7] The university also altered its previous admission criteria, examining applicants' educational records from the prior three years of high school rather than four, in effect lowering Stanford's selectivity.[8] As a result, university officials believed Stanford was "drifting into paths that could lead to hopeless mediocrity."[9]

Tresidder hoped to reverse the university's decline, beginning with a weekend meeting at the Ahwahnee Hotel in Yosemite National Park on December 5, 1941. Guests, including members of the faculty, the Board of Trustees, and wealthy alumni, discussed the desirability of acquiring contracted research projects as a way to improve both the university's financial status and its national reputation.[10] As representatives of an institution closely associated with Stanford graduate and former Republican president Herbert Hoover, however, participants found the idea of developing a relationship with the New Deal administration of President Franklin D. Roosevelt unappealing. Instead, the group agreed to further the university's connections with private industry. As participants began developing strategies for doing so, however, news of the attack on Pearl Harbor abruptly ended the meeting.[11]

The rapid mobilization of national resources following America's declaration of war on December 8, 1941, had profound consequences for colleges and universities throughout the nation. Although higher education administrators began planning for U.S. involvement in World War II prior to the attack on Pearl Harbor, the lowering of the draft age to 18 in 1942 and the elimination of a broad deferral for college and university students decimated higher education enrollments, leaving colleges and universities without desperately needed tuition dollars.[12] As with many institutions throughout the United States, Stanford University responded by identifying alternative sources of revenue in wartime contracts with the federal government, the armed forces, and defense industries. Stanford's leaders established the University Services Office in Washington, DC, as a base of lobbying operations and proceeded to negotiate a number of important defense research projects while also seeking agreements with federal agencies to take advantage of the university's suddenly underutilized facilities and personnel. Stanford's adoption of the Engineering Science Management War Training program through the U.S. Office of Education and the Army Specialized Training Program through the U.S. Department of War are two of the most evident examples of contractual arrangements that successfully alleviated the university's financial difficulties.

By contracting for war-related research and programs, Stanford's administrators increasingly aligned the university's work with national defense priorities—a development personified in 1943 by the passing of the presidency from Wilbur, a physician and administrator who desired that the university remain independent from contractual research obligations, to Tresidder, a businessman who strongly fostered Stanford's ties to industry.[13] This process, however, was more complicated than simply converting Stanford into an arsenal of democracy. Although administrators justified the university's involvement in the war effort by reinterpreting Stanford's founding charter to "promote the public welfare," many faculty members strove to maintain the university's prewar commitments to liberal education. In 1942, *Time* magazine again placed Stanford in the national spotlight by announcing the establishment of the university's new School of Humanities, an event understood by many as running directly counter to wartime trends in higher education. "Last week," proclaimed *Time*, "as liberal arts colleges all over the nation rushed to accelerate the arts of war (mathematics and science), President Wilbur and trustees announced that Stanford, which has never had a liberal arts college, will start one next fall."[14]

World War II undoubtedly heightened the emphasis that colleges and universities placed on technical training and applied curricula, a trend that transformed higher education research agendas throughout the United States. As this chapter's opening quote from U.S. presidential candidate Wendell Willkie suggests, however, many Americans believed that the United States was at war precisely for the purpose of preserving democratic ideals and urged colleges and universities to maintain their historic commitment to conceptions of higher education that transcended the immediate national crisis. At Stanford University, such seemingly dichotomous developments as the enthusiastic adoption of war-related programs and the establishment of a School of Humanities reveal the relatively unexplored complexity of higher education's divergent responses to the forces of mobilization during World War II.

Higher Education and National Defense

Even prior to December 1941, Ray Lyman Wilbur encouraged students to remain at Stanford until called up for active duty. Aware that a U.S. declaration of war would result in a significant decline in university enrollments, he also requested that the faculty support his position.[15] After reminding faculty members that "under the selective draft, and for national service, each individual is of value to the country in proportion to his or her educational attainments," Wilbur suggested that impatient students be informed of the university's efforts to speed up the academic program, allowing most to complete their degree requirements in three years rather than the usual four.[16] "The School of Engineering, for the first time," Wilbur reported, "will offer summer courses to make possible the completion of the twelve-quarter course in three years. Similarly, the other schools of the University will offer distinctive training to complete their requirements in a shorter time."[17] To students, Wilbur directed an equally pragmatic justification for remaining at Stanford. "It is not mere force that wins modern wars," Wilbur informed students, "but force plus brains.... That means that the universities and the student bodies in the universities have become predominant in importance; that everybody with enough brains to go into such fields as physics, chemistry, biology, meteorology, medicine, engineering, etc., must not be tempted to go off and do something that other people can do."[18]

As Figure 2.1 shows, Wilbur's desire that students remain on campus was initially satisfied, with university enrollments remaining fairly stable during the 1941/42 and 1942/43 academic years. Following the lowering of the draft age from 21 to 18 in November 1942, however, there was little Wilbur could do to slow the eventual exodus of predominantly male students and their financial support from Stanford.[19]

Many institutions of higher education shared Stanford's experience during the war years. On January 3–4, 1942, the Baltimore Conference on Higher Education and the War brought college and university presidents together to discuss the impact of America's involvement in the conflict on their institutions' financial resources and future development.[20] Sponsored by the United States Office of Education and the American Council on Education's National Committee on Education and Defense, the conference was reported to be the largest of its kind ever held in the United States. Delegates

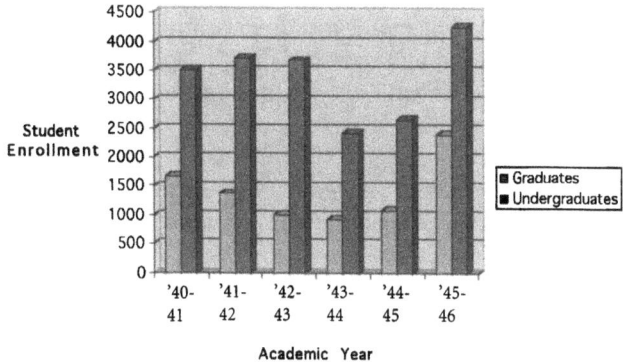

Figure 2.1 Stanford University enrollment, 1940/45

Source: Stanford University Bulletin, Annual Registers, 1940/46 (Stanford: Stanford University Press).

discussed how to resolve the problem of declining revenues and developed several proposals urging the federal government and industry to award contracts that both employed universities in war-related research and supplemented the use of university facilities and personnel.[21]

The Baltimore conference was one of a series of efforts on the part of higher education administrators to make their institutions' needs and resources known to the government and armed forces. The previous February, the American Council on Education convened more than 500 individuals representing 370 colleges from 40 states for the Organizing Higher Education for National Defense conference in Washington, DC.[22] Participants called for colleges' and universities' increased involvement in defense preparation. Five months later, Stanford hosted a similar conference for higher education administrators in the western United States. Chaired by Ray Lyman Wilbur, the meeting concluded with a proposal to establish a commission to "study, plan and propose far-reaching policies designed to unite higher education centers in the area in contributing to national defense and general social welfare."[23] Again, participants generated and distributed a list of concerns relating to the impact of mobilization on America's campuses and declared their willingness to support the war effort.

In July 1941, one month following Stanford's gathering, the National Committee on Education and Defense and the National Education Association brought together college administrators and government officials, including those representing the Office of Civil Defense, the U.S. Army and Navy, and the Civil Aeronautics Administration, for a meeting entitled, "Higher Education Cooperates in National Defense."[24] Touted as an opportunity for participants to engage in an informal dialogue, the conference resulted in a general agreement that the nation's colleges and universities would eventually play an important role in such varied areas as pilot training, morale, research, and civilian protection. Participants, however, did not develop specific plans for how to utilize higher education facilities and personnel to achieve these ends. In response, administrators like Wilbur continued their public outcry for the government to take advantage of the resources that institutions of higher education, such as Stanford, offered. The nation's universities were, according to

Wilbur, "valuable assets in winning the war and the peace that follows."[25] Emphasizing that the longer the government delayed, the more serious wartime challenges confronting colleges and universities would become, Wilbur insisted that "some means need to be devised for continuing to lend financial support to institutions of higher learning."[26] Indeed, how to make up for financial losses resulting from the draft was colleges' and universities' central challenge during World War II. When government and industry leaders finally offered assistance, it came in the form of contracts awarded specifically for the purpose of advancing the war effort. Taking primarily two forms, the contracts were designed to employ the university in research and to supplement the use of university facilities and personnel.[27] Stanford was well situated to take advantage of both.

In *Creating the Cold War University: The Transformation of Stanford*, historian Rebecca Lowen details Stanford's evolution into a government and industry contract-driven research university beginning with World War II.[28] As Lowen describes, Stanford's leaders desired to exploit the "wonderful opportunity" that wartime defense research contracts presented through increased reputation and financial resources.[29] Having generally avoided contractual obligations under Wilbur's leadership, however, pursuing a defense research agenda required reframing Stanford's prewar educational mission in the national interest, allowing university administrators to claim they were acting in the best traditions of the university while fundamentally reshaping the institution's previously stated civic purpose. Stanford's General Secretary Paul Davis, for instance, asserted that by seeking out federal and industrial patronage the university was simply broadening its founding charter to "promote the public welfare" to include "High Service in all forms."[30] According to Lowen, "Davis, as well as administrators at other universities, had eagerly sought to bring their universities to the service of the nation, and Davis recognized early on that such service conferred institutional prestige. He wanted Stanford to continue to play the role of a service institution after the war.... Tresidder... took seriously Davis' suggestions."[31]

Professor of Education Paul Hanna, who was actively involved in promoting Stanford's lobbying efforts, also urged a redefinition of the university's educational mission during World War II. Hoping to capitalize on Stanford's location in the western United States, Hanna outlined a vision that involved developing Stanford into a "regional university." Writing to Wilbur in February 1942, Hanna proposed that faculty members focus on solving social problems stemming from wartime mobilization in the West, including "the development of water and electrical energy, improvement of schools and colleges, improvement of agricultural crops . . . and improvement of municipal, county and state government, etc."[32] Hanna reminded Wilbur that public institutions, including Stanford's local rival, the University of California, Berkeley, were compelled to focus on state issues to secure funding from legislators. He then suggested that, as a private institution, Stanford was free to "take the initiative and make itself ready to play the dominant role in the West in integrating the research and projecting the master plans as they will be called for by government and private enterprise."[33] According to Hanna, "The next logical step is the creation of an institution to serve the region, and I cherish for Stanford University this role. Such a regional rootage would give our students more significant opportunities for service and would greatly increase the total good our University would render the people of this nation."[34]

Davis and Hanna were both greatly satisfied with what occurred at Stanford over the next several months. In a "Statement of Principle" issued to faculty in October 1942, the Committee on University Services wrote:

> The problems confronting the nation at war require that institutions of higher learning re-appraise their activities in order to ascertain if they may better contribute to the welfare of the country. It would seem clear that the immediate objectives of Stanford should be to turn its facilities for study and research into those channels which will make for the winning of the war and the successful foundation of a constructive and enduring peace. The first step is to make its full research staff and facilities available to the government, its agencies, and the governing bodies in the western areas to perform those tasks the government now deems most necessary. All research in areas which do not specifically contribute to the war effort or bear directly on the problems which immediately will follow should be suspended.[35]

By declaring that suspending research not specifically contributing to the war effort would best serve the "welfare" of the country, the committee clearly strove to adjust Stanford's founding charter to wartime demands. The university administration affirmed this effort the following month when it approved a plan to reorient "the Resources of Stanford University for Greater Public Service" by carrying out "a vastly augmented program of service on a contractual basis" that would bring "substantial additional income to the University."[36]

Although ultimately trailing behind institutions such as the Massachusetts Institute of Technology and Harvard University in the total number of research projects acquired during the war, Stanford negotiated 25 contracts totaling over a half-million dollars with the federal Office of Scientific Research and Development (initially the National Defense Research Council).[37] What Stanford did not achieve fiscally in the area of contracted research, however, it made up for by negotiating with the U.S. Office of Education to offer courses through the Engineering, Science, and Management War Training program and the Department of War in order to provide coursework to military recruits through the Army Specialized Training Program.[38]

Engineering, Science, and Management War Training

As early as 1939, many Americans acknowledged their nation's lack of necessary technical expertise to win a war in which the United States might someday be involved.[39] A study conducted in that year by the U.S. Office of Education, for instance, demonstrated that only one-tenth the number of engineers qualified to engage in defense production in the Pittsburgh area were currently available.[40] In response to this perceived lack of brainpower, the U.S. Congress proposed contracting with the nation's colleges and universities to provide additional training, an idea that came to fruition in October 1940 with the establishment of the Engineering Defense Training program (EDT).[41]

Although the EDT program was initially designed to alleviate an engineering personnel shortage, the federal government quickly recognized America's need for scientists, particularly chemists, physicists, and production supervisors, to meet the growing demands of mobilization. As offerings in all three fields evolved, the program's name was changed to Engineering, Science, and Management Defense Training. After the United States declared war, the program's name was changed again, to Engineering, Science, and Management War Training (ESMWT). Public or tax-exempt colleges and universities offering four-year degrees in certified fields qualified for contracts with the federal government to provide ESMWT courses.[42] Federal education officials selected Stanford as one of approximately 230 institutions to offer the courses.

Stanford University served as an ideal site for the ESMWT program. In addition to a respected school of engineering, the university had a nationally recognized science program and business school. If these qualities were not enough to merit the attention of the U.S. Office of Education, Stanford University School of Engineering Dean Samuel B. Morris served as the Northern California-Nevada Regional Advisor for the ESMWT program. Not surprisingly, Stanford received substantial ESMWT contracts throughout the war, with university administrators welcoming the generous revenues these agreements generated.[43]

Government officials announced that ESMWT was not intended to provide a complete engineering, scientific, or business education but rather to "give specific, intensive training to meet specific and definitely determined needs of defense and war industries."[44] Stanford met this requirement by offering short courses of "college grade"—a designation that symbolized the challenge Stanford confronted in distinguishing these courses from those offered as part of their degree-granting programs as well as from other vocational offerings administered and funded by the U.S. Office of Education. In advertising the program, Stanford specified that ESMWT was "not a general college program but training for a specific activity" and used the term "college grade" to refer to the "character and content of the course" as well as to an academic standard "customarily required of college and university students in the same field."[45]

Stanford divided its course offerings into four divisions. The first two consisted of part-time courses, 12 to 16 weeks in duration, offered in the evenings from 7:30 to 9:30 p.m. Labeled Part-Time In-Plant, the courses in the first division included those "tailor-made for upgrading on jobs within a war plant or essential civilian activity," such as Strength Calculations for Ship Structures. The university usually held these classes in defense plants, making them easily accessible for workers and allowing plant equipment to be used for instruction.[46]

The second division consisted of Part-Time Open courses designed to meet specific needs common to a group of industries. These classes, such as Engineering Vibration Problems, were offered at "war-training centers" and were labeled as open because there were either too few students to provide instruction in-plant or because the curriculum allowed students from various agencies, military and industrial, to take the same course.[47] Most of these classes were held on campus or at extension sites, including those in San Francisco, Sausalito, San Mateo, and Eureka.[48]

The third and fourth divisions were full-time and required daily attendance from 8:00 a.m. to 5:00 p.m.[49] The courses in the third division were for women, veterans, and men designated 4-F (signifying disqualification for the draft mostly due to medical and physical disabilities) who were "to be trained to assume responsibility for certain specific tasks in the engineering and production offices and in industrial laboratories." Stanford called these Full-Time Pre-Employment courses, such as "Industrial Accounting," and held them on campus along with courses in the fourth division, Full-Time Special-Purpose.[50] This last set of offerings, which included courses such as Quality Control by Statistical Methods, was designed to provide "up-to-date information, about recent technological developments, to key personnel of war industries and the armed forces." All of the courses in the fourth division were the product of specific requests by defense plant executives or military officials.[51]

Stanford's ESMWT offerings in November 1943 included 54 classes, with approximately one-third directed toward employees of specific defense plants or branches of the armed forces and the other two-thirds open to any individual meeting the necessary prerequisites. Thirty-seven of the 54 courses offered were in engineering, 16 were in production supervision, and one was in science. The members of the regular faculty taught only 7 of the 54 courses, with Stanford subcontracting for the services of non-Stanford professionals for the other 47 courses.[52] Women enrolled in many of these courses, and Stanford had in fact designated some courses for women only, such as the full-time programs in Engineering Drafting and Technical Calculations.[53] In addition, Stanford's Chemistry Department offered Chemical Analyst Training for Women, while the Graduate School of Business offered Fundamentals of Industrial Management for Women.[54]

Prior to the program's termination on June 30, 1945, enrollment in ESMWT courses at Stanford totaled 19,894 students, with 400 course sections offered and more than 10,000 individuals enrolled.[55] In a summary assessment of the program, Stanford's ESMWT representative, Professor Eugene L. Grant, noted the contributions he believed the university made to the war effort by participating in the program, including "helping to meet acute shortages of technical and supervisory personnel through upgrading training" and introducing defense plants to "various new ideas and techniques" in industrial processes.[56] For Stanford, Grant claimed an enrichment of future university instruction as the result of "closer contacts of many of the faculty with the changing problems of technology and industry."[57] Grant was especially enthusiastic regarding the financial advantages the program provided Stanford, including equipment purchased, alterations and improvement of buildings, and contributions to university salary and maintenance budgets.

In a memo detailing the material rewards Stanford received through its involvement in ESMWT, Grant cited as exemplary a radio program that the university developed for the Signal Corps. Through this single contract, Stanford received funding for $9,900 worth of building alterations that allowed the university to create three new laboratory rooms, an equipment room, three small classrooms, and three small offices out of a building that had previously been considered too dilapidated to use. "This program," Grant noted, "has also financed the purchases of some $15,000 worth of radio instruction equipment."[58] In an accompanying report, Grant noted the ESMWT budget for the 1942/43 academic year as $200,000, no small portion of the university's total budget for that year.[59]

It was in Stanford's enlarged and elevated reputation, however, that Grant believed Stanford made its greatest strides through the ESMWT program. He emphasized the positive effect on university public relations achieved through Stanford's participation and noted that this was "not only in relations with industries served and with trainees enrolled, but also through a general public knowledge of this contribution to the war and through the prestige gained in those fields in which we have done a particularly successful job."[60] Impressed by what he perceived as the short- and long-term institutional benefits ESMWT generated, J. Hugh Jackson, dean of Stanford's Graduate

School of Business, concurred. Jackson identified several prominent businessmen in the ESMWT courses offered through the business school, including a "Mr. Rath," whose company had produced $126 million in sales the previous year. Jackson suggested that Rath's new status as "alumni" of a Stanford program would permit the university to approach him and others like him for support in the future. "All in all," Jackson informed Tresidder, "I have become convinced that these ESMWT courses sponsored by the University represent one of the finest pieces of public relations work that is being done in the University at the present time."[61]

By acknowledging benefits to both the war effort and to Stanford, Grant and Jackson identified a lesson learned by many college and university administrators during World War II—serving the national interest equated with serving higher education's needs. The discovery of this powerful formula had a profound influence on the way these administrators conceived of their institutions' purposes throughout the war and afterward. The U.S. Office of Education's final report on ESMWT, however, identified another equally important contribution that the program made to higher education. "ESMWT set a pattern," it noted, "for relationships between the Federal Government and the colleges in a federally sponsored educational program, which many observers feel has important implications for the future."[62] Clearly visible at Stanford, ESMWT's adoption established a precedent for using university resources to "train" individuals actively involved in mobilization, whether civilian or military. It was hardly surprising, then, when Stanford administrators agreed in 1943 to contract directly with the U.S. Department of War to provide instruction to thousands of military recruits through the Army Specialized Training program.

Army Specialized Training Program

As with the Student Army Training Corps, its World War I predecessor, the Army Specialized Training Program (ASTP) was rooted in an assumption that it was in the national interest to educate America's soldiers even while on active-duty.[63] Officials, therefore, designed the ASTP to provide recruits with both the necessary skills to fulfill their military responsibilities and training for future leadership roles.[64] Until the Army announced the establishment of the ASTP on December 17, 1942, however, over a year after America's entry into World War II, college and university administrators were uncertain as to whether the armed forces would implement a program reliant upon their institutions, as it had during World War I. When the program's description was finally released, they delivered a cumulative sigh of relief. "The purpose of the Army Specialized Training Program," reported Colonel Herman Beukema, director of the Army Specialized Training Division, "is to meet the need of the Army for specialized technical training of soldiers on active duty for certain Army tasks for which its own training facilities are insufficient in extent or character."[65] With great satisfaction, higher education leaders understood Beukema to mean their institutions would employ both their human and material resources. Participating colleges and universities anticipated receiving substantial compensation from the Department of War for their involvement.

Stanford University had strong programs in the ASTP's three central training areas—engineering, foreign languages, and medicine. President Ray Lyman Wilbur had good reason to believe, therefore, that the Army would choose his institution to participate. As a physician and university president, moreover, Wilbur was asked by Beukema to serve on a nine-person ASTP advisory committee.[66] Wilbur accepted and attended the first committee meeting in February 1943.[67] Three weeks later, he received notice that Stanford had been selected as an ASTP site.[68]

Wilbur immediately set out to mobilize the campus, announcing the expected arrival of the first 400 ASTP students to Stanford in early April. He reaffirmed the university's wartime operating schedule of four 12-week quarters, with four one-week vacations, and requested that faculty interested in teaching mathematics, chemistry, physics, engineering drawing, surveying, or engineering mechanics as part of the program identify themselves.[69] Throughout much of this planning, however, Wilbur hedged, uncertain as to what extent the Army would actually utilize the university's facilities. Wilbur had cause to be skeptical. The Department of War previously dashed his hopes for Stanford's financial salvation when, after the U.S. Navy informed him of its intention to turn Stanford into the "Annapolis of the West," the Department unceremoniously dropped such plans.[70]

Wilbur's skepticism increased in April 1943 when Stanford's representatives in Washington, DC, Paul Hanna and Paul Davis, informed him that the ASTP might not be implemented at all. Citing an effort on the part of the "line officers in the Army" to sabotage it, Hanna reported on the "mess and confusion" of the program, writing to Wilbur that "there is a faint possibility that the program on which Beukema has been working may be scrapped entirely."[71] One month later, Hanna's assessment was confirmed by a *New York Times* headline that read, "Army's College Program Is Reported Bogged Down." The *Times* reported the ASTP as being hampered by a "mass of administrative difficulties" and "still struggling to get under way" despite the scheduled date of March 1 to begin operations.[72] Nevertheless, by the end of the month Stanford's board of trustees received a contract offer for the ASTP stipulating that trainees would begin arriving on campus on May 3, 1943, with instruction commencing on May 10.[73] On May 11, training at Stanford began.

Faculty taught an ASTP curriculum consisting of a basic phase and an advanced phase.[74] The basic phase consisted of three 12-week quarters, considered the equivalent of the first one-and-a-half years of university study. Although the basic curriculum included coursework in mathematics, physics, chemistry, English, history, and geography, the program included a focus on engineering, including classes in "engineering specialities" such as surveying, internal combustion engines, and communications.[75] The ASTP's advanced phase opened with courses normally found in the second half of the sophomore year and usually lasted no longer than four quarters. It was a highly specialized program that included branches in Foreign Area and Language Studies; Engineering; Premedical, Predental, and Preveterinary Studies; and Psychology. A central objective of the advanced phase was to ready military personnel to serve overseas prior to and immediately following the occupation of enemy territory.[76] The ASTP described the Foreign Area and Language Studies branch, for instance, as providing the training necessary "for duty with all arms of the Army Ground Forces, and for duty with Military Intelligence Services, the Provost Marshall General's Department, and the Signal Corps. A common interest of these arms and services is that the soldier be fluent in one or more modern foreign languages, know the area in which the languages are used, and have insight into the elements which favor or endanger relations between the Army of the United States and the people in that area."[77] At Stanford, this included training in the language, geography, and history of European nations such as Germany and Italy, as well as Asian nations such as Japan.

The ASTP subdivided the advanced engineering branch into Chemical, Civil, Electrical, Mechanical, Sanitary, and Marine Transportation Engineering, with Stanford offering the first four. The Premedical, Predental and Preveterinary branches were also subdivided into the Preprofessional Stage, lasting five quarters, and the Professional Stage, which represented the standard curriculum prescribed by accredited schools of medicine, dentistry, and veterinary medicine. Of these, Stanford offered the Premedical program, hosting between 30 and 60 trainees per session.[78] Finally, Stanford offered the Psychology program, albeit inconsistently, throughout the war's duration. Primarily a personnel psychology program providing training in the "techniques and procedures" employed in selecting, classifying, and assigning military personnel to their duty stations, it involved nine courses spread over two quarters.[79]

The ASTP had a significant influence on collegiate life at Stanford. Over the course of the war years, the university trained 11,928 military personnel as part of Army Specialized Training Units.[80] The technical training aspects of the program, accompanied by the arrival on campus of literally thousands of members of the armed forces, had the effect of militarizing the university (see Figure 2.2). As reported by a United Press correspondent in October 1943, "The first Army-approved inspection of the program disclosed that these soldiers—3,000 strong—have virtually taken over Stanford University.... The Stanford Quadrangle resounds with young soldiers going to class in formation, books and slide rules under their arms, shouting the 'Hut-two-three-four' cadence, instead of the 'Rah-Rah' of former college days."[81]

The average Stanford ASTP trainee age of 26 dramatically transformed the characteristics of the university student population. During the 1943/44 academic year, for instance, the total number of military personnel present at Stanford was 3,726, easily outnumbering the 2,412 undergraduates.[82] These soldiers used the athletic fields for drill, marksmanship, and in some cases artillery training, and they attended class sometimes as early as 7:30 a.m. and as late as 11:00 p.m.

Figure 2.2 Uniformed students—Members of the Army Specialized Training Program on the history corner steps during World War II
Courtesy, Stanford University Archives

The university even renamed the fraternity houses and dormitories in which military personnel resided during their stay in honor of presidents of the United States.[83]

Charles Philips attended Stanford as an ASTP trainee in 1944. His recollections of the time emphasized both the heightened military presence on campus as well as the dramatically altered university culture.[84] Philips first learned of the ASTP from an army recruiter in his hometown of Phoenix, Arizona. Knowing he would soon be drafted and wanting to join the program, Philips took summer classes, graduating from high school one semester early. In January 1945 he enlisted and several weeks later received orders to report to the Fort MacArthur army base in southern California.[85]

The army sent Philips to Stanford University almost immediately. "We moved into Encina Hall," Philips recalled, "which until that time had been a student dorm. They sent us up to the Presidio [army base] in San Francisco to get our uniforms, and they brought us back down, and the next day we went to our first classes."[86] Philips enrolled in the basic ASTP curriculum and remembered marching in uniform to and from classes that were segregated from civilian students. "There were no Stanford students in our classes, just military," he recalled, "And we had a pretty busy schedule. We took chemistry, history, advanced algebra, physics, and English. It was a lot of work." Yet Philips did not spend all his time at Stanford studying. He also remembered playing French horn in the Stanford Band; "We played at all the swim meets for the Stanford girls. We played for all the girls' athletic things because there were no men's athletics at all during the war." Indeed, Philips had difficulty remembering any male students on campus at the time. "There were women everywhere, just everywhere," he stated, "but you just never saw any men."[87]

Clyde Marshall had similar recollections. After graduating from high school in northern California in 1941, Marshall attended San Mateo Junior College for a year, and upon turning 18, enlisted in the Army. Before receiving his orders, however, Marshall transferred to Stanford University. "I was not a very serious student," he recalled. "I drank a lot and had a good time, knowing I would be in the war soon."[88] Marshall clearly recollected the military presence programs such as the ASTP brought to campus. "There were all sorts of programs to train officers and enlisted men," he remembered. "Some were going to occupy places in Europe, others were trained for special roles in the infantry. They even trained with artillery on Stanford's fields. They had those old World War I pieces—that was the old horse-drawn artillery—and, God, they went careening through the eucalyptus trees at Stanford."[89]

Impressed by the sight of the military on campus, Marshall was unaware that he, too, would soon be training on Stanford's grounds.

At the end of his first semester at Stanford, Marshall received orders to report to Fort Ord in Monterey, California. Soon after arriving, he volunteered for the ASTP and returned to Stanford. His time on campus was short-lived, however, for after "careening through the eucalyptus trees" himself for several weeks, Marshall's commanding officer ordered him to report to the University of California, Berkeley, for specialized training in engineering.[90]

The profound effect that the ASTP and similar military programs had on Stanford's institutional culture was equaled only by the financial benefits the university reaped through its participation.[91] In May 1943, for instance, Stanford received a program "activation expense" that included $18,935 for alterations to facilities, $53,736 for required equipment (including anything from baking tins to furniture), and a 3 percent general administrative expense, for a total of $74,851. Moreover, for the 2,827 trainees at Stanford between October 11 and November 8, 1943, Stanford's reimbursements included $13,439 for the use of facilities, $96,360 for instructional expenses, $96,892 for trainee texts and other equipment, $3,259 for medical services provided to trainees, $114,153 for trainee subsistence, and $29,028 for maintenance and operation. Although the number of trainees at Stanford varied throughout the year, at this rate the military would have reimbursed the university for an estimated annual cost of $4,237,572.[92] With gross expenditures of $6,215,595 in 1943, Stanford relied heavily on the ASTP for its fiscal health. Given such lucrative arrangements, it is hardly surprising that university Financial Vice President Frank F. Walker reported in December 1943 that although Stanford had expected an operating deficit of $174,000 by the end of 1943, the university budget was "actually in the black."[93]

As with the ESMWT program, the ASTP provided Stanford an opportunity to engage in positive public relations by claiming that the university was directly supporting the nation's military objectives. Indeed, by offering coursework in so many of the ASTP's training areas, Stanford distinguished itself among western colleges and universities.[94] Of the 28 western institutions of higher education participating in the ASTP, only nine offered both the engineering and the language and area studies programs. Stanford was one.[95] Moreover, of all participating institutions, Stanford offered the broadest field of language instruction, including Dutch, French, German, Italian, Russian, Spanish, Chinese, and Japanese.[96]

Unlike with the ESMWT program, however, Stanford's reputation was temporarily threatened in 1944 by the Army's examination of ASTP trainees. Ironically, Stanford had initially benefited from the Army's decision to evaluate ASTP recruits, contracting with the military to develop 21 examinations for 11 ASTP courses.[97] When the results of the basic curriculum examinations were released in January 1945, however, Stanford's standing in comparison to other institutions offering the same coursework was dismal:

- Chemistry: 30 out of 33
- English: 41 out of 43
- Geography: 39 out of 40
- History: 31 out of 34
- Physics: 43 out of 45
- Mathematics: 38 out of 40[98]

Upon learning of the results, Paul Hanna immediately contacted Tresidder, warning him of the implications of the low scores.[99] Although the Department of War had no plan to publicly release the results, Hanna and Tresidder were concerned that the information might leak and be published or that the Army might use the results to justify withdrawing its contracts. Tresidder quickly countered the ASTP director's charge of "poor quality instruction" at Stanford, arguing that the university maintained a far lower attrition rate for its trainees than other participating colleges and universities. The discrepancy, Tresidder claimed, was not the result of poor instruction but of vague Army policies regarding what constituted a trainee's "failure."[100]

The accuracy of Tresidder's position was ultimately left unchallenged, for not long after the examination scores became known the Army began curtailing ASTP operations in anticipation of the war's end. Nevertheless, Tresidder's apprehension regarding Stanford's scores indicated how quickly the university's reputation had become fused with wartime programs. In effect, Stanford's embrace of both ESMWT and ASTP contracts demonstrated the degree to which the university had become a willing competitor in the race to achieve distinction in the midst of national crisis. By 1945, Stanford administrators' prewar anxiety over its academic reputation had been sidelined and replaced by more immediate concerns over how the public would view the university's role as an arsenal of democracy.

A clear expression of the enthusiasm with which Stanford's leaders embraced promoting the national interest, the university's adoption of ESMWT and ASTP nevertheless caused concern among some members of the faculty. Liberal and fine arts professors, in particular, were concerned that the university was departing radically from Leland and Jane Stanford's founding desire for their institution to be one "where any person can find instruction in any study."[101] The dramatic expansion of the university's commitment to defense research and the sudden distinction of academic fields relating to technical and managerial training led some faculty members to perceive their disciplines, and their departments, as losing broad support. Partially in response to this wartime attack on the liberal arts, Stanford University took a somewhat unusual, and in President Wilbur's words, a "bold step . . . in the midst of a war where the emphasis is upon other phases of education and culture."[102] In the fall of 1942, the university opened a School of Humanities.

The School of Humanities

Following the outbreak of war in Europe in 1939, the esteemed novelist and essayist C.S. Lewis delivered his sermon "Learning in Wartime," in which he addressed the seeming hypocrisy of continuing academic study while war raged in Europe.[103] Wasn't doing so analogous to "fiddling while Rome burns?" Lewis asked his students rhetorically, "How can you be so frivolous and selfish as to think of anything but the war?" In response, Lewis suggested that the European conflict created no new dilemma in students' lives but, instead, simply aggravated the already tenuous state of humanity, so much so that it could no longer be ignored. "Human life," said Lewis, "has always been lived on the edge of a precipice," yet unlike insects that first seek "the material welfare and security of the hive," humanity chooses to ignore the threats posed to it, pursuing truth in the face of extinction. "Plausible reasons," he preached, "have never been lacking for putting off all merely cultural activities until some imminent danger has been averted or some crying injustice put right. But humanity long ago chose to neglect those plausible reasons. They wanted knowledge and beauty now, and would not wait for the suitable moment that never comes."[104]

Lewis's lecture reflected many scholars' anxiety that the war crisis would undermine non-technical disciplines. Their apprehension was well founded. "The immediate occasion of this book is the war," wrote Mark Van Doren of Columbia University in his wartime defense of the liberal arts, "which in the United States has almost completely suspended liberal education."[105] Van Doren did not overstate the case. When the *New York Times* reported on the formation of the ASTP, it headlined the announcement, "New Plans Suspend Liberal Education" and quoted Secretary of War Henry Stimson as stating, "The immediate necessity is to win this war, and unless we do that there is no hope for liberal education in this country."[106] *Time* magazine put the issue even more bluntly, "War has," it reported, "violently discombobulated the teaching of the liberal arts."[107]

Colleges and universities across the United States dramatically curbed liberal arts offerings as higher education institutions became increasingly militarized during the war years. "In all sections of the country," noted *New York Times* reporter Benjamin Fine, "the emphasis now is upon technical training."[108] In some cases, higher education administrators altered academic programs to meet perceived war needs, while in others student interest catalyzed curricular modifications.[109] At the University of Wisconsin, for instance, *Time* reported that the "biggest change" on campus in 1941 was the decrease in students studying the humanities, down 33 percent, while engineering was up more than 25 percent.[110] By 1943, Western Reserve University registered a 250 percent increase in freshman enrollments in science and technical courses, with chemistry enrollment registering its highest rate in the institution's 117-year history.[111] At Colgate University, an institution with a traditionally strong liberal arts program, enrollments in physics rose 76 percent, in chemistry 60 percent, and in mathematics 100 percent.[112] Whether through administrative edict or student choice, humanities programs throughout the United States suffered from a perceived lack of relevance during World War II.[113]

The issue of relevance was not unfamiliar to humanities scholars. Debates in the United States regarding the utility and practicality of the humanities long predated the attack on Pearl Harbor.[114] Yet during the First World War, humanities faculty were no less likely than scholars of scientific disciplines to offer their services to the state in return for extrinsic rewards. As historian Carol Gruber has indicated, "Not only scientists but humanists and social scientists as well sensed in the war situation an opportunity to win confidence in their disciplines, to stimulate interest in them, and to accomplish necessary reorganization and reform."[115] Historians, in particular, used wartime conditions to promote their field of study and establish newly defined "public" identities.[116] Although later criticized for their active participation in promoting government propaganda through organizations such as the National Board for Historical Service, historians nevertheless represented the zeal with which many humanists pursued supporting the nation's military aims.[117]

Faculty support of the Allied effort during World War I corresponded with an equally significant development in liberal arts education—the "Western Civilization" course.[118] As historian Gilbert Allardyce has demonstrated, World War I fostered a shared sense of identity among the United States, England, and Western Europe as a "great Atlantic civilization, formed from a common history, challenged by a common enemy, and destined to a common future."[119] This new conception of America, which contrasted dramatically with previous portrayals of the United States as a "pioneer" nation "formed by the frontier experience," combined with prewar ideas related to curriculum reform in higher education to give birth to a course in Western Civilization at Columbia University in 1919.[120] Eventually spreading to colleges and universities throughout the nation, including Stanford University, "Western Civ" became the central requirement of many institutions' course offerings, bolstering the disciplines that comprised the course and increasing the institutional investment in those departments.[121]

Following the attack on Pearl Harbor in 1941, liberal arts faculty at Stanford University seemed to initially follow the path of their World War I predecessors. Philosophy Department Chairman Harold Chapman Brown, for instance, noted the important contribution he believed his field might make to this new war effort by informing Wilbur, "The Department does not consider itself as remote from service as the layman might be inclined to believe, for a part of our regular work is the investigation and clarification of ideologies lying behind political, ethical, and social conflicts."[122] Yet unlike during World War I, when the conflict energized liberal arts faculty and their disciplines, World War II put liberal education "on the defensive."[123] As Gruber writes, during World War II "the complexities of the relationship between intellect and power were exposed" when, among other instances, scholars resigned from positions in the Office of War Information (OWI) because "they were *not* permitted to tell the truth about the war as they saw it" [emphasis original].[124] As a result, Elmer Davis, head of the OWI, informed President Roosevelt that the "intellectual" conceived of OWI policies as "an intolerable limitation on his freedom of thought and speech," and that "you cannot do much with people who are convinced that they are the sole authorized custodians of Truth."[125]

Partially in response to these developments, members of the Stanford faculty in the School of Letters, consisting of the departments of Classics, English, Germanic Languages, Religion, Romance Languages, and Slavic Languages, joined with members of the departments of History, Philosophy, Music, Graphic Arts, and Speech and Drama to support the opening of a distinct undergraduate school dedicated to the study of the humanities.[126] At first glance, Stanford's establishing a School of Humanities during the war crisis seemed an anomaly. Indeed, *Time* magazine prefaced its announcement of the school by reporting that the university's "shrewd" president and trustees knew "how to take advantage of a trend by going against it."[127] In actuality, the school's founding has a discernible history that was rooted in both prewar and wartime events and situated in a national context.

In 1943, the American Council of Learned Societies, an organization concerned with the "place of the humanities in education at all levels," published *Liberal Education Re-examined: Its Role in a Democracy*.[128] Issued in the midst of the war, the report declared the United States "urgently in need of liberally minded and well-educated teachers in charge of programs of study which offer students a sound liberal education as a preparation for responsible citizenship and human living."[129] Seemingly a defense of the liberal arts during World War II, *Liberal Education Re-examined* actually grew out of a symposium on humanistic studies held at the council's annual meeting in 1936.[130] Conference participants proposed a study inquiring into the status of humanities education in schools, colleges, and universities throughout the United States.[131] Council members specifically directed the investigating committee *not* to formulate a "defense of the humanities," but instead to make a "positive and constructive effort to develop the full values of the contribution that the humanities must make to education and life."[132]

The authors of *Liberal Education Re-examined* drew conclusions that revealed the concerns many scholars shared prior to World War II that the United States had developed into an industrial bureaucracy plagued by a "lack of genuine culture."[133] Proclaiming liberal education the only solution to the "superficiality of many of our standards, the poverty of many of our individual experiences, and the inadequacy of our social consciousness," the authors asserted, "humanistic faculties have lost their way and forfeited public confidence."[134] America's educational institutions, according to the report, were failing to preserve and transmit the nation's cultural heritage to succeeding generations. Combined with an increasing concern over higher education's curricular direction (including, among other issues, the elective system and the rise of vocational and professional training), this sentiment led many colleges and universities to reemphasize the importance of the humanities during the interwar period. In a 1940 survey of academic programs in higher education, for instance, Patricia Beesley of Columbia University indicated that colleges and universities throughout the United States had created more than 30 humanities courses between 1928 and 1940, a clear indicator for Beesley of what she labeled the "current revival of the Humanities in American education."[135]

Conditions of war, then, beginning in Europe in 1939 and extending to the United States in late 1941, did not cause the nation to reexamine liberal education as much as it accelerated those discussions by posing an immediate threat to the study of the liberal arts in higher education. As with the American Council of Learned Societies, which began its work prior to the outbreak of hostilities in Europe, Stanford University's board of trustees voted to establish the School of

Humanities on July 22, 1941, five months prior to America's declaration of war. And like the work of the council, Stanford founded the school, not in an effort to defend the humanities, but rather as an assertion of their fundamental place in undergraduate education.[136] As a result, the rationale for the school's establishment initially reflected a discernible detachment from wartime events.[137] "It is clear," noted Wilbur in explaining the school's origin:

> that some reasonable balance must be maintained in education between the pressure for early specialization and the need for a coherent view of human activities—the need also to train critical minds capable not simply of acting but also of distinguishing that which is excellent from that which is second rate. The power to make enlightened choices will result from a coordinated curriculum in the liberal arts designed to train the student through guidance and personal supervision to think clearly and coherently; to have a many-sided grasp of the past development of our civilization and its relation to the philosophic, social, and cultural forces shaping the modern world. The interlocked and co-ordinated planning toward this end by the combined departments of the School of Humanities . . . makes possible a School program so synthesized as to be both comprehensive and unified. Its aim is the unified education of a man or woman.[138]

Yet when *Time* magazine announced the opening of Stanford's School of Humanities several months later, it did not locate the school's roots in scholarly concerns over the nature of students' humanistic development. Instead, the magazine proposed that Stanford's leaders were responding directly to wartime conditions by acting "on the belief" that future national security was wholly dependent upon a liberally educated citizenry.[139] Indeed, as the development of a defense research agenda and the establishment of programs such as ESMWT and the ASTP further aligned Stanford's educational purposes with the nation's military objectives, university administrators increasingly defined the school's role as a citadel of democracy. By the time it began enrolling students for the fall of 1942, for instance, Wilbur had modified his rationale for the school to reflect the significance that Americans ascribed to liberal education as an essential contributor to democracy's survival in the postwar era. "With the marked emphasis now given to technological education in our universities, due to the war," Wilbur claimed, "we are in danger of losing sight of the great importance of the humanities and the social sciences in the training of our men and women. We hope to win the war with technologically trained men, but certainly without the humanities and the social sciences, we are likely to lose the peace."[140]

Throughout the war years, numerous public figures voiced concerns that a war won at the cost of liberal education would put democracy's future, and the nation's future security, at risk. "The destruction of the tradition of the liberal arts at this crisis in our history," declared Wendell Willkie, "would be a crime comparable, in my opinion, with the burning of books by the Nazis. . . . Burn your books—or, what amounts to the same thing, neglect your books—and you will lose freedom as surely as if you were to invite Hitler and his henchmen to rule over you."[141]

California Governor and future Supreme Court Chief Justice Earl Warren concurred with Willkie, declaring in a 1943 commencement address:

> History leaves no room for doubt that the greatest civilizations have always been those with the best understanding of the broad scope of application necessary for progress—in other words the best liberal education.
>
> In a technological age such as this there arises a danger that the full meaning of the word education will become obscured by the urgent occupational demands of immediate objectives. . . .
>
> For us to permit the educational specialization necessitated by war to become the permanent pattern of our educational future would be no more than placing reliance for our future advancement upon mechanical achievements. It would mean the abandonment of knowledge as an accomplishment to be enjoyed, the forsaking of the humanizing influence of broad understanding for the perfection in materialistic distortions which ignore man's individuality.[142]

Harvard University President James B. Conant echoed Warren's sentiment, writing in the *New York Times*, "Those who express grave concern about the future of the country if the liberal arts were destroyed are entirely right. For there can be no question that the basis of a free society is the education which that society provides."[143] General Omar Bradley, reflecting on his troops' understanding of the "political and philosophical origins" of their country, similarly observed, "When I recall the political illiteracy of our young troops at the start of the war, I am moved to charge education with gross dereliction in its responsibility to teach knowledge of the human values at issue in the world.... Good citizenship springs from an appreciation of the great values of our institutions and from active participation in them."[144]

Appearing in a wide range of popular publications, statements such as these demonstrated broad concerns over the decline of the humanities during the World War II period and directed the public's attention toward it.[145] The resulting national dialogue over the value of the liberal arts in promoting civic mindedness among students led historian and philosopher I.L. Kandel to declare the war years "one of the most significant and fruitful periods in the history of colleges and universities because of the nation-wide discussion and the extensive literature on the meaning of a liberal education and the methods for achieving it."[146]

Participants in this discussion employed a range of strategies to examine the status of humanities education in the United States. Organizations such as the Association of American Colleges appointed commissions to study how liberal education was being "blacked out" as a result of the war.[147] Private foundations conducted studies of the potential "rebirth of liberal education" following the war, such as the one produced by Fred B. Millett of Wesleyan University for the Humanities Division of the Rockefeller Foundation.[148] At Harvard University, President Conant appointed a committee "to consider the infusion of the liberal and humane tradition into our entire educational system," resulting in the widely distributed *General Education in a Free Society*.[149] And colleges and universities throughout the nation held academic conferences to investigate the war's influence on the study of the humanities, with Stanford University serving as the primary location for these meetings in the western United States.

On May 7–8, 1943, Stanford held its first of a projected series of annual humanities conferences. "The Humanities Look Ahead" attracted 175 delegates from throughout the western states, no small number given the travel restrictions in place during World War II.[150] Organized around the theme "The Humanities in the War and Postwar World," conference papers focused on the war period as a defining moment in the survival of the humanities in higher education. "If the speakers represent a fair sampling of humanists in America," claimed one observer, "it is clear that the present period of war has been interpreted as a call to attack, not to maintain a forlorn hope."[151] One reviewer reported the conference as "characteristically American," with delegates engaged both in "self-criticism" of humanities programs in the United States and in asserting the necessity of American leadership in the postwar era.[152] "Now that the arts, true science, and philosophy are all 'dislodged and beaten almost beyond surviving there in Europe and Asia,'" the reviewer quoted one delegate, the United States "had leadership in this field thrust upon her."[153] Although higher education institutions held similar conferences in other regions of the country, such as Vanderbilt University in the South, some considered Stanford's the "most notable" effort to engage scholars in examining the role of the humanities in educating for democracy in wartime.[154] More importantly for the university itself, the meetings provided Stanford an opportunity to showcase its newest school's academic program.[155]

When the School of Humanities opened in the fall of 1942, it offered coursework for students majoring either in the humanities or a "constituent department."[156] Stanford placed freshmen and sophomores in the school's Lower Division and introduced them to a curriculum rooted in the "fundamental fields of human interest."[157] Lower Division courses were organized into three groups, Arts and Letters, Natural Sciences and Mathematics, and Social Sciences, with students responsible for fulfilling requirements in each of these groups. Once they completed these requirements, students moved to the school's Upper Division, where humanities majors began required coursework offered by newly appointed humanities faculty. Grouped under the theme "The Development of Modern Man," the school's first three upper-level courses, "The Nature of Man," "The Nature of Civilization," and "The Nature of Personality," examined "the study of man as a rational and artistic being seeking to understand himself and the world in which he lives."[158]

To teach these courses, Stanford appointed four new faculty members in the humanities: Assistant Professors Arthur Bestor, Jeffery Smith, and Desmond Powell, and Professor Lewis Mumford.[159] Of the four, recognized historian, sociologist, urban planner, and architectural critic Lewis Mumford provided Stanford with a nationally respected figure and defender of the humanities' role in fostering democratic and humanitarian values. Proclaiming him "no intellectual opportunist," *Time* magazine quoted Mumford as envisioning at Stanford "a chance for me to put into practice the concept of education I have had for many years, which is that the humanities and science are not in inherent conflict but have become separated in the 20th Century. Now their essential unity must be re-emphasized."[160] Mumford developed this theme in his courses and made it a central element in his description of the school. "The re-integration of the human personality and the re-establishment of our whole civilization on a stable co-operative basis are two co-ordinate parts of the same problem," Mumford claimed. "They rest on our capacity, as educable human beings, to experience and understand life as a related whole. . . . In the light of this general statement, we are perhaps in a position to understand better the role of the new School of the Humanities at Stanford."[161]

Not even as outspoken a critic of the war's impact on higher education as Mumford, however, could completely defend the School of Humanities from the pressures of mobilization. Consisting of courses detached from the war in curricular content, the school's academic program nevertheless became increasingly rationalized by its potential contribution to the war effort. Following the military's request that the university train recruits for service in occupied nations, for instance, Wilbur remarked:

> There is a proposal now to train men to act as administrators of territories taken over from the enemy. This means peaceful organization and requires a knowledge of the language, literature, folklore, social customs, economic life, religion and government of the peoples involved. . . . Yet for the most part these subjects are now considered secondary, are classified as "liberal education" which must step aside during the war period. As I see it, there has never been a more important period for Stanford to emphasize the humanities than the one that is just ahead of us.[162]

Wilbur's rhetorical reorientation of the school's mission was undoubtedly strategic. In November 1941, he wrote a letter of support to accompany a Rockefeller Foundation grant proposal in which he asserted Stanford's reliance on the School of Humanities to implement military programs that included instruction in foreign languages, geography, and history.[163] Although this role for the school had powerful appeal—the following May Wilbur accepted a three-year, $47,500 grant from the foundation—it nevertheless had serious consequences for the university's historic role of educating students to take their place as competent citizens in American society.[164]

Conclusion

What began as a rhetorical reorientation of the School of Humanities' founding purpose soon took the very real form of wartime programming. Increasing its emphasis on war-related studies, the school began offering full-time, intensive Japanese courses "to supply more rapidly the demands of the government for persons able to use the Japanese language."[165] In session six days a week, the course consisted of three hours of classes in the morning, three hours of conversation drill in the afternoon, and a four-hour exam each Saturday. Moreover, the School of Humanities' first dean, John W. Dodds, announced his intent to establish a "regional major" through which students might study the "language, literature, philosophy, art, history, religion, geography, social customs, governmental organization, and the cultural geography of one country or region."[166] Addressing a memo to humanities faculty in November 1942, Dodds proposed the regional major as "a small part of Stanford's war effort," promoting it on the grounds that it could provide training for recruits to participate in the reconstruction of Axis nations.[167] "A regional major might well be defended merely as a valid major in general education," Dodds wrote, "but its point for young people today would be by way of preparation for service during the war and post-war period in occupied or liberated territories, as well as in other countries where there may be a need for Americans with a rich background in national cultures."[168]

Further capitalizing on wartime needs, Dodds requested an additional appropriation from the Rockefeller Foundation to develop a program in "Oriental Studies," asserting:

> It is becoming clearer all the time that the problems which the program attacks will not be solved with the coming of peace, but will be continuing problems, demanding a totally new cultural reorientation. The United States will have mighty responsibilities in the post-war Orient, and in our present depths of insularity we are but poorly equipped to deal with them. . . .
>
> Already various government services are searching desperately for people whose knowledge of the Far East—linguistic, geographical, cultural—equips them for service in the theatres of war. Those who can be of use there must have a deep understanding of Oriental cultures, traditions. . . .
>
> It might be thought by some that in critical times a university should postpone an extension of its program into these fields. But if the concept of the School of Humanities at Stanford is valid, such an extension toward the Orient, as well as the traditional concern with Europe, is implicitly necessary—and more than ever necessary now, in the light of world history in the past year.[169]

Although Rockefeller declined Dodds's request, by June 1943 the School of Humanities had nevertheless begun satisfying the demands of military mobilization, offering the regional major to students interested in concentrating their studies in the Far East as well as Central Europe, France, Hispanic America, the Western Mediterranean, Greece, and Russia.[170]

In his final presidential report, Wilbur explained the School of Humanities' partial realignment with wartime needs, writing, "It was inevitable that the work of the school . . . should have been severely affected by the increasing pressures of war and the necessity of adapting university curricula and programs to the needs of the various Army training programs which have come to Stanford."[171] Prior to his departure from Stanford's presidency, Wilbur further glossed over his previous claim that the university had established the school to educate students "to have a many-sided grasp of the past development of our civilization and its relation to the philosophic, social, and cultural forces shaping the modern world."[172] Instead, he suggested that Stanford had anticipated the military's need to train recruits in foreign language and area studies and had devised a curricular program in the humanities in part to meet this demand.

In December 1944, Donald Tresidder issued his first presidential report. Breaking tradition with Wilbur's established format for the publication, Tresidder opened with an extensive letter to the Board of Trustees. "At the end of my first year as president," Tresidder wrote:

> the activities and purposes of Stanford University revolve, as do those of all the nation, about the securing of a complete Allied victory. The preservation of our democracy depends upon our winning the war; so too does the preservation of freedom of teaching and research in our institutions of higher learning, for without victory there can be no such freedom. Until victory comes, then, Stanford will continue to devote its resources to the country's war effort.[173]

A strong proponent of increasing Stanford's ties to industry and the federal government, Tresidder's inauguration ushered in a renewed sense of urgency in reorienting Stanford's campus-wide operations towards serving as an arsenal of democracy. For the School of Humanities, this meant exploiting its location on the West Coast by developing a "Pacific-Asiatic-Russian" study program, a fully developed successor to Dodds's initial Oriental Studies proposal. The program, which led to a bachelor of arts degree in the humanities with a concentration in either China, Japan, Russia, or Southeast Asia and the Pacific, was specifically intended to prepare military officers to govern occupied enemy lands through the Army's Civil Affairs Training School, which Stanford began hosting in 1944.[174]

As with many college and university administrators who confronted declining student enrollments and tuition revenues during World War II, Stanford's leaders recognized the financial reward and institutional prestige associated with war service and negotiated defense contracts with industry, the federal government, and the military. The ESMWT program provided the medium through which war-related disciplines were financially supported and paved the way for other, even more lucrative, contracts with the federal government and the armed forces. In turn, programs such as the ASTP had a profound impact on the university, militarizing, at least in the short run, Stanford's collegiate environment and campus culture. Over the long term, World War II provided a catalyst for the university to more clearly define and expand its defense research agenda. Although Stanford had not obtained as many research contracts during the war years as administrators had hoped, university officials had by 1945 positioned the institution to broaden its defense research program.

The evolution of its School of Humanities, however, particularly the multiple objectives university administrators assigned it between 1941 and 1945, reveals the complexity of the challenges confronting institutions of higher education during World War II. As a product of the nationwide reexamination of liberal education begun in the 1930s, the School of Humanities sought to reaffirm the importance of the humanities in fulfilling Stanford's prewar educational mission. Yet almost immediately upon America's declaring war, Stanford's leadership reconceptualized the school's previously articulated institutional purpose. At first the university claimed, as did many in the United States, that winning the war while destroying liberal education would ultimately lead to democracy's defeat in the postwar era. As administrators delineated more practical wartime roles for specific disciplines within the humanities, however, rhetorical support for liberal education shifted toward contributing more directly to the war effort. Recruits were "trained"—not "educated"—in foreign languages, history, and geography, with the explicit understanding that such training would prove beneficial in military positions abroad. Although the school continued to act as a citadel of democracy throughout the war years, pragmatic war aims consistently eroded its civic function.

University leaders demonstrated the value they attached to war-related purposes in a bulletin issued by Stanford's external relations and development personnel during World War II. Entitled "Stanford and the War," the bulletin publicized work being conducted at Stanford and highlighted the university's many wartime achievements, dramatically claiming, "Stanford today is a university at war, training experts in a score of fields, including chemistry, biology, physics, engineering and medicine. Every few months another quota of these trained technicians leaves the campus to take a place in the civilian or military war service of the nation. That is one of our country's greatest needs in the technological war which we are fighting."[175]

After reviewing the contributions that the schools of Physical Science, Engineering, Health, and Law were making to the Allied cause, the bulletin publicized the achievements of the School of Humanities, although in a manner that indicated institutional confusion over its exact wartime role. Emphasizing the humanities as "one of the outposts to keep alive an awareness of the civilization our country is fighting to defend," the bulletin proclaimed that "unless we can keep alive such fundamental American concepts, any military victory, however glorious, will be barren."[176] In the very next paragraph, however, the bulletin proposed a strikingly different purpose for the school. "Meanwhile," it reported, "there is immediate need for young men and women trained in the much-neglected Japanese, Chinese and Russian languages, as well as in the better-known foreign languages, and we are therefore emphasizing that aspect of our program."[177] The message to potential donors was clear; the university was actively engaged in national service by directly assisting the Allies in winning the war and the School of Humanities was a part of this undertaking. The final page of the publication solidified this ideal: "Gifts to Stanford, unrestricted or designated, serve the country's war effort as well as the university, for with strengthened resources Stanford will do an even better war job than it is now doing."[178]

Ultimately, Stanford's correlation of victory in the war and support for the university gave birth to an important institutional legacy. What Tresidder set out to accomplish when he called a meeting in Yosemite the weekend of December 5, 1941, eventually came to pass.[179] Stanford developed into an internationally respected university in the postwar era, investing its human and material resources in federal and industrial research and acquiring millions of dollars worth of contracts during the Cold War. By 1960, 39 percent of the university's operating budget came from federal support, with 80 percent of that amount going directly to research in engineering and physics.[180] The acquisition of these contracts significantly influenced Stanford's educational mission and was a clear result of university administrators' strategic efforts to tap into suddenly available, resource-rich opportunities generated by war-related demands. Although many at the time conceived of serving the national interest as an inherently positive development, this legacy would return to haunt Stanford less than two decades later as a new war forced the university's leadership to reconsider both its investment in national defense and the security-oriented institutional purpose it had adopted.

3

Palo Alto Schools at War

When the schools closed on Friday, December 5, they had many purposes and they followed many roads to achieve those purposes. When the schools opened on Monday, December 8, they had but one dominant purpose—complete, intelligent, and enthusiastic cooperation in the war effort. The very existence of free schools anywhere in the world depends upon the achievement of that purpose.[1]

—The Educational Policies Commission, 1942

During World War II, U.S. educational leaders and professional organizations issued a series of policy statements signifying their eagerness to transform public schools into arsenals of democracy.[2] This chapter's opening quote, from a report entitled "A War Policy for American Schools," illustrates the speed and conviction with which many embraced the idea of modifying public education to meet the demands of mobilization. Drafted by the Educational Policies Commission immediately following the United States' declaration of war, the proclamation is notable both for its bold assertion of schools' "one dominant purpose" and for the way it broke with the commission's previously articulated position. Published in 1940 under the title "Education and the Defense of American Democracy," the commission had urged that schools "come to grips with the needs of the hour" by redirecting resources towards "increasing the civic understanding, the loyalties and the intellectual competence of millions of citizens." The commission, moreover, had recommended that each school accomplish this objective *without interfering with its regular program* [emphasis added]."[3]

Through a case study of the Palo Alto Unified School District, this chapter investigates the extent to which wartime secondary schools actually transformed their operations to reflect a single dominating purpose.[4] Beginning with an examination of the degree of curricular modification that occurred in Palo Alto High School as a result of wartime pressures, the chapter's first section demonstrates how the district expanded the school's curricular program to include war-related classes such as aeronautics and adjusted prewar classes such as physical education to provide military training. These alterations, however, occurred almost exclusively in classes peripheral to the school's core academic curriculum. Indeed, an analysis of the wartime academic program reveals a high degree of constancy rather than change, belying educational leaders' claims that they would significantly alter the secondary school program to serve the nation's wartime needs.

The chapter's second section examines school officials' efforts to provide students with greater vocational preparation for employment in defense industries and for service in the armed forces. Applying for generous federal grants through the Vocational Education for National Defense program, Palo Alto established its first vocational day school during World War II—the Peninsula Defense Training Center—offering pre-employment and pre-induction training for enrolled secondary school students and those who had dropped out of school as well as supplementary employment training for adolescents and adults already working in defense plants and shipyards. The success of this wartime vocational experiment convinced district leaders that vocational education would be an essential component of any comprehensive school system in the postwar era. They also believed that as the end of the war approached, demand for specific forms of training would recede and be replaced by the need for a more diversified vocational program to serve the district's non-college bound students and returning veterans seeking to advance their educational attainment through the G.I. Bill. As part of their postwar agenda, therefore, school officials proposed establishing a junior college consisting of grades 10 through 14 to provide "terminal-technical training" for non-college bound students as well as a liberal arts curriculum for those continuing on to higher education.

Although not Palo Alto's first effort to establish a junior college, district officials believed that wartime conditions created a timely moment to bring such a proposal to fruition. Palo Alto residents, however, perceived the wartime expansion of vocational education solely as an emergency measure, effective in meeting the demands of mobilization but unnecessary in peacetime. The conflict that developed between the district's advocacy of an institutionalized vocational program, even in the context of a junior college, and residents' eventual refusal to support this proposal illuminates the enduring dilemmas surrounding the role of vocationalism in American public education.

In contrast to the considerable debate within Palo Alto over how to meet the academic and vocational needs of college bound and non-college bound students in the war and postwar era, there was general agreement regarding the appropriateness of modifying secondary school extracurricular activities to advance the nation's war effort. Students bought and sold war stamps and bonds, joined aviation and Junior Red Cross clubs in record numbers, and worked to harvest crops in the midst of a wartime labor shortage. The final section of this chapter investigates these undertakings, relying primarily on student-produced evidence such as newspapers and yearbooks as well as oral history interviews conducted with homefront veterans who were Palo Alto students during the war years.

The experience of the Palo Alto Unified School District between 1941 and 1945 illustrates the tensions associated with reorienting public education in the United States towards meeting the demands of a national crisis. The community's secondary schools provided students with opportunities to simultaneously participate in the Allied cause and prepare for a role on the homefront or the battlefront following graduation. The schools' actions led to a modification of extracurricular activities as well as a temporary expansion of vocational education in Palo Alto. Constancy in the high school's core curriculum, however, and residents' ultimate rejection of the junior college proposal reflected the community's dedication to students' broader civic education. To many, Palo Alto High School's academic program represented a democratic project on which residents were unwilling to compromise. Their commitment indicates the sturdiness of an American attitude towards secondary schooling rooted in long-standing social values and beliefs regarding public education's central purpose in preparing students for democratic citizenship, even in wartime.

Constancy and Change in the Wartime Curriculum

"Palo Alto" takes its name from the Spanish for "high tree," a redwood that was a landmark for eighteenth century expeditions into what is now known as the San Francisco Bay Area.[5] Although settlements in the region were established throughout the 1800s, the founding of the city of Palo Alto was mostly a product of Leland and Jane Stanford's desire for a retreat from San Francisco city life. The 8,000 acres of their "Palo Alto Stock Farm" would eventually provide the site on which they would build a university in memory of their only son—Leland Jr.—who became ill and died at the age of 15 while traveling with his parents in Europe in 1884. The Stanfords' initial plans, however, included more than simply an institution of higher education. They envisioned an educational enterprise incorporating a system of schooling from kindergarten through graduate study and a village that would serve as a home to students, administrators, and faculty.[6] Although the Stanfords eventually scaled back their building plans, their vision for Palo Alto nevertheless became a reality.

By 1940, Palo Alto was, indeed, a small municipality consisting of predominantly native-born, relatively well-educated white residents and a small number of other racial and ethnic groups, including Asian Americans, African Americans, and Chicanos.[7] Palo Alto's school district consisted of eight elementary schools, one junior high school (David Starr Jordan Junior High—named in honor of Stanford University's first president), and one high school. District enrollment that year was 2,912 students, with 70–75 percent of Palo Alto High School's graduates going on to some form of higher education, several of them literally across the street to Stanford University.[8] Students attended well-financed schools in a district that increased its assessed valuation of taxable property over a million dollars a year between 1936 and 1944; a 50 percent total increase over this eight-year period, it represented more than triple the corresponding percent increase in student attendance.[9]

On December 7, 1941, however, community members were suddenly jolted out of their suburban bliss as reports of the Japanese attack on Pearl Harbor began filtering into the city.[10] Eleven-year-old Sally Allen was lying in bed listening to the radio when she heard reports from Oahu. "Boy, I woke up so fast," she recalled. "It was really, really something. And then I woke my sisters up and we just sort of listened to the radio and called our friends."[11] Joan Paulin, who was also 11 at the time, remembered that her father enthusiastically urged U.S. intervention in the European conflict long before the attack. Having befriended a young Jewish girl recently arrived in Palo Alto with her parents as refugees from Austria, Paulin embarrassingly recalled being overjoyed when she heard the news from Hawaii.[12] Paula Berka also had vivid memories of the morning of the attack. "We kids got up fairly early and played baseball. And I remember somebody coming out to the field and saying, 'The Japs attacked us.' So I went home and found my parents listening closely to the radio."[13]

Prior to that day, the school community's biggest news had been the announced departure of district superintendent J. R. Overturf and his replacement by Charles W. Lockwood. Although not formally assuming the superintendency until January 1942, Lockwood announced his plans for Palo Alto's schools in late 1941. In reference to the district he had supervised in southern California over the previous several years, Lockwood declared, "In Laguna Beach schools we have taken a definite stand in an effort to teach the basic subjects—and if we are accused of having overlooked the capital 'P' aspects of Progressive Education we shall have to plead guilty."[14] By slighting the Progressive reform movement in American education, Lockwood implied his commitment to "traditional" school programs emphasizing the "three R's" while rejecting Progressive methods developed to meet the "needs and interests" of the student. Immediately following the attack on Pearl Harbor, however, Lockwood shifted his rhetorical stance, publicly claiming that he would redirect the city's school system "to meet any needs dictated by the war."[15]

Lockwood's conversion was hardly exceptional. In 1942, U.S. Commissioner of Education John Studebaker called on "the schools of this country" to "engage in an all-out campaign to help win the war, even though it would mean drastically modified curricula."[16] That same year the editor of *The American School Board Journal* issued a similar declaration while assessing schools' national progress in revising curricular programs. "No schools," he wrote, "can be conducted during this war year 'as usual'. . . . All schools and particularly the high schools have revised their courses of study. Aviation education, new emphasis on mathematics and the sciences, physical education for all pupils, industrial arts of a purposive type, and direct training for essential mechanical trades are more thorough and more rapid than ever were dreamt possible by schoolmen."[17] Moreover, in January 1943 the Educational Policies Commission again proclaimed the importance of altering the nation's secondary school curricula in response to the war. "To expect that the secondary-school program can be retained substantially as it was," wrote the commission, "with superficial additions here and there to acknowledge the fact that the United States is engaged in a war of survival, is to avoid reality. . . . The war must profoundly modify the entire program of secondary education."[18]

A report released in December 1942 by the research division of the National Education Association suggested that such wartime policy proposals were being implemented.[19] The study claimed that over 70 percent of respondents indicated an "increased emphasis" on war-related subjects such as science, mathematics, and physical education, while between 30 and 40 percent noted a similar increase in social studies, home economics, and commercial subjects.[20] Although suggesting that wartime educational reform was being undertaken nationally, this data conflicted with a similar study of California's secondary schools conducted by the Stanford University School of Education.[21] In the Stanford report, comparatively fewer schools reported war-related changes to their academic courses of study, with 52 percent of schools indicating modifications to health and physical education programs, 47 percent to mathematics courses, 43 percent to the social studies program, and 36 percent to science offerings.[22] Regardless of popular rhetoric urging the revolutionary transformation of secondary school curricula to meet wartime demands, modifications to core academic programs throughout California seemed relatively minor. This was especially true for Palo Alto.

In 1943, more than a year after Lockwood became superintendent, the Palo Alto High School student newspaper, *The Campanile*, announced the district's intention to dramatically modify school curricula. Under the headline "Curriculum Changes Disclosed to Seniors; Four Classifications Offered to Students," the newspaper reported, "Wartime changes in the Palo Alto High School curriculum were disclosed to senior students. . . . These changes provide an opportunity for students in the junior and senior years to face realistically their obligation to their country. The specific courses to be offered will prepare them for a definite place in the war program after their graduation from high school."[23] The community's local newspaper, the *Daily Palo Alto Times*, also announced the curricular revision, noting that the focus of the school curriculum for the duration of the war would involve "courses to prepare students for essential war industries or community service."[24]

The new school program reportedly divided the curriculum into four categories: Pre-Induction, College, Industry, and Community Service. Although courses in each of the categories overlapped, students were advised to self-select one of the four classifications. Administrators, for instance, recommended that girls whose academic achievement indicated they would not attend college, prepare for war industry or community service. Courses such as Fundamentals of Electricity, Automotive Mechanics, and Radio were reportedly offered to students preparing for military service, while those training for war industry had the opportunity to take classes in Aircraft Sheet-Metal, Acetylene Welding, and Blueprint Reading. Students planning on community service work were encouraged to choose courses "leading to employment in offices, stores, and in food production jobs."[25] The school's administration also announced the creation of nine-week classes related to the war, including First Aid, Problems of War and Peace, Map Reading, Forest Fire Control, and Harvest Labor Training."[26]

Had these reported modifications reflected actual reforms in the Palo Alto school district, the impact of the war on the city's secondary schools would have been remarkable. An analysis of course offerings between 1939 and 1945, however, indicates that although the Palo Alto High School curriculum did undergo some change as a result of wartime pressure, the school's core academic program remained relatively constant throughout the duration of the conflict.

Using data from the "October Reports," filed annually by the Palo Alto Unified School District with the California State Department of

Education, Table 3.1 reports the number of class periods of each subject offered per week at Palo Alto High School in October of the years 1939 to 1945.[27] As the data indicate, required English classes dominated the school program prior to and during World War II, with approximately 130 periods of English taken by students each week in 26 separate classes. The number of English electives offered also remained constant during the war years, with courses in journalism recording a minor increase while creative and free writing classes registered an equivalent decline.

In mathematics, the average number of periods of all levels of algebra offered prior to and during World War II remained constant, at roughly 47. The number of periods of geometry offered, however, increased from approximately 23 to 35. A two-class addition to the school schedule, this rise was most probably a result of the well-publicized need for engineers and other technical experts throughout the war years.[28]

Similarly, although science offerings declined overall from an average of 73 class periods per week prior to the war to 58 per week during the conflict, the greatest decline in this field of study occurred in biology. Physics offerings, on the other hand, remained constant. Like geometry, between 1942 and 1945 physics course taking was encouraged throughout the United States in an effort to increase the number of high school students with the basic mathematical and scientific preparation necessary to engage in further war-related technical training.

Foreign language offerings, extremely popular at Palo Alto High School before the war, with an estimated 112 class periods offered per week, remained relatively constant throughout the war, declining minimally to 98 class periods between 1942 and 1945. There was, however, a marked decrease in the total number of classes of French, German, and Latin offered. In contrast, the number of Spanish classes taken by students rose from 49 before the war to 56 during the war, reflecting the emphasis the United States placed on fostering greater "Inter-American" relations with Latin America nations during World War II.[29]

U.S. history offerings declined after 1941 from a prewar high of 60 class periods per week to a wartime low of 45. Social studies teachers, however, offered several courses explicitly addressing war-related

PALO ALTO SCHOOLS AT WAR   69

Table 3.1 Number of class periods offered per week, Palo Alto High School, 1939/45

- 1939/45 data represents the number of class periods offered per week, per course, in October of the year identified.
- Each class was held five periods per week and was 55 minutes in length.
- "Avg. '39–'41" and "Avg. '42–'45" represent the average number of class periods offered per week, per course, in October of the year identified.
- "Chg." represents the increase or decrease in the average number of class periods offered per week, per course, in 1942/45 compared with 1939/41.

Course Name	1939	1940	1941	1942	1943	1944	1945	Avg. '39–'41	Avg. '42–'45	Chg.
Aeronautics	–	–	–	5	–	–	–	0.0	1.25	+1.25
Auto Mech.	10	15	5	5	5	30	30	10.0	17.5	+7.50
Auto Skills	–	–	10	10	15	–	–	3.33	6.25	+2.92
Drafting	–	–	–	20	20	15	15	0.0	17.5	+17.5
General Shop	10	5	–	–	–	–	–	5.0	0.0	-5.00
Landscaping	5	–	5	–	–	–	–	3.33	0.0	-3.33
Mech. Draw.	5	10	20	–	–	–	–	11.67	0.0	11.67
Ad. Mch. Drw.	5	–	–	–	–	–	–	1.67	0.0	-1.67
Printing	5	10	10	5	5	5	5	8.33	5.0	-3.33
Radio	–	–	–	–	–	–	5	0.0	1.25	+1.25
Woodwork	5	10	10	10	5	5	5	8.33	6.25	-2.08
Ad Woodwork	5	–	–	–	–	–	–	1.67	0.0	-1.67
Bank Practice	10	10	10	10	15	15	10	10.0	12.25	+2.25
Bookkeeping	10	10	10	10	5	5	5	10.0	6.25	-3.75
Office Trng.	–	–	–	5	–	–	5	0.0	2.5	+2.5
Public Spkng.	5	–	5	5	5	–	5	3.33	3.75	+0.42
Retail Selling	–	–	–	–	–	–	5	0.0	1.25	+1.25
Typing I	25	25	20	20	20	20	20	23.33	20.0	-3.33
Typing II	10	5	5	5	–	–	5	6.67	2.5	-4.17
Typing III	–	–	5	–	–	–	5	1.67	1.25	-0.42
Shorthand	10	15	10	10	10	5	5	11.67	7.5	-4.17
Ad. Shorthand	5	–	5	5	10	5	5	3.33	6.25	+2.92
Homemaking	–	–	–	10	5	5	5	0.0	6.25	+6.25
Child Care	–	–	–	5	–	–	–	0.0	1.25	+1.25
Family Rel.	5	5	5	–	5	–	–	5.0	2.5	-2.5
Foods	15	_	5	5	5	10	5	6.67	6.25	-0.42
Clothing	5	10	15	10	10	15	15	10.0	12.5	+2.5
Clothing III	5	–	–	–	–	–	–	1.67	0.0	-1.67
Color & Dsgn.	5	5	5	5	5	5	5	5.0	5.0	0.0

Table 3.1 (continued)

Course Name	1939	1940	1941	1942	1943	1944	1945	Avg. '39–'41	Avg. '42–'45	Chg.
Community Art	5	–	5	–	5	5	5	3.33	3.75	+0.42
Costume Dsgn.	10	5	5	5	5	–	5	6.67	3.75	-2.92
Crafts	5	5	_	–	–	–	–	3.33	0.0	-3.33
Int. Decoration	5	–	–	5	–	5	5	1.67	3.75	+2.08
Painting	–	–	–	–	–	–	5	0.0	1.25	+1.25
Photography	5	5	10	5	–	5	5	6.67	3.75	-2.92
Poster Work	5	–	–	–	–	–	–	1.67	0.0	-1.67
Sketching	10	10	10	5	–	–	5	10.0	2.5	-7.5
A Cappella	15	–	–	–	–	–	–	5.0	0.0	-5.0
Band	5	10	5		–	5	5	6.67	2.5	-4.17
Choir	10	_	10	10	10	10	5	6.67	8.75	+2.08
General Music	5	–	–	–	–	–	–	1.67	0.0	-1.67
Ind. Music Instr.	5	5	5	15	–	5	10	5.0	7.5	+2.5
Music Apprec.	5	–	–	–	–	–	–	1.67	0.0	-1.67
Orchestra	5	5	5	–	–	5	5	5.0	2.5	-2.5
El. Voice Trng.	5	–	–	–	–	–	–	1.67	0.0	-1.67
Voice Training	5	–	5	5	5	5	5	3.33	5.0	-1.67
Ad. Voice Trng.	5	–	–	–	–	–	–	1.67	0.0	-1.67
Crtv. Writing	5	–	–	–	–	–	–	1.67	0.0	-1.67
Drama	10	10	5	10	10	5	5	8.33	7.5	-0.83
English Grmr.	5	–	5	5	–	5	–	3.33	2.5	-0.83
English III (10)	40	55	50	55	50	55	55	48.33	53.75	+5.42
English V (11)	40	45	50	40	40	50	50	45.0	45.0	0.00
English VII (12)	30	40	40	25	30	35	45	36.67	33.75	-2.92
Free Writing	5	–	5	–	–	–	–	3.33	0.0	-3.33
Journalism	10	–	10	10	15	5	5	6.67	8.75	+2.08
Ad. Journalism	5	–	–	–	–	10	5	1.67	3.75	+2.08
Reading Skills	–	–	5	–	–	–	–	1.67	0.00	-1.67
World Lit.	5	–	–	–	–	5	5	1.67	2.5	+0.83
French I	5	10	5	5	5	5	10	6.67	6.25	-0.42
French III	10	10	10	5	5	5	5	10.0	5.0	-5.0
French V	10	5	5	5	–	–	–	6.67	1.25	-5.42
German I	5	5	5	5	5	5	10	5.0	6.25	+1.25
German III	10	5	5	5	5	5	5	6.67	5.0	-1.67
German V	5	5	5	–	–	–	–	5.0	0.0	-5.0

Table 3.1 (continued)

Course Name	1939	1940	1941	1942	1943	1944	1945	Avg. '39–'41	Avg. '42–'45	Chg.
Latin I	5	10	5	5	5	5	5	6.67	5.0	-1.67
Latin III	10	10	10	10	5	10	10	10.0	8.75	-1.25
Latin V & VII	5	5	5	5	–	5	5	5.0	3.75	-1.25
Spanish I	15	25	25	25	25	25	25	21.67	25.0	+3.33
Spanish II	5	–	10	–	–	–	–	5.0	0.0	-5.0
Spanish III	10	20	20	20	20	25	20	16.67	21.25	+4.58
Spanish V	10	5	–	10	10	10	10	5.0	10.0	+5.0
Biology	25	30	20	20	10	15	15	25.0	15.0	-10.0
Chemistry	30	30	30	25	20	25	30	30.0	25.0	-5.0
Gen. Phy. Scn.	5	5	–	–	–	–	–	3.33	0	-3.33
Physics	10	10	15	10	20	10	10	11.67	12.5	+0.83
Physiology	5	–	5	5	5	5	5	3.33	5.0	+1.67
Amer. Dem.	–	–	–	–	–	–	5	0.00	1.25	+1.25
Economic Prob.	5	–	–	5	–	–	–	1.67	1.25	-0.42
Politics	5	–	–	–	–	–	–	1.67	0.0	-1.67
Psychology	5	5	5	5	–	–	–	5.0	1.25	-3.75
Social Prob.	5	–	5	5	5	–	–	3.33	2.5	-0.83
U.S. History	50	55	60	45	50	45	50	55.0	47.5	-7.5
World Affairs	5	5	5	–	–	10	5	5.0	3.75	-1.25
World Civ.	10	5	5	5	5	10	10	6.67	7.5	+0.83
Algebra I	25	20	20	20	20	20	15	21.67	18.75	-2.92
Algebra III	15	–	20	15	15	20	20	11.67	17.5	+5.83
Inter. Algebra	15	–	–	–	–	5	10	5.0	3.75	-1.25
Ad. Algebra	10	10	5	10	10	–	–	8.33	5.0	-3.33
General Math	5	5	–	–	–	–	–	3.33	0.0	-3.33
Geometry	15	–	–	15	15	10	10	5.0	12.5	+7.5
Geometry I	20	–	35	20	20	20	30	18.33	22.5	+4.17
Math Fund.	–	–	–	–	–	5	–	0.0	1.25	+1.25
Shop Math	–	–	–	10	5	–	–	0.0	3.75	-3.75
PE 10	40	35	40	35	30	40	30	38.33	33.75	-4.58
PE 11	35	35	35	35	35	25	40	35.0	33.75	-1.25
PE 12	45	45	35	40	30	35	40	41.67	36.25	-5.42
Hygiene	15	–	10	10	10	5	10	8.33	8.75	+0.42
Hygiene II	20	–	10	10	10	10	15	10.0	8.75	-1.25

Table 3.1 (continued)

Source: California State Archives, Dept. of Education. Bureau of School Apportionments and Reports Records, October Reports, 1915–21, 1924–52:

- F:3601:1143, Education–School Apportionments and Reports, J-35, P-Q, 1939. "October Report of Secondary School Principal, October 13, 1939–Part Two, Palo Alto Senior High."
- F:3601:1160, Education–School Apportionments and Reports, J-35, High Schools, P, 1940. "October Report of Secondary School Principal, October 18, 1940–Part Two, Palo Alto Senior High."
- F:3601:1174, Education–School Apportionments and Reports, J-35, P-Q. 1941. "October Report of Secondary School Principal, October 31, 1941–Part Two, Palo Alto Senior High."
- F:3601:1195, Education–School Apportionments and Reports, J-35, P-Q. 1942. "October Report of Secondary School Principal, October 30, 1942–Part Two, Palo Alto Senior High."
- F:3601:1226, Education–School Apportionments and Reports, J-35, Santa Clara-Santa Cruz County, 1943. "October Report of Secondary School Principal, October 29, 1943–Part Two, Palo Alto Senior High."
- F:3601:1244, Education–School Apportionments and Reports, J-35, High Schools, San Luis Obispo-Santa Cruz counties. 1944. "October Report of Secondary School Principal, October 18, 1944–Part Two, Palo Alto Senior High."
- F:3601:1266, Education–School Apportionments and Reports, J-35, Santa Clara County, 1945. "October Report of Secondary School Principal, October 30, 1945–Part Two, Palo Alto Senior High."

issues. Teacher Frank Colombat taught a course in economic problems to juniors and seniors addressing "labor problems . . . international trade and tariff policies, reconstruction following the present war . . . and a stronger League of Nations to enforce peace by means of an international police force."[30] Among other projects, students in the class created a chart entitled, "The War Time Self-Sufficiency of the Major Nations" and posted the project on the bulletin board near the school's main office.[31] Another class, entitled World Affairs, examined "problems of war and peace" and was reported to "give those who will soon be fighting on the battle front a clearer conception of what the war is all about."[32]

Fine arts subjects did not fare well during the war years, with the number of class periods in subjects such as sketching, band, and costume design decreasing in number.[33] Also, in spite of Principal Ivan

Linder's proposal to expand the high school's "general education" program in 1942, the number of class periods offered in courses such as psychology and family relationships actually declined.[34] Linder's desire that Palo Alto High School increase its "non-academic" offerings was also never fulfilled. Commerce classes, such as bank practice, retail selling, and shorthand, declined from 70 periods offered per week between 1939 and 1941 to 64 between 1942 and 1945. Even the number of typing classes, which girls throughout the United States were encouraged to take to meet the secretarial needs of the federal government and defense industries during World War II, declined. Other "non-academic" course offerings targeted specifically toward girls, such as childcare, family relations, and foods, remained fairly constant throughout the war years, although homemaking registered an approximately one-class-period-per-day increase.

Although the total number of boys' vocational class periods offered at Palo Alto High School between 1939 and 1945 remained relatively steady, this set of courses underwent two significant changes following America's declaration of war. First, the number of periods of drafting offered recorded the greatest increase of all courses at the high school, rising from zero prior to 1941 to approximately 18 between 1942 and 1945. Again, defense industries' well-publicized wartime needs undoubtedly catalyzed the increase. Second, Palo Alto High School did not change the overall number of vocational class periods it offered because the district established a vocational day school for secondary students during World War II. Explained in greater detail in the next section of this chapter, the Peninsula Defense Training Center was a wartime vocational school distinct from the regular operation of the senior high school. Fully funded by the federal government and serving mostly adult students, this center's vocational opportunities help explain district officials' dramatic claims regarding the reorganization of the secondary school program to meet wartime needs.

The two secondary school course offerings receiving the greatest national publicity during World War II were aeronautics and physical education.[35] In response to concerns that schools in the United States were not preparing students for a place in the world's first air war, districts across the country were encouraged to offer aviation instruction so as to "air condition" students for a role over the battlefront.³⁶ A cover illustration for the September 1942 issue of *The American School Board Journal* with the caption "From Small Beginnings" revealed the importance that school officials' assigned aeronautics during the war years. The image depicted a towering pilot, with "American Air Supremacy in War and Peace" written across the front of his flight jacket, looking over the shoulders of two young boys and their teacher as they construct a model airplane. Behind them, a sign reading "Aviation Instruction in the Schools" emphasized the necessity of educating students in the principles of aviation from an early age.³⁷ *Time* magazine also highlighted the importance assigned to aviation instruction in 1942 when it reported, "A fourth R, pre-flight training, is now part of many curricula."³⁸ Indeed, by October of that year, 60 percent of California's secondary schools reportedly offered courses in aviation, with many of the remaining 40 percent introducing "preflight aeronautics units" in science courses.³⁹

At Palo Alto High School, science teacher Henry Martin began offering an aeronautics course for boys and girls in the fall of 1942. About the course, Martin remembered:

> There was a lot of work in aviation. We went to a big high school in San Francisco. I forget how many times a week. And took aviation ground school. This got the teachers and the students interested in aviation. At the end of this time, we went over to Oakland and then they gave us airplane rides to work it out. Also during this time we had field trips to Treasure Island, which was a big center for electronics. All kinds of electronics training went on there, and signal, and Morse Code.⁴⁰

Although satisfying the district's declared obligation to prepare secondary school students for war, Martin never found his aeronautics class in great demand. It was offered one period per day in 1942 and then dropped from the school's program.

As a result of the large number of draft deferments issued due to military recruits' poor physical conditioning, physical education (PE) programs also received glaring public attention during World War II.⁴¹ Placing the blame for the reportedly poor health of the nation's adolescent males on the front steps of secondary schools, many

Americans proposed that PE prepare male students for pre-induction military training.[42] Consequently, the "Cadet Corps," a program established by the California State Legislature in 1911 to train public and private school students in military drill, physical exercise, and marksmanship, was either adopted or re-adopted by many school districts in California as an appropriate modification of physical education courses.[43]

As early as 1940, the Palo Alto School Board unanimously rejected a proposal to adopt the Cadet Corps at the secondary level, responding to community pressure that such a program was unnecessarily militaristic. Simultaneously, however, the board acknowledged the need to "toughen up" potential recruits at the high school level through rigorous physical education courses.[44] Two years later, district officials tempered their opposition to direct military training as part of the high school's physical education classes for boys, agreeing to include an obstacle course, calisthenics, and "basic marching tactics as set up by the army and navy."[45] As the national trend towards military training continued throughout the war years, the board reversed its initial decision and in 1944 implemented the Cadet Corps in grades 10 through 12.[46]

Beginning in the fall semester of 1944, 307 Palo Alto High School boys put on brown khaki uniforms and gathered twice a week to drill under the command of Army Colonel R. E. Fletcher (retired).[47] With selected seniors serving as corps leaders, training included "calisthenics and cadence exercise" during the month of October, "organized games and runs" in November, "practice ceremonies and an obstacle course" in December, and "preparatory rifle marksmanship and tumbling" in January.[48] The Cadet Corps continued throughout the 1944 academic year as part of Palo Alto High School's regular physical education curriculum. As World War II drew to a close in the summer of 1945, however, district officials dissolved the program.

Aeronautics and physical education were undoubtedly the most visible curricular modifications made to the secondary school program during World War II, yet they were far from representative of the changes that occurred in Palo Alto's schools. Despite district officials' public proclamations to "meet any needs dictated by the war," students at Palo Alto High School experienced relatively minor alterations in their course of study between 1941 and 1945. For instance, neither Sally Allen nor her future husband Peter Edmondson, who was also a Palo Alto student during the war years, recalled the war explicitly influencing what they studied in their academic classes. In fact, reflecting on the time, they now wish teachers had brought the war into the classroom in a more meaningful way. "Probably," noted Allen, "we would have been much more interested in what was being taught."[49]

Allen and Edmondson's educational experience during World War II was undoubtedly a common one for the 70–75 percent of Palo Alto High School students planning to continue on to higher education. For a portion of the 25–30 percent of graduates who would not go on to college, however, wartime educational developments in Palo Alto—*outside* of the high school building—were dramatic. For these students, pre-employment and pre-induction vocational training received significant support from the federal government during World War II. Even in the Palo Alto Unified School District, with its historically college-bound student population, the opportunity to establish a vocational education program funded by the federal government was too tempting an opportunity for school officials to ignore.

The Peninsula Defense Training Center

Calling vocational education's contribution to the war effort "real and widely admired," historian Herbert Kliebard has demonstrated how Americans hailed vocational training during World War II as a central component in the Allied victory over the Axis powers.[50] At the annual convention of the American Association of School Administrators in 1942, for instance, one participant celebrated what he believed to be vocational education's significant wartime achievements, declaring:

> In the past we have not faced reality. We have considered ourselves unconquerable. Gradually we are realizing that this is no child's play in which we are engaged. . . . We and our allies have experienced in the weeks since Pearl Harbor reverses greater than any ever suffered in all our history as a nation. . . . The story of the response of the American schools to the crisis first of national defense and now

offense constitutes one of the glorious chapters in the history of American education.[51]

"At the heart" of this response, continued the speaker, was a program of vocational education that demonstrated accomplishments "without parallel in the history of our American education."[52]

Enthusiasm for vocational education was partially rooted in what historian David Kennedy has called President Roosevelt's "breathtakingly ambitious production goals" for 1942 and 1943, which included 185,000 aircraft, 120,000 tanks, 55,000 antiaircraft guns, and 16 million deadweight tons of merchant shipping.[53] Even prior to Roosevelt's announcement, however, indeed as early as May 1940, government and military officials understood that a national defense program would necessarily involve vocational training for unemployed and unskilled laborers.[54] The remarkable speed with which legislation for vocational education became law reflects the priority that government officials assigned this form of defense preparation. On May 29, 1940, the U.S. Office of Education submitted a report to President Roosevelt entitled "Training for National Defense" that promoted the use of existing public school facilities for vocational education.[55] After only minor revision, the President forwarded the report to Congress, which passed the "Defense Training Act" less than a month later. Roosevelt signed the bill, which included a $15 million appropriation for the vocational training of defense workers, into law on June 27. Just four days later, instruction began.[56]

As described by Commissioner Studebaker, "Immediately after the passage of this appropriation, the public vocational schools of the Nation, ordinarily closed for the summer months, became the scene of bustling activity. Instructors were called back from vacations. The doors of the schools were thrown open. Within 2 months enrollments had passed the 100,000 mark."[57] Studebaker's description was not overstated. In the 19 months between July 1, 1940 and January 31, 1942, the total number of men and women—from teenagers to retirees—receiving training in public vocational facilities for employment in defense industries was 2,211,585.[58]

Public Law No. 668 created the Vocational Education for National Defense (VEND) program, which by the end of the war provided approximately $375 million for vocational education and defense training.[59] The structure of VEND intentionally mirrored the Smith-Hughes

Act of 1917 and the George-Deen Act of 1936, previous landmark vocational education legislation.[60] Yet the VEND program was distinct from these forerunners in two important ways.[61] First, VEND training applied solely to employment "essential" to national defense; for this reason, schools offering prewar vocational coursework were generally unable to draw on VEND funding to simply finance previously existing programs.[62] Second, in contrast to the Smith-Hughes and George-Deen Acts, there was no requirement for states to provide matching funds under VEND. Schools, therefore, could initiate vocational education programs and expect to be fully reimbursed for instructors' salaries and teacher training as well as for equipment purchased and the cost of renting facilities to house the program.[63]

Palo Alto school officials' response to the opportunities that the VEND program offered initially emulated the district's previous approach to the Smith-Hughes and George-Deen Acts. The city's secondary schools provided students with no federally reimbursed vocational courses in 1940, in part because of a decision that district leaders made in 1922 to establish an Evening High School.[64] Over time, the Evening High School became popular because, according to city Superintendent J. R. Overturf, it had both "avocational value," offering such classes as pottery, badminton, and lip reading, and "direct vocational value," with such diverse offerings as real estate law, metal craft, and radio maintenance.[65] As a result of making these courses available to students and adults through the Evening High School, however, the district avoided establishing vocational day programs at either the junior high school or high school level. Throughout 1939 and 1940, school officials kept with tradition, increasing vocational offerings at the Evening High School but leaving the secondary school program untouched.[66]

Expanding defense offerings at the Evening High School met the needs of some Palo Alto residents. However, it failed to serve two important groups: those not free to take courses in the evening, and students who desired to take vocational classes as part of their daytime educational program. As communities across the nation took advantage of VEND funding, Palo Alto district administrators came to realize the weakness of their vocational education strategy and held a special meeting with John C. Beswick, the state director of vocational education and state director of vocational training for war production workers, to address what was called the "problem" of vocational and defense education in Palo Alto.

Meeting with the Palo Alto School Board on April 2, 1941, Beswick urged board members to draw on Smith-Hughes and George-Deen funding to further expand the district's Evening High School, and he expressed his support for establishing a defense training center in Palo Alto.[67] Beswick said his office could be used as a resource in identifying a suitable location for the center and in laying the necessary bureaucratic groundwork for its establishment. Of particular interest to those present at the meeting was Beswick's claim that, in addition to federal reimbursement for teachers' salaries and facility rental costs, any equipment purchased for the undertaking would become district property. Following the war, Beswick reported, the equipment "could be installed in this community for a permanent program of vocational education."[68] Given such a financially advantageous solution to meeting the community's vocational education needs, the Palo Alto School Board immediately and enthusiastically set out to establish such a center.[69] It rented the "Jack-Heintz" building, owned by Stanford University and located three miles from campus, and opened the Peninsula Defense Training Center in time for the fall semester 1941.[70]

As Figure 3.1 indicates, expenditures for vocational education in Palo Alto skyrocketed as a result of the center's establishment, from $5,913 during the 1940/41 academic year to $127,577 for 1942/43.[71] The center's courses, which included Aircraft Mechanics, Industrial Drafting, and Aircraft Riveting, were generally offered from 8:00 a.m. to 4:00 p.m., satisfying the desires of students, young and old, to attend daytime classes. Moreover, in an effort to encourage Palo Alto High School students to enroll in the center, senior boys and girls began tours of the facility in September 1942.[72]

The center's overwhelming popularity, as measured by average daily attendance (ADA), is depicted in Figure 3.2. Initial enrollment at the center for the 1941/42 academic year was 344 students, almost three times that of the Evening High School at any time prior to or immediately following the war. That year also marked the first wartime decline in Palo Alto High School's enrollment. During the 1942/43 school year, as the high school's enrollment continued to decline, the center's ADA increased to 429 students.[73]

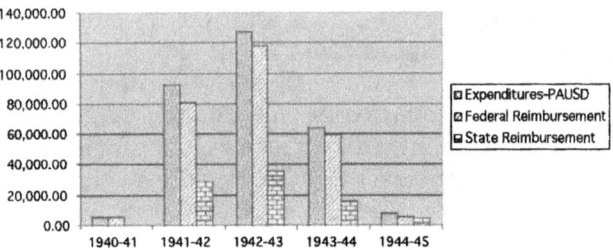

Figure 3.1 Palo Alto VEND expenditures, 1940/45

Note: Funding for the 1940/41 academic year consisted of only three months of expenditures. In addition, for that year only, federal and state reimbursements were combined in the district's accounting. The two are represented here by "Federal Reimbursement." Although the state was not obliged to provide appropriations under the VEND program, the California Commission for Vocational Education chose to participate in the National Defense Training Act by providing ADA (average daily attendance) allowances because the program was deemed to be "guaranteeing to the state and national governments trained employees who create taxable wealth." See California State Archives, F3752: 1998, Department of Education–Vocational Education, Commission for Vocational Education, 1931–42. "Minutes of a Meeting of the Commission for Vocational Education, January 7, 1942."

Source: C. R. Holbrook, "Palo Alto Unified School District Financial Report for 1944–1945," (Palo Alto, CA: Palo Alto Unified School District, 1945).

As World War II progressed, Palo Alto's efforts in support of vocational education seemed increasingly justified. At the annual conference of the American Vocational Association in December 1942, Brigadier General Frank J. McSherry (reported to be the "father" of the VEND program) declared that over 6 million additional workers would be needed for war industries in 1943, most of whom would be trained by America's schools.[74] This development had three significant consequences for school districts across the United States. First, vocational education stormed onto the educational landscape during World War II in ways previously unimagined, leading Stanford School of Education Dean Grayson N. Kefauver to write in 1943, "We have never before witnessed as great an effort to strengthen and to extend the program of vocational education in the schools of this country."[75] Second, combined with the lure of well-paying defense work, vocational education provided a legitimate avenue for students to leave school prior to graduation and begin full-time employment.[76] Third, the strong demand for vocational education during the war led

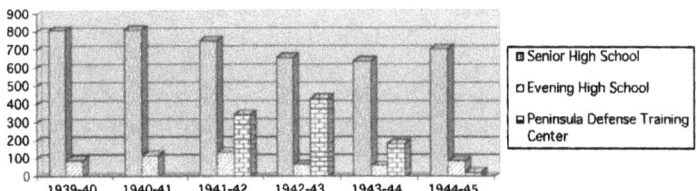

Figure 3.2 Palo Alto average daily attendance, 1939/45

Note: Nationwide, total enrollment in federally funded VEND or War Production Training programs from 1940/45 was estimated at more than 11,500,000 workers. See Arthur F. McClure, James Riley Chrisman, and Perry Mock, *Education for Work: The Historical Evolution of Vocational and Distributive Education in America* (London: Associated University Press, 1985), 92.

Source: C. R. Holbrook, "Palo Alto Unified School District Financial Report for 1944–1945," (Palo Alto, CA: Palo Alto Unified School District, 1945), 19.

many to believe that vocational programs would remain a central component of students' education in the postwar world. "A new era of education is being ushered in," declared J. C. Wright, assistant U.S. commissioner for vocational education, in late 1942. "Future educational programs will concentrate to a greater extent than formerly on teaching men and women to work with their hands as well as their heads."[77]

Partly in response to such proclamations, Palo Alto school officials conceived of a postwar educational program designed to institutionalize many of the district's wartime vocational advances.[78] The school board hoped to provide a broad selection of vocational education courses to serve high school students and graduates, returning military personnel, displaced war workers, and adults in the community, while also unifying the Senior High School, Evening High School, and Peninsula Defense Training Center into one institution.[79] To achieve these objectives, board members proposed establishing a junior college as part of the Palo Alto Unified School District.[80] The plan involved reorganizing district schools into a "six-four-four" arrangement, with elementary school remaining grades one through six, junior high school becoming grades seven through ten, and the junior college providing for grades eleven through fourteen. According to the district's proposal:

> Educational experts and the citizens of California ... have determined that in order to meet the needs of society, and to provide for the improvement of democracy, the State minimum program of education should extend through the 14th grade. ... This committee agrees with these conclusions and finds that there is a need for more vocational training in grades 11 and 12 and a special need for terminal and technical courses preparing for specific vocations after most of our youth have completed the 12th grade. It is, therefore, proposed to extend the school system upward two more years and offer terminal-technical training for specific vocations, as well as the two-year liberal arts course which will provide the kind of educational services needed for all the youth and adults in this area.[81]

Further justification for Palo Alto's embrace of this educational reorganization was provided by Principal Ivan Linder, when he informed the Palo Alto School Board in November 1944 that he believed the high school program was "well adapted to the needs of from 20 to 25% of the pupils; fairly well adapted to the needs of from 55% to 65% of the pupils; and not at all suited to the needs of from 15% to 20% of the pupils."[82] Linder's assessment led him to conclude, "All of this adds up to the conviction that our High School is a very good school for the upper 50% of our students, a mediocre to poor school for the lower 50%."[83] District leaders, however, had yet another reason for wanting to establish a junior college. Prior to the end of the war, Stanford University announced that it planned to construct laboratory facilities in the Jack-Heintz building housing the Peninsula Defense Training Center.[84] The district, which hoped to retain the vocational training equipment it had acquired through the VEND program, believed that by receiving quick approval for a junior college from the California Department of Education, the state would contribute to the cost of constructing a new facility.[85]

The idea of a junior college affiliated with the school district was not new for Palo Alto residents. In 1927, the Palo Alto Union High School District created a junior college division, enrolling 60 students taught by individually selected Palo Alto High School faculty. In March of the following year, however, the Palo Alto School Board voted to dissolve the fledging college because of financial difficulties.[86] In 1936, the effort to establish a junior college was renewed but again abandoned by the district due to lack of community support.[87] By 1944, however, district leaders claimed that the immediacy of the junior college proposal was a direct outcome of wartime developments. "The establishment of the War Production Training Program at the Peninsula Defense Training Center," wrote the district's Junior College Committee, "with its extensive training program for several thousand youth and adults in vocational fields has awakened an interest in vocational education, not only in Palo Alto itself, but particularly in the area surrounding Palo Alto which may be served by such an institution."[88]

In March 1944, just five months prior to resigning his position as Palo Alto's superintendent, Charles Lockwood wrote to Dr. Walter F. Dexter, California Superintendent of Public Instruction and Executive Officer of the Commission for Vocational Education, requesting state support in undertaking the establishment of the junior college in Palo Alto.[89] Dexter's enthusiastic reply came several days later, informing Lockwood that he was "Personally . . . very much interested" in the proposal.[90] Soon after, in a meeting of the Commission for Vocational Education, Dexter discussed his support for postwar funding of vocational education programs in junior colleges, identifying Palo Alto specifically:

> We do need to move into the junior colleges and see that they receive aid if they need it. We need to be concerned with vocational programs in the junior colleges because some have neglected it. I have asked others to study . . . the whole State of California and recommend the establishment of junior colleges in areas not now served. For instance, Palo Alto, and perhaps three or four in the northern part of the state so that we will have a complete system of these institutions.[91]

Given such strong state support for a junior college in Palo Alto, school officials were stunned to discover equally strong opposition to the proposal from community members. The local newspaper, the *Daily Palo Alto Times*, provided a forum for debate in the weeks leading up to the Palo Alto School Board vote on the issue. Residents' concerns included an improper allocation of resources from elementary school buildings to the junior college, a potential increase in class size in grades one through twelve as a result of funding the new initiative, the harm that might be brought to neighboring junior colleges by drawing on their enrollments, and the failure of Palo Alto's first junior college effort.[92]

On March 21, 1945, one day prior to the board's vote, the local newspaper, the *Daily Palo Alto Times*, conducted an opinion poll on the proposal. Of the 682 votes tabulated, 570 demonstrated opposition to the junior college.[93] The following day, a group calling itself the "Citizens' Fact-Finding Committee" confronted the school board and presented a petition with 150 signatures. It stated:

> We . . . respectfully request that the members of the Board of Education do not pass at this time any resolution which would result in the establishment of a junior college for Palo Alto, but instead that the Board of Education and the school administrators concentrate their energies and all available resources on the development of SUPERIOR educational opportunities for ALL youth on the elementary and high school levels. We believe that such a procedure would result in the maximum benefits to the greatest number of individuals of this community [emphasis original].[94]

Palo Alto High School student George Morris, Chairman of the Public Relations Committee of the school's student body, also addressed school board members, presenting the results of a student survey indicating that 82 percent of the high school's students opposed the proposal.[95] Given an overwhelming lack of support, the board unanimously voted to postpone the junior college plan indefinitely.[96]

Extracurricular Activities

By the time Commissioner Studebaker addressed the National Education Association (NEA) in June 1942, elementary and secondary schools had already begun playing an important part in civil defense. Studebaker informed the organization's membership that public schools were serving as:

> centers for adult discussion of war aims and problems; for civilian defense activities which involve school participation with the whole community in cooperative wartime projects. . . . Schools are helping to raise funds to finance the war effort through the sale of War Savings

Stamps and Bonds. . . . They are safeguarding the health and safety and increasing the physical fitness of their youthful charges; conducting classes in first aid, home nursing and nutrition; sponsoring school and other home garden projects; and in a score of other ways contributing to the war effort.[97]

Although Studebaker's description emphasized how, as institutions, schools had developed into wartime community centers, his reference to their "helping to raise funds to finance the war effort" identified just one of the many ways that students became directly involved in homefront mobilization. Indeed, student participation through extracurricular activities was a significant element of many schools' overall contribution to World War II.

Although Palo Altans may have differed with school officials over the curricular and organizational arrangement of postwar public schooling in their district, residents frequently welcomed opportunities for schools to advance the Allied cause by reorienting students' extracurricular programs to support the war effort. Although open to girls and boys, the Junior Red Cross served as one of the few organizations at Palo Alto High School dedicated to female participation.[98] Girls participated by wrapping bandages and sponsoring fund drives for Red Cross projects.[99] During one week in November 1943, for instance, members raised $226.23 by challenging each classmate to contribute 25 cents to the drive.[100] Frequently exceeding their goals, students used the money they raised to carry out their "box-a-month" war project, sending packages containing "cigarettes, toilet articles and other comfort items" to servicemen recuperating from wounds suffered on the battlefield.[101]

Sometimes girls' involvement in the Junior Red Cross helped alter their stated plans for the future. One senior, Millie Post, claimed that prior to her involvement with the organization she had hoped to become a director of religious education. Upon graduating, however, she chose to enroll in pre-nursing at Stanford University.[102] Carolyn Field also partly credited involvement in the Junior Red Cross with influencing her career plans. In an interview with a student reporter from *The Campanile* following the battlefield death of her brother, Field announced her intention to enlist in the Cadet Nurse Corps, stating, "It will be a proud day for me when I receive my R.N. and know that I can carry on the fight that took the life of my brother."[103]

Although students and faculty reoriented many extracurricular activities to assist in the war effort, schools also established new clubs and projects directly concerned with wartime issues. Some of these received support from the federal government. In the summer of 1942, Robert A. Lovett, Assistant Secretary of War for Air, contacted Commissioner Studebaker concerning the imminent impact of the lowering of the draft age from 21 to 18 years of age. Both men agreed that the U.S. Office of Education needed to develop policies that would ease the shock to be felt at the high school level. Government forecasts suggested that 80 percent of the country's "1,300,000 high school boys between 16 and 18 would enter the armed forces shortly after graduation."[104] Although military service, precipitated by either the draft or volunteering, was a normal expectation for most high school males, the change in the draft age made many of the anxieties felt by these future soldiers more immediate. Lovett and Studebaker believed they could develop and implement a federal program that would relieve some of this anxiety. By September, the "High School Victory Corps" had been established, with goals that included:

> (1) the training of youth; (2) the active participation of youth in the community's war effort while they were yet in school . . . and specifically, (a) guidance into critical services and occupations; (b) wartime citizenship; (c) physical fitness; (d) military drill; (e) competence in science and mathematics; (f) pre-flight training in aeronautics; (g) pre-induction training for critical occupation; (h) community services.[105]

"The Office of Education," according to scholar Richard Ugland, "hoped that the Victory Corps would give substance to the idea of the high school student as reservist."[106] Indeed, the conception of the high school as a way station for young men prior to basic training was fully featured in the Victory Corps' characteristics. The program consisted of general membership and five special divisions; land, sea, air, production, and community service. Students within two years of graduation were permitted to join on a voluntary basis, though girls were encouraged to join the latter two divisions due to their probable non-enlistment in the armed forces.[107] The criteria for membership included participating in a physical fitness program, involvement in at least one wartime service activity (such as assisting with childcare or salvaging scrap metal), and enrollment in subjects useful to the war effort.[108] Each division had its own insignia and members were encouraged to wear the Victory Corps' uniform—a white shirt with dark trousers for boys and a white blouse and dark skirt for girls.[109]

When first instituted in Palo Alto High School in October 1942, the Victory Corps was widely popular. School administrators selected a "Victory Council" consisting of seven girls and six boys to run the organization. These student leaders were continually highlighted in both the school newspaper and the yearbook. A student editorial in a January 1943 issue of *The Campanile* indicated that some students thought of the Victory Corps as the primary mechanism through which they could directly participate in the war effort. "All in all," the writer claimed, "war is the headline in the minds of every high school student. Studies are important but they come under war, too. The best effort the Palo Alto High School can offer towards victory is its Victory Corps.... Join the Victory Corps and help yourself as well as your nation."[110] As the war progressed, however, the organization quickly fell in popularity and soon dissolved.

Palo Alto High School's experience with the Victory Corps mirrored the nation's. At first it seemed as if the program was going to meet planners' expectations. Seventy percent of high schools surveyed within one year of the Victory Corps' inception reported having adopted the program. The number of students participating declined rapidly, however, so much so that less than one-third of the nation's high schools were estimated to have some form of the program still in place at the end of the war. Scholars have offered three central reasons for the Victory Corps' rapid decline. First, state and local school administrators were charged with adopting and managing the program. Although this was a pragmatic decision on the part of federal officials who did not want to violate the tradition of local control in public education, it required local and state officials to commit to yet another civil defense responsibility initiated by the war. For many, this was one program too many. Second, the program's attempt to replicate the military hierarchy within the school was seen by some as "artificial and unrealistic" and by others as too "militaristic," reminding them of a "Fascist-type organization."¹¹¹ Finally, federal funding, promised when the program was initially announced, never materialized.¹¹²

The overall significance of the Victory Corps is difficult to determine. The organization is strongly criticized by some as a "piece of wartime Washington folly," while others give it at least some credit as a catalyst in stimulating high schools to shift their extracurricular emphasis to a greater wartime footing.¹¹³ Palo Alto High School science teacher Henry Martin's two war-related extracurricular clubs serve as good examples.¹¹⁴ Martin's Morse Code Club was extremely popular, requiring him to limit the number of students involved.¹¹⁵ Martin also developed an Aviation Club (with colleague Richard Nolte) designed for students hoping to join the Army Air Corps and other aviation organizations after graduation. Meeting weekly, students studied aviation, meteorology, and aerodynamics as well as the role of aviation in warfare. Noting the interest of both boys and girls in joining the group, a student journalist reported in December 1943, "The air-minded hopefuls will meet to discuss job openings for women in the field of aviation."¹¹⁶

Although organizations such as the Junior Red Cross and Henry Martin's clubs often met during breaks in the school day or immediately after the school day ended, schools also coordinated student participation in the war effort outside of school hours. As the armed forces continually absorbed able-bodied men into their ranks, fewer were left to work in the nation's fields and factories. The resulting labor shortage became a serious problem by 1943, as defense plants scrambled to find workers and farmers pleaded with local and state governments for assistance in harvesting crops. As the labor shortage deepened, state governments encouraged local communities to look to the last abundant labor pool in the immediate vicinity, the student body. Schools responded by providing organized access to this labor supply.¹¹⁷

Palo Alto students were encouraged to work during the war so long as employment did not unnecessarily interrupt their schooling. "By obtaining a job and working Saturdays or after school," wrote the editor of the school newspaper, "you will not only be setting a man free for active service or more important work which is an aid to your country but you will be earning yourself some spare cash and extra money for war bonds. . . . Each and every one of us must realize, although he or she cannot actually handle the gun out on the front lines, that we can strengthen the home defense by being the 'man behind the man behind the gun.'"[118] Years later, Peter Edmondson remembered answering this call. "We all worked," he recalled, "Kids did a lot of work that the adults normally did. We worked after school, on weekends, during vacation, and even during school."[119] Indeed, *The Campanile* reported in 1943 that "Palo Alto High Schoolites, like highschoolers everywhere, are aiding extensively in the war program, especially by outside employment. The files in the office are filled with a variety of work and hours put in by Palo Alto High School students in addition to their school courses."[120]

One of the greatest needs for student labor during World War II was in harvesting. Traditionally, agricultural regions across the nation relied on local and transient labor. With the draft and better paying positions in defense industry pulling workers away from the fields, however, farmers became reliant upon students to save their crops from rotting on the vine. In Palo Alto, students worked to harvest fruits and vegetables in nearby Mountain View and Santa Clara during the school year and vacation periods, with the full support of parents and district officials.[121] Sally Allen remembered school-sponsored trips to the fields to pick the ripened fruit. "The yellow school bus came by the school and picked up the kids and took them to whatever orchard or berry farm, or whatever farm needed labor, because most of the labor was working in the factories or building ships."[122] Peter Edmondson remembered receiving 17 cents a bucket for his labor.[123] Paula Berka recalled harvesting crops as a junior high school student; "I remember going out one day, getting up at dawn, and being transported to pick green beans! Backbreaking work! And then cutting apricots."[124]

The labor shortage became so severe that in September 1942, the Palo Alto High School administration held an all-school assembly for the purpose of registering students to work in the fields. Reporting on the event, *The Campanile* urged, "This story comes as an earnest appeal to the student body of this institution, loyal to their school and loyal to their country, to forget their football games, their dances, and their good time for just a short while, and devote themselves and their leisure time to the heaviest and most urgent task ever to confront a high school generation, that of saving the crops that feed America and the army defending it."[125] Although the appeal was quite zealous, the description might not have been far from reality. The *Daily Palo Alto Times* reported one month later, "Palo Alto High School students are certainly doing their share of harvesting crops! Every morning truckloads of volunteer boys and girls leave the school for farms and ranches."[126] By 1943, Superintendent Lockwood enthusiastically reported that 213 of Palo Alto High School's 779 students had worked to harvest crops during the previous year.[127] In fact, farmers in northern California became so heavily reliant upon student labor that State Senator Byrl R. Salsman of Palo Alto introduced legislation into the state assembly proposing to waive physical education class if students worked in the fields. Students, in response, seemed delighted to have the opportunity to simultaneously contribute to the war effort, earn money, and skip PE.[128]

Although many educators supported students' wartime employment, some found this distraction from school disturbing. In response, administrators and school board members developed a justification for student labor by portraying the supposed educationally beneficial characteristics of students' work. The cover art of the May 1943 issue of *The American School Board Journal* depicted this rationale by portraying a smiling youth hoeing a field of lettuce with the caption, "A Vital Crop to be Raised."[129] Behind the boy, the sign "City High School Vacation Farm Helpers" indicated that the student was not working during school hours, while labels on the various heads of lettuce implied that the student was fortunate to reap the "benefits" of "hard labor" while gaining "experience" and a "broader knowledge and outlook."

As Commissioner Studebaker's 1942 address to the NEA suggested, another popular method of student participation in the war effort was the purchase and sale of war stamps and bonds. To finance the war, the Roosevelt administration urged Americans to make long-term voluntary loans to the federal government in the form of small denomination Series-E Bonds issued for sale to the general public. The cost of these bonds was disaggregated into stamps, making an individual stamp affordable to almost every American.[130] The federal government quickly recognized the role that students might play in marketing the stamps and bonds and immediately set out to foster enthusiasm among the nation's children and youth.[131]

In cooperation with the Treasury Department, the U.S. Office of Education organized the "Sharing America" program to coordinate student buying and selling of war stamps and bonds across the United States.[132] Palo Alto High School students responded enthusiastically, challenging nearby Sequoia High School to a "War Stamp Duel."[133] At the height of the duel, Palo Alto students purchased $350 worth of stamps and $125 worth of bonds in one day, with *The Campanile* reporting that "The number of bonds sold exceeded expectations . . . several classes went over the top with the entire class buying 100%."[134] Over 50 years later, Joan Paulin remembered the stamp and bond sales and the central role the school played in their organization; "We all bought stamps and put them in a little book. They were sold through school. Sometimes it set a goal and we tried to meet it."[135] Peter Edmondson remembered the stamps' value. "$18.75 would get you a $25.00 bond," he recalled. "And everyone bought them. You did it for patriotism."[136] Paula Berka remembered school rallies, held to encourage student involvement in buying and selling the stamps. "It seems to me," Berka remembered, "that there were monitors in the classroom who collected the money and handed out the stamps. There was a lot of enthusiasm."[137]

Excitement over competing with a rival school diminished when students learned they could "purchase" military equipment through yet another federal program designed to motivate school war stamp and bonds sales. In 1943, Palo Alto High School students began their first drive to obtain $75,000 in stamps and bonds towards the purchase of a pursuit plane. By the end of the first day, the *Daily Palo Alto Times* reported that students, "spurred by visions of a pursuit plane soaring through the skies with 'Palo Alto' painted across its nose" raised $14,750 in stamp and bond sales.[138] Before the end of the war, Palo Alto High School students financed the purchase of two of these planes and raised an additional $175,000 to purchase a B-25 bomber. When a picture of "Palo Alto's" bomber arrived, students were thrilled to see the high school's name and "Li'l Viking"—the school's mascot—painted across the airplane's fuselage.[139]

Conclusion

In June 1944, a student presented President Franklin Roosevelt with a trophy listing the nationwide student contribution in war stamps and bonds for the 1943/44 school year. The trophy read:

> To President Franklin D. Roosevelt
> Commander in Chief of our Armed Forces
> AMERICA'S
> SCHOOL CHILDREN
> are proud
> to present
> 13,500 PLANES
> 44,700 JEEPS
> and other war equipment to the value of
> $510,000,000
> through the purchase of War Bonds
> during the school year ending June 1944[140]

This was no small accomplishment on the part of the nation's children and youth, and it was an important component of the federal government's effort to finance America's role in World War II. Most notable, however, was the enthusiasm with which students involved themselves in war stamp and bond sales as well as the many other extracurricular activities reoriented to support the war effort. Student entries in school newspapers and yearbooks from this time suggest that students experienced a great sense of achievement through their participation. "America has given us our chance to help," wrote one student. "After all the times we high school students have been told that 'Modern Youth Is Soft,' we are being given a chance to prove otherwise. Our parents will have to hold their tongues from now on. So we're off to work, and I'll see you next summer."[141] Indeed, for many students school was the primary institution through which they became directly involved in World War II.[142]

In 1942, Federal Security Agency Administrator Paul V. McNutt articulated the important responsibility that many Americans believed public schools held during wartime, writing, "It is quite clear that the school and its staff will play a still larger role in the community as the war goes on. Schools must continue to be centers of learning, but they must also be centers of community service. Schools must be the company headquarters of the homefront."[143] In keeping with this belief, educators, school administrators, policy makers, government officials, and citizens across the country urged public elementary and secondary schools to become arsenals of democracy.

Palo Alto was no exception. Residents embraced a role for their secondary schools in advancing the Allied cause by supporting the district's efforts to increase vocational opportunities. Hoping to more thoroughly prepare students for war work and service in the armed forces, school officials expanded course offerings at the Evening High School and then took advantage of the lucrative Vocational Education for National Defense program to establish the Peninsula Defense Training Center. Moreover, district leaders and community members encouraged students' involvement in war-related activities through an extracurricular program that included, among other things, laboring in agricultural fields and raising funds to purchase war matériel. Not surprisingly, students themselves welcomed these opportunities to participate in what was perceived by most at the time as the nation's single most important undertaking. Evidence produced by students during the war years indicates that many believed their efforts made a significant contribution to United States military success abroad. As a result, students experienced a high degree of efficacy through their genuine contributions to the Allied cause.

In keeping with proclamations by educational leaders and professional organizations that schools should be transformed to meet a single dominating purpose during the war years, Palo Alto school officials hoped to extend wartime modifications of the schools' vocational and extracurricular programs to the district's secondary school curriculum. School administrators militarized physical education for boys and began offering war-related courses such as aeronautics. Throughout World War II, however, the high school's academic core curriculum remained relatively unaltered. What changes were instituted were limited in scope, involved relatively few students, and were short-lived. Moreover, when school board members attempted to institutionalize wartime vocational developments through a secondary school reorganization culminating in the establishment of a junior college, their plan met fierce community opposition.

School officials misconstrued the exceptional state of educational affairs during World War II as causing a significant shift in Palo Altans' attitudes towards vocational education. By providing an emergency justification for the expansion of vocational offerings, the war did urge a reconsideration of the role of secondary schooling in Palo Alto, as it did throughout the nation. As proposed by district officials, however, the schools' newly defined postwar role conflicted with many residents' previously conceived notions of the academic and civic purposes of public education. Tensions ultimately arose between community members' commitment to a liberal arts oriented institution and the district's proposed rearrangement of the secondary school program. These tensions were not easily resolved, reflecting larger national dilemmas over what constituted a liberal democratic education in the postwar era.

Even in the midst of a national calamity, Palo Alto residents conceived of their schools as citadels of democracy—places that fostered the academic studies necessary for students to become competent citizens during and following World War II. Palo Altans' faith that their public schools could achieve this aim was a product of long-standing social values and beliefs concerning the role of education in the United States. Given the war's relatively minimal impact on their city, it was a conception that residents could afford to nurture well into the future.

4

"An Avalanche Hits Richmond"

> I think it was pretty exciting [to teach] during the war. It was a challenge to say the least. And I don't think we thought much about it. We just went ahead and did it because here were all these children and you just go ahead and do your job. . . . There were all kinds of kids all together . . . and they didn't seem to fight or have a problem. . . . I don't remember there being a problem with the kids of various races and so forth. . . . We had principally black and white children and they all got along fine. I had all kinds of kids in my classes and it was fine.[1]
> —Richmond Elementary School Teacher Marian Sauer

Marian Sauer began teaching at Woodrow Wilson Elementary School in Richmond, California, in 1942. Her first years in the classroom were strikingly unusual. During World War II, Richmond's population skyrocketed as a direct result of homefront mobilization, from 23,642 residents in 1940 to 93,738 only three years later. School enrollments grew sixfold, dramatically overtaxing the capacity of the city's public schools.[2] Simultaneously, emigration transformed the demographic characteristics of Richmond's student population. Many of the migrant families who moved to Richmond came from the South and Midwest, bringing with them customs unfamiliar to one another and the city's native residents. Black migration, in particular, altered the relative homogeneity of the prewar population, with the number of Richmond's black residents increasing over 5,000 percent between 1940 and 1947.[3]

In 1944, Robert D. Lee, Mayor of Richmond, described the "avalanche" that hit his city in a report both summarizing the impact of World War II on Richmond and outlining the city's desperate need for state and federal support in coping with the war boom:

> In 1940 progress was normal in the city of Richmond.... In 1941 the first avalanche of shipyard construction struck the city. By 1942, disruption in municipal affairs became commonplace.... But the real avalanche—of Liberty ship and Victory ship construction, of nearly 100,000 shipyard workers in a city of less than 100,000 persons—was just gathering speed. By 1943 its full force crashed upon Richmond and overwhelmed it. No small city with its limited civic resources could withstand such a savage, roaring impact of urgently concentrated, highly specialized, all-out response to the Nation's critical war needs.[4]

Lee's rhetoric may seem extravagant, but his description of the war's impact on Richmond was not. Between 1940 and 1945, cities and towns in the United States experienced the "roaring impact" of wartime mobilization as they were transformed into centers of defense production. With tens of thousands of migrants suddenly moving to these areas in search of well-paying defense work, local officials were unable to keep pace with the dramatically changing needs of their communities, often leading them to feel they were losing control of their cities.[5]

Plagued by a dramatic lack of classroom space, a sudden teacher shortage, and confronted by a growing number of academically impoverished students, Richmond's public elementary and secondary schools struggled to simply remain in operation throughout the war years. Yet as trying as their working conditions were, many of Richmond's educators considered their racially, ethnically, and culturally diverse pupils desperately in need of a good education and considered it their professional, wartime "duty" to educate "all" students—terms revealing both the patriotic self-sacrifice and color-blind ideology that infused Richmond educators' approach to public schools as citadels of democracy during World War II.

Given the significant degree of racism and discrimination practiced in the United States throughout the war years, it seems puzzling that teachers such as Marian Sauer would strive to treat "all kinds of kids" fairly. Yet as this chapter's opening quote suggests, Sauer and many of her colleagues adopted what I will call "civic-professionalism" in their occupations between 1940 and 1945, leading city teachers and administrators to conceive of the public school as a place where civic-mindedness and democratic principles were both modeled for students and explicitly instructed.[6]

The confluence of three well-documented and interrelated social, political, and educational developments produced the civic-professional ideal during World War II. First, racial oppression in the United States became an increasing source of embarrassment in the late 1930s and 1940s as the federal government openly repudiated fascist treatment of ethnic minorities. As a result, President Roosevelt issued at first rhetorical statements, and then policy proposals, promoting tolerance and equality of opportunity for Americans, regardless of race, color, or creed.[7] Second, theories of race-blind liberalism, developed earlier in the century and popularized during the 1930s, came to fruition during the war.[8] Culminating in the 1944 publication of Gunnar Myrdal's *An American Dilemma*, race-blind liberalism developed out of the work of social scientists such as Ruth Benedict, who asserted the primacy of cultural difference over biologically determinant categories (including race) and called for the application of these theories in the nation's public schools.[9] Third, many California educators expanded their previous conception of the teaching profession as class-blind so that it now included race, ethnicity, and culture.[10] Promoted through the work of California State Department of Education officials such as Helen Heffernan and university professors such as University of California at Los Angeles's Corinne Seeds, a color-blind approach to schooling, practically realized through "intercultural" curricula and pedagogy, allowed California teachers and administrators to claim equal treatment of their students as individuals in a democratic society.[11]

As a result of the civic-professional ideal, racial mixing in Richmond's classrooms was common, school district policies directed specifically towards minority students were rare, and hostility toward migrants, explicit in the broader community, was attenuated for students in public schools. As practiced in Richmond, however, civic-professionalism cut both ways. By attributing prejudice to the attitudes of individuals instead of power differentials between social groups, Richmond's educators ignored race, ethnicity, and culture as elements of subordination in American society. Employing a shallow conception of difference in a nation tormented by its racist social and institutional structures, teachers and administrators denied students' personal identities and social realities. The joining of a series of social forces, moreover, influenced Richmond's schools during the war years. Although teachers such as Marian Sauer and administrators such as School Superintendent Walter Helms adopted civic-professionalism in their work lives, racist practices and beliefs embedded in the surrounding community—finding expression in, among other areas of life, segregated public housing, defense industry discrimination, and a Jim Crow army—shaped the school institution.

Civic-professionalism dissolved during the late 1940s and 1950s, a victim of conservative backlash and rapid economic change during the Cold War. Although native white residents judged the arrival of blacks into Richmond during World War II as creating conditions that made the city "ripe for a racial holocaust," most believed this social disruption to be a temporary wartime necessity.[12] Indeed, a climate of wartime national unity provided fertile soil for the civic-professional ideal to flourish. As the war drew to a close, however, Richmond's black migrants did not abandon their new homes. Instead, as concerns over economic conditions replaced anxiety over Axis victories and patriotic zeal resulting from the war crisis dwindled in the United States, blacks increasingly lobbied for fair treatment in areas such as housing and employment. In response to black demands for social justice, racial conflict intensified.[13] In the postwar era, public schools in Richmond, as elsewhere throughout the United States, became one of the primary battlegrounds in the fight for civil rights.

This denouement, however, should not detract from the accomplishments of Richmond's teachers and administrators during World War II. Although innate contradictions in white liberals' view of race at this time in United States history led to the insufficient and inadequate implementation of the civic-professional ideal—thus limiting its effectiveness in bringing democratic principles to fruition in Richmond's public schools—much can be learned from the ways that it permitted teachers and administrators to resist historically defined patterns of discrimination. In recent years, color-blind ideology has fallen out of favor with liberals and is currently employed by conservatives as a strategy through which to deny minority demands for equal access. As Americans continue to vigorously debate the legacy of the landmark Supreme Court decision in *Brown v. Board of Education*, a case in which the National Association for the Advancement of Colored People (NAACP) relied heavily on color-blind ideology to argue against the legal segregation of public schools, examining the implementation of civic-professionalism in wartime Richmond illuminates persistent struggles in developing a public school program that attends to student diversity without abandoning integration as a worthy goal in a democratic society.[14]

"The Quintessential War Boom Town"

Palo Alto and Richmond's distinct prewar histories foreshadowed the cities' dramatically different experiences during World War II. If Palo Alto arose as a home for the members of a newly developing educational community, Richmond was established, in the words of its founders, as the "Pittsburgh of the West." The city was intended to be the Pacific Coast's industrial heart, drawing employees from nearby metropolitan areas into its chambers and pumping economic prosperity back out to the western United States.[15] This vision, first proposed by Oakland land developer Augustin S. Macdonald, relied on Richmond's deep coastal waters, abundance of cheap land, and location just north of Oakland and northeast (across the bay) from San Francisco as the necessary prerequisites for industrial development.[16]

Although minor businesses operated in the region known as Point Richmond since 1894, Macdonald promoted the area east of the Point by convincing Santa Fe Railroad officials to locate the western terminus of their rail line in Richmond.[17] With the railroad established, Macdonald lobbied representatives of Standard Oil to build a refinery in the town. Agreeing to the generous terms offered by local officials, the company constructed the facility and the first oil ceremoniously came through the line on July 4, 1902.[18] By 1904, the Standard Oil refinery in Richmond was the second largest in the world.[19] Well on its way to becoming an industrial center, Richmond's commercial and residential development began to increase rapidly, culminating in the town's incorporation in 1905.[20]

By 1912, Richmond had grown to a city of about 12,000 residents. Local officials claimed a capital investment of over $40 million and pointed to the city's new public library, constructed with a grant from the Carnegie Foundation, as evidence of Richmond's civic development.[21] Moreover, although initial planning for the educational needs of Richmond's children was poor, leading some classes to be held in the basement of the local Methodist Church and even the loft of a barn, the city eventually established its own school district, enrolling 1,275 students in four elementary schools and one high school.[22] In 1901, city officials made what was probably their most important educational decision when they hired Walter Helms as supervising principal. Promoted three years later, Helms held the position of superintendent until 1949, a 45-year term and the longest in California history.[23]

Although Richmond's continued growth seemed certain, especially after public officials obtained federal funds to modernize the city's port facilities, Richmond's rate of industrial development declined throughout the 1920s.[24] To stimulate business investment, the city further expanded its port to service steamships from the Fred D. Paar Terminal Company.[25] Richmond officials were rewarded in 1928 when the Ford Motor Company agreed to construct a $5 million assembly plant in Richmond to take advantage of the city's port facilities and railways.[26] The automobile manufacturer quickly became a major source of employment for Richmond's residents, second only to Standard Oil.[27] By the time the Ford plant opened in 1931, however, it was no longer viewed as a symbol of economic growth but of survival. As was the case throughout the nation, Richmond's economy stagnated during the early years of the Great Depression.

By the end of the 1930s, Richmond had renewed its drive to become an industrial hub, attracting over 50 manufacturing and processing factories. Its port grew to the second largest in the West in tonnage (17th in the nation), and its population increased to approximately 23,000 residents.[28] By 1940, the city had an elementary district and a high school district; Walter Helms was superintendent of both.[29] The Richmond City School District served 2,987 students in 11 elementary schools, including those in the cities of Richmond, El Cerrito, and the Kensington area southeast of El Cerrito. Consisting of two junior high schools, one senior high school, and one junior-senior high school then under construction, the Richmond Union High School District served 3,430 students, including those from the Richmond City School District and the San Pablo, Pinole-Hercules, and Sheldon Elementary School districts.[30] Richmond's schools were relatively well-funded, due in part to the city's substantial industrial tax base. Between 1920 and 1930, Richmond's assessed valuation increased at approximately the same rate as the school population, so that by 1940 annual elementary school expenditures were $133 per pupil, greater than the average financial support received by California's public schools as measured by assessed valuation per unit of average daily attendance.[31]

By 1940, however, many of Richmond's elementary schools were also over 25 years old and several were in desperate need of repair, plagued with problems such as flooding in winter.[32] Moreover, Walter Helms was a notorious pinchfist, often leaving Richmond's schools with only the barest operating essentials. The districts' elementary schools and the top floor of the high school, for instance, had no electric lighting. Parents rallied in 1939 for lights to be installed, but Helms argued that the schools' natural lighting was within state regulations. Both of Richmond's school boards allowed Helms's decision to stand, answering any question as to who maintained authority over the city's schools.[33]

On the eve of World War II, then, Richmond was reported to be a "law-abiding, financially sound" city, with "good schools and a good government."[34] These qualities continued to convince officials that Richmond would assume a position of industrial dominance in the West, especially considering the number of federal defense contracts being let to industries in the San Francisco Bay Area. "U.S. Pours Millions in the East Bay" declared a headline in the *Richmond Independent*, the city's newspaper, referring to the dramatic increase in federal defense expenditures directed toward northern California.[35] Only one week later, however, the paper's headline cautioned, "Richmond Has Scored Zero in Defense Funds."[36] Fearing that the federal government would bypass their city completely, public officials formed the "Richmond National Defense Committee" to seek defense contracts.[37] Little did committee members realize they would come to regret their success as events unfolded in the ensuing weeks. On January 14, 1941, the Todd-California Shipbuilding Corporation, later renamed Kaiser Corporation, broke ground for the construction of a shipyard on Richmond's harbor. Only one month earlier, city officials had convinced Henry J. Kaiser to fulfill a $50 million, 30-ship contract from the British Purchasing Commission by building a shipyard on 90 acres of "boggy marshland" in Richmond.[38] On October 27, 1941, Kaiser launched his first ship in the record time of 125 days on the ways (where ships were constructed prior to being launched), followed by 72 days at the outfitting docks.[39] By applying Henry Ford's assembly line techniques to the construction of large ocean-going cargo vessels, Kaiser revolutionized shipbuilding during World War II. As in Ford's automotive plants, workers with little or no skill were employed, quickly trained in seven- to ten-day courses to perform one small element of the shipbuilding process, and then put to work building ships more efficiently and cost-effectively than Kaiser's competitors.[40]

In April 1941, Kaiser negotiated the construction of a second shipyard in Richmond to meet the demands of a 24-ship, $46 million contract from the U.S. Maritime Commission. In November, Kaiser received yet another multimillion dollar contract. To city officials, Kaiser Corporation's arrival and subsequent growth signaled the final stage in Richmond's economic rise. Yet already by December 1941, the city was beginning to experience growing pains as people flowed into the area seeking the relatively high wages Kaiser offered.[41] Having little idea of what was about to overtake their city, local officials identified only a minor need to increase the provision of "general information, civic publicity and advertising" and improve "traffic rates and other necessary services" for Richmond's new residents.[42]

Shipyard officials, on the other hand, believing the burden of providing housing, municipal services, and schooling for the newcomers rested with the city, clearly understood the ramifications of what was happening in Richmond. Two days prior to the Japanese attack on Pearl Harbor, Kaiser's general manager, Clay Bedford, confronted the city's Chamber of Commerce, stating, "Frankly, one of our principal concerns is the ability of the city of Richmond to expand fast enough to absorb all the people we want to put to work.... We do not want to accept inferior personnel because the best personnel can live more economically and comfortably somewhere else."[43] City officials, although relishing the revenues that 13,000 shipyard employees were already bringing to Richmond's businesses, ignored Bedford's concerns.

At this point, Richmond's story becomes one of almost unimaginable growth. This "sleepy little town," in the words of historian Gerald Nash, became the "quintessential war boom town in America."[44] By 1943, Kaiser's shipyards and the conversion of many of Richmond's more than 50 industries to defense production drew tens of thousands of people from across the nation. In 1944, a special census of the San Francisco Bay Area indicated that although one-third of wartime migrants came from within California, two-thirds came from outside the state.[45] Of the latter, the greatest number came from the "West South Central" region of the country, including Oklahoma, Arkansas, Texas, and Louisiana.[46] Among these migrants were many blacks.[47] In 1940, there were 270 black residents in Richmond. By 1947, there were 13,780 or 14 percent of the city's total population.[48]

The consequences of wartime migration were visible everywhere in Richmond. Small business revenues in the city increased four to five times, while the circulation of the local newspaper, the *Richmond Independent*, rose from 6,000 to 35,000 daily.[49] As Richmond's population mushroomed, the number of houses and dwelling units available increased from 7,000 prior to the war to nearly 40,000.[50] Of these, most were constructed with funding from the federal government. Cumulatively, these housing developments represented the nation's largest public housing program up to that time.[51] Still, a housing shortage led many workers to sleep in cars, tents, and "hot beds" that were rented by the hour and never unoccupied.[52] Drawing on these newcomers as a source of labor, the Kaiser shipyards launched 727 ships, including 20 percent of the "Liberty ships" produced in the United States, and at "peak production" employed 90,634 people or over 7 percent of California's industrial employees during World War II.

Overcrowding and the Teacher Shortage

As a result of war-worker migration, annual city government expenditures rose from $800,000 in 1940 to $1,800,000 in 1944 in Richmond. Yet income from property taxes increased from $700,000 to only $1,070,000 during the same period, leaving the city without the finances necessary to sustain the municipal services, such as police, fire protection and sanitation, necessary for a safe, healthy, and livable community.[53] This weakness was nowhere more evident than in the public schools, with school enrollments between 1940 and 1945 reflecting Kaiser company officials' estimate of an average of three children "per family unit of in-migrant families" into Richmond.[54] During this period, the number of students in the Richmond Union High School District increased from 3,430 to 7,921, overwhelming the city's four secondary schools.[55] It was the increase in the number of elementary school students, however, from 2,987 to 13,112, that sent shock waves through city schools, leading one scholar to write that during World War II Richmond's schools "were in a state little short of chaotic disaster."[56]

The Federal Works Agency assigned public schools a low priority during the war years.[57] Prevented from acquiring the necessary federal financial support and rationed building materials, Helms was unable to construct classrooms to keep pace with skyrocketing enrollments. In 1940, there were 133 secondary school classrooms in Richmond, for an average enrollment of 26 students per room. By 1944, district officials obtained funding and construction materials approval for only four additional secondary classrooms, increasing this average to 58 students per room. As extreme as this was, the situation in the city's elementary schools was worse. With a prewar total of 132 classrooms, average enrollment in the elementary district was 23 children per classroom. With the construction of only 60 additional rooms by 1944, the average elementary school enrollment rose to 67 children per classroom.[58]

Richmond's native residents seemed oblivious to the extent of their city's boom when, in September 1941, an editorial in the *Richmond Independent* suggested that city schools could assimilate the growing migrant population: "The family that comes to a city with children is much more likely to become part of the community.... The children in the school first become a part of the community through the friendships with other pupils. Through the outside events of the school, they interest their parents and their parents, too, become oriented into the new surroundings."[59] Only days later, however, the paper reported that Richmond's schools were already struggling to adjust to the influx of such a great number of new students. "We are speedily reaching a saturation point," Walter Helms claimed, "and it is possible that measures to cope with the situation may have to be taken before the end of September."[60]

This was not the first time Helms publicly addressed the issue of overcrowding in Richmond's schools. Two months earlier he had called a meeting of city officials and the regional director of the Works Projects Administration to discuss the potential impact of defense worker housing then under construction.[61] The city's first federally subsidized project, Atchison Village, was relatively small, with 450 units of "permanent design" constructed near the Kaiser shipyards.[62] Early in the war, public officials decided they would contain the impact of war-worker migration in one area of the city by locating public housing close to the Kaiser shipyards and other defense industries.[63] The Richmond Housing Authority (RHA), which acted both as an agent of the federal government in public housing construction and management and as the city's watchdog committee on wartime housing, agreed to provide public housing during the war years at a ratio of one black family to every three white families (in practice the ratio was one to four).[64] The RHA then effectively segregated these units, assigning blacks to only the most poorly constructed developments.[65]

Not only did the "permanent design" of Atchison Village housing meet city officials' expectations, but because defense worker demand for the units far exceeded supply, members of the RHA were in a position to select the tenants who occupied the units, choosing primarily white, skilled workers. City officials were also pleased with the financial arrangements resulting from the housing. Under the provisions of the "Community Facilities" or Lanham Act of 1940, which funded the construction of public housing for defense personnel, the federal government provided the total $1,575,000 cost of building Atchison Village.[66] By directly purchasing the land on which public housing was constructed, however, the federal government removed the property from local tax rolls.[67] The Lanham Act, therefore, also provided for "payments in lieu of taxes" to local governments. These payments approximated the local revenues that would have been derived from the property had it been assessed and taxed at the local rate for private real estate. In the case of Atchison Village, the RHA agreed to accept 5 percent of the units' gross rental receipts as payment in lieu of taxes, which, in turn, were used to finance municipal services for the residents of these units.[68] Walter Helms signed a similar agreement with the federal government, accepting the districts' share of these in-lieu payments in order to finance schooling for the children and youth residing in Atchison Village.[69]

Not long after these arrangements were made, however, city officials learned that Richmond's first lucrative foray into federally subsidized housing would not be repeated. Between 1941 and 1943, the steady flow of migrants into Richmond became, as the city's mayor called it, an "avalanche."[70] To house these newcomers, the Federal Works Agency (FWA) constructed over 24,000 units at a cost of $50 million.[71] As the need for housing in defense areas expanded throughout the United States, however, the War Production Board imposed rationing restrictions on building materials. The federal government, in turn, abandoned funding permanent housing designs, such as those comprising Atchison Village, and began constructing temporary units designed as "war apartments" and "dormitories."[72] By the end of the war, 97 percent of Richmond's public housing was classified as "temporary" and over 50 percent of the city's residents lived in it.[73]

Problems stemming from temporary housing in Richmond arose as early as 1942. The poorly constructed, high-density units inverted the generous financial agreement the city had first entered into with the federal government concerning Atchison Village. By increasing the number of residents per acre while decreasing the assessed value on each of the units, temporary housing effectively decreased per capita rental receipts.[74] Moreover, because the federal bureaucracy processed these receipts at a typically slow pace compared to the speed of construction, Richmond received no in-lieu payments until well into 1943.[75] Finally, in 1942 the federal government amended the Lanham Act, permitting the Federal Housing Authority to deduct the cost of providing utilities, streets, and sewers to serve the residents of the units.[76] The financial loss suffered by the city government as a result of these developments was significant, leading the executive director of the Richmond Housing Authority to claim, "we don't believe if it were carried out to the limit that we would get anything."[77]

Simultaneously, Richmond lost a significant portion of its potential war-worker housing revenues by a technicality that removed almost 15,000 units from taxation. Housing constructed by the Maritime Commission (rather than the War Department) did not qualify under the Lanham Act for in-lieu payments of any kind. Whereas cities directly involved in the production of military materiél, such as nearby Vallejo, received substantial subsidies from the armed forces, Richmond did not qualify for an equal share of these subsidies for much of the war. City Attorney Thomas Carlson revealed the frustration that Richmond officials felt towards this situation during congressional hearings investigating the impact of mobilization on congested areas. "We want the influence of Congress with the Maritime Commission," proclaimed Carlson, "so that they will adopt Richmond the same as the Navy has adopted Vallejo. . . . We have nobody in the Maritime Commission that we can go to to sponsor us with the various Federal agencies to get the things necessary for our community."[78] As if these losses were not enough, following the United States' declaration of war, the U.S. government federalized Kaiser's shipyards as vital to the nation's military objectives. By taking control of the shipyards, the federal government removed a multimillion dollar industry from Richmond's tax rolls.[79]

Richmond's inability to increase city revenues at the same rate as its population put the city's two school districts in an almost impossible situation. By January 1942, with residents streaming into Atchison Village and more war housing under construction, school enrollment rose by 600 students, "the greatest increase in the history of Richmond schools," pronounced the *Richmond Independent*.[80] Walter Helms, having received no response from the federal government for a funding proposal he had submitted the previous July, announced that students would begin holding class in condemned parts of Lincoln Elementary School. "With almost every school in the district crowded to capacity," proclaimed Helms, "and enrollment still going upward, a search is being launched for additional space for classrooms."[81]

Although all of Richmond's wartime schools experienced some strain, those serving the city's war-worker housing developments faced the greatest challenges. As the percentage of children in kindergarten through grade eight who resided in public housing more than doubled (rising from 23.1 percent of Richmond's school enrollment during the 1942/43 school year to 53.3 percent the following school year), the four elementary schools located closest to the shipyards—Nystrom, Lincoln, Pullman, and Stege—became remarkably overcrowded.[82] In January 1943, Nystrom Elementary School, which normally enrolled 245 students, held 518. Lincoln Elementary, which normally served 210 students, enrolled 729. Pullman Elementary, which prior to the war served 105 students, enrolled 171. And Stege Elementary, which normally held 315 students, enrolled 622.[83] In October, the *Richmond War Homes Weekly*, a bulletin published by the Richmond Housing Authority, declared the city's school enrollment in excess of 18,000 students. "Leading the field," reported the *Weekly*, "is Nystrom school which had a total enrollment of less than 300 pupils three years ago and now, with a 30-room addition, has a total enrollment of 3,005, or more than a 1000 percent increase."[84]

To manage these enrollments, Walter Helms adopted a two-pronged strategy. First, he announced that several schools would begin double sessions or "shifts" during which half of the schools' students would arrive at 8:30 a.m. and depart at 12:30 p.m. Ten minutes later, class would begin for the other half of the student body and end at 4:40 p.m., essentially cutting in half the length of the school day.[85] By 1944, Nystrom Elementary had 72 classes on double session, Pullman had 28, and Stege had 60.[86] Over 50 years later, Marian Sauer recalled the difficulty this scheduling and a lack of adequate school facilities posed for teachers and students in Richmond:

> My first assignment was at Woodrow Wilson School, which at that time was 52 second graders on shift. I was the morning shift, eight o'clock, and another teacher took it over in the afternoon. Incidentally, there were no lights in Woodrow Wilson School in the classrooms . . . so if you had an eight o'clock group of children, you had to pretty much wing it until it got light.[87]

Alice Brimhall, who taught both first and third grade in Nystrom during the war, similarly recalled the challenges posed by the burgeoning student population:

That first day of school I'll never forget. . . . We were out in the yard and there was this mass of children, like a herd of cattle, and we held up signs. I held up third grade and they were to follow the signs if the children were in third grade. And when I got to my room I had 112 children, and 50 desks. So we took turns—who would sit in the desk and who would sit on the floor—and that lasted about three days and then I got down to 60, and usually you had people absent.[88]

Brimhall's colleague at Nystrom, Evelyn Haag, confirmed Brimhall's recollections, remembering the challenges of double sessions and the way the district coped with a shortage of classrooms:

I was hired in Richmond and went to work in September of '44, in a school, which before I got there, had made the big jump from a six or eight room school, to a school which must have had 50 teachers at least. We taught shift. I never had more than 49 children. Never hit 50, never hit 50—but it was in the high 40s. I know the first day of school you never knew how many you were going to have, and kindergarten teachers at the end of a few hours would come in and they had, that morning, had a hundred children to process in their room. . . . Mr. Helms was the superintendent for many, many years when all of a sudden he was faced with a sort of really different situation . . . and they built some new schools. The first part of that school [Nystrom Elementary] had been built in 1908. The first semester I taught in one of those old buildings. And then there was an annex to that which was still very old, built in the 30s, and then the new school, which had been built in '43. It was very nice, good facilities.[89]

As poor as their working conditions were, Sauer, Brimhall, and Haag escaped the worst classroom experiences in the city. In January 1944, one class at Stege Elementary enrolled 82 students and several classes went on quadruple session.[90]

Both the *Richmond War Homes Weekly* reference to a "30-room addition" to Nystrom Elementary School and Haag's memory of a "new school" on the Nystrom site indicated the second method Walter Helms employed to address the shortage of classroom space in Richmond. Continually frustrated in his efforts to receive funding and building material approval through the Lanham Act, Helms directly approached the agencies constructing war housing in Richmond in early 1943.[91] In response, the RHA agreed to finance the construction of a ten-room school near a new 806-unit housing development in an area of Richmond known as Harbor Gate.[92] The

U.S. Maritime Commission also assured Helms that it would build a 30-room school adjacent to Nystrom Elementary to serve a new 6,005-unit housing project.[93] Over the next three months, however, none of these commitments were fulfilled.

Just when it seemed matters could not get worse, on March 5, 1943, Roosevelt Junior High School was set ablaze. The fire destroyed 30 classrooms and forced Helms to put Richmond Union High School on double sessions so as to house the junior high school students in the high school building.[94] One month later, Helms's anger over the fire was still apparent when he issued an ultimatum to a congressional subcommittee. "A recent fire destroyed the classroom building of the Roosevelt Junior High School," Helms declared to the committee members. "This deprived us of 30 classrooms which were being used twice daily. Since the auditorium, shops, gymnasium and cafeteria buildings of this school were saved it is absolutely necessary that permission be given to reconstruct the classroom building."[95] To the *Richmond Independent*, Helms was even more forthright, asserting, "Even with the Roosevelt junior high school building restored our situation would still be acute. We are operating schools in Richmond on double sessions with classes ranging upwards from 60 pupils and still more coming in. It is not a question of whether or not the teacher can teach the youngsters anything. It is simply a question of whether she can maintain discipline."[96]

Finally, during the summer of 1943, financing for new classrooms and building material approval from the War Production Board began trickling in. By September, the U.S. Maritime Commission completed the promised 30-room school at the Nystrom site. In 1944, when Helms reported on the condition of the districts' schools, he indicated that there were an additional 50 classrooms being built, including those for a new junior high school, and another 23 classrooms approved for construction.[97]

Even among boomtowns, Richmond schools' over-enrollment and inability to obtain financial support to expand classroom space was extreme. As Congressman George Bates indicated in April 1943, "Here is a community ... which, I think, is undoubtedly the worst we have run across in the entire country in these congested areas. I don't think there is any comparison between your problems in Richmond and any other city even though the other cities are bad."[98] Walter

Helms ultimately held these developments responsible for limiting students' wartime educational attainment.⁹⁹ He acknowledged, moreover, the burden that the war boom placed on Richmond's teachers and how, in response, many abandoned their classrooms to obtain better paying defense work.

As the U.S. unemployment rate declined between 1940 and 1944, and males between the ages of 18 and 35 were drafted away from fields, factories, and even public schools, a nation-wide labor shortage developed.¹⁰⁰ Desperate for workers, defense industries turned to women, so much so that during the war years 49 percent of women working in factories and shipyards had not been employed prior to 1940 while 27 percent left behind lower-paying occupations, such as teaching school, to enter the mostly male workforce.¹⁰¹ Indeed, the National Education Association reported that a shortage of between 50,000 and 60,000 teachers existed in the nation at large as early as 1941.¹⁰² As the war progressed, this shortage grew at an alarming rate.¹⁰³ By June 1943, the rate of teachers leaving the profession rose from a national average of about one in ten, or 93,000 per year, to 189,000 a year.¹⁰⁴ In September, *Time* magazine reported that "half a million children may be locked out" of public and private school classrooms as a result of the shortage.¹⁰⁵ Moreover, as the number of teachers resigning their positions increased, the number of women planning on entering the teaching profession declined. Although during 1943/44, women's overall enrollment in institutions of higher education decreased to 67.1 percent of 1939/40 enrollments, in teacher preparation "normal schools" this decline was even more substantial, to 46.6 percent of prewar enrollments.¹⁰⁶

Richmond's teacher shortage mirrored trends both throughout California and the nation.¹⁰⁷ In 1941, Richmond's beginning "Class I" teacher's salary was $1,580 a year.¹⁰⁸ This contrasted dramatically with an unskilled shipyard laborer's starting salary of $2,375 a year.¹⁰⁹ Whereas the average annual salary of a shipyard worker was $3,090, the highest pay to be received on Richmond's two districts' salary scales was $2,865 a year.¹¹⁰ To counter the lure of shipyard wages, in May 1941 the Richmond Union High School District Board of Trustees voted to raise secondary school teachers' salaries by five dollars per month in addition to the regular annual increase of five dollars per month for the 1941/42 school year.¹¹¹ Implemented as an incentive for teachers to remain in their classrooms, the increase clearly failed to bring teachers' pay into parity with wages being offered by the Kaiser Corporation. Under pressure from a loosely coordinated group of teachers, the Board of Trustees again voted in 1942 to raise teacher salaries, this time adding ten dollars per month to the regular annual increase.[112] One year later, the then well-organized "Secondary Teachers' Association" lobbied for and received a 30-dollar monthly salary increase over and above the regular annual increase.[113]

While Richmond implemented pay increases in an effort to maintain its teaching force, Walter Helms publicly requested that retired teachers return to the city's classrooms.[114] Prior to the war, Helms succeeded in recruiting student-teachers while still in college. By 1943, however, with normal school enrollments declining, this labor pool became too shallow to rely on.[115] By convincing retired teachers to return to the classroom for the duration of the war, Helms hoped to alleviate Richmond's rapidly growing teacher shortage. In May 1944, however, at the same moment that the city's student enrollment peaked, Helms received 80 teacher resignations.[116] Desperate, Helms began to hire personnel from two remaining sources of labor, married women emigrating to the city with their husbands in search of war work and single women willing to journey to California.[117]

Helms successfully recruited teachers from across the nation as well as from the public housing projects surrounding the shipyards. Evelyn Haag observed the results of Helms's recruitment efforts in the characteristics of Nystrom Elementary School's wartime staff:

> Many, many of the teachers were, not temporary, but emergency credentials. My best friends came from Pennsylvania, Minnesota, Oklahoma. . . . They had been recruited. And they heard too that the money was out here. Some of them, I know one husband had come out to work in the shipyard industry, but the others were single young women. And my roommate who taught in the morning in the class was from Pennsylvania with, I think she probably had about six or seven years of experience.[118]

A survey of the Richmond public schools conducted two years following the end of the war confirmed Haag's impression of her colleagues. By 1947, only 25 percent of Richmond's teachers had five or more years of experience in the city's schools. Most were from other parts of California, the Great Lakes, and the Great Plains regions, and a large majority had taught in their home districts before moving to Richmond.[119]

Although Helms succeeded in increasing the size of the Richmond teaching force during the war years, he had neither the funding nor the number of applicants necessary to maintain the districts' prewar pupil-teacher ratios. Between September 1938 and June 1941, an average of 25 students were assigned to each teacher in kindergarten through grade eight in Richmond.[120] During the 1944/45 school year, this ratio peaked at approximately 50 students per teacher. To maintain its prewar pupil-teacher ratio, Richmond would have had to employ 780 teachers in the elementary grades in 1944. Instead, 315 teachers worked in the elementary district that year.[121]

By 1945, more than a third, or approximately 350,000, of the teachers employed at the beginning of the war had left the profession. In that same year, the U.S. Office of Education estimated that 109,000 teachers nationally were working under an emergency credential.[122] In Richmond, this included 25 percent of the teaching force.[123] That so many teachers abandoned their classrooms for employment in defense industries was indicative of both the low status attributed to teaching and the correspondingly low wages teachers received for their work.[124] In boomtowns such as Richmond, poor working conditions generated by overcrowded classes provided yet another incentive for teachers to seek greater occupational rewards elsewhere.

Civic-Professionalism

Although double sessions, school construction, and teacher recruitment eventually eased the challenges confronting Richmond's districts, these strategies did not resolve the question of whether schools should adjust for the transformed racial, ethnic, and cultural characteristics of their students. Walter Helms's response proved noteworthy. At a moment when city officials segregated public housing and defense industries spurned minority applicants and segregated workplaces, Helms chose not to mirror these patterns in school enrollments. Instead, the children of migrant families, black and white, attended the same schools and were taught in the same classrooms by the same teachers. As a result, children and youth from across the United States attended many of Richmond's schools during the war years and experienced what one could call a cross section of America's racial, ethnic, and cultural traditions.

In 1942, documentary photographer Dorothea Lange captured wartime developments in Richmond's schools on film. Familiar with the city's boomtown transformation, Lange chose to photograph Richmond because it represented the dramatic changes taking place in the San Francisco Bay Area during World War II.[125] Although much of her work depicted adult and family life, in 1942 Lange also photographed two classes of Richmond elementary school students. Assembled in a rough semicircle, students looked up toward Lange, who took the picture from an elevated position. Prior to snapping the shot, Lange asked the students to raise their hands in response to the question, "How many of you were *not* born in California?" The resulting photograph captured the overwhelmingly migrant nature of the group as well as the substantial degree of racial, ethnic, and cultural mixing that occurred in the city's schools as a result of Walter Helms's administrative policies.

Helms's leadership on issues involving migrant students arose from a sense of civic-professionalism anchored in both prewar and wartime developments and shared by many of Helms's colleagues—teachers and administrators alike. Seemingly at odds with prevailing social trends, civic-professionalism did not so much depart from precedent as it mirrored earlier patterns relating to race and education evolving throughout the western and northern United States for more than a decade—patterns that led school segregation, for instance, to be declared unconstitutional in the state of California soon after the end of World War II.

In June 1947, Governor Earl Warren formally ended *de jure* school segregation in the state of California. Only seven years later, as Chief Justice of the Supreme Court, he would read the Court's decision in *Brown v. Board of Education*, which ended segregation in public schools.[126] Warren repealed the state's segregation codes because of the Ninth Circuit Court of Appeals' upholding of the federal district court's decision in *Mendez et al. v. Westminster School District of Orange County*.[127] On February 18, 1946, Judge Paul J. McCormick had ruled in favor of five Mexican-American plaintiffs who sued the state for "unconstitutionally discriminating" against their children by requiring them to attend racially segregated schools.[128] On appeal, the seven-justice unanimous decision affirmed McCormick's ruling that segregating Mexican-American students in schools separate from whites violated their Fourteenth Amendment rights.[129]

Historian Charles Wollenberg writes that McCormick's decision in the *Mendez* case reflected "significant social and intellectual movements which produced a remarkable change in educational and judicial attitudes on matters of segregation and race," with "much of the social and educational theory" cited by McCormick anticipating "Earl Warren's historic opinion in the Brown case."[130] During the 1930s and 1940s, this "remarkable change" led many liberals to view segregation not as sound educational practice, as had previously been the case, but as a violation of the democratic principle of equality. Although *de facto* segregation continued to exist in California long after the *Mendez* decision, and indeed remains to this day, Wollenberg asserted that the *Mendez* ruling represented "a virtual revolution in educational thought," leading "spokesmen for California's educational establishment" to "vigorously condemn school segregation."[131]

As with the "movements" that bred Wollenberg's "virtual revolution," during World War II three social and intellectual developments intersected to inform the evolution of the civic-professional ideal.[132] The first of these was a reaction to the rise of fascism and the corresponding treatment of ethnic minorities in Europe during the 1930s. According to historian Richard Weiss, the rise of European totalitarianism, personified by the dictatorships of Hitler and Mussolini, resulted in "a sustained debate over ethnicity" in the United States that "produced a major assault on xenophobic and racist traditions."[133] Although this assault initially encouraged tolerance of ethnic groups of European descent, such as Jews, it eventually included blacks and other non-European minorities. "The situation in Europe became a touchstone for discussions of minority problems in America," writes Weiss. "In the 1930s, the tables were turned, the immigrant and to a lesser degree the black were seen as victims rather than threats. Racists replaced races as the villains in the social drama."[134]

Following America's entrance into the war, however, contradictions between racial oppression in the United States and the federal government's opposition to racist policies adopted by totalitarian governments became increasingly problematic. In response, President Roosevelt urgently promoted racial and religious tolerance.[135] In his State of the Union address in January 1942, for instance, Roosevelt declared, "We must be particularly vigilant against racial discrimination in any of its ugly forms. Hitler will try again to breed mistrust and suspicion between one individual and another, one group and another, one race and another."[136] Historian David Kennedy has suggested that Roosevelt's proclamations were not simply those of a "pragmatic wartime leader" striving to unify his people, but that "countless Americans" shared such sentiments.[137] As historian Ronald Takaki has made clear, however, Roosevelt's rhetoric frequently became reality only when minority groups in the United States, particularly blacks, forced his hand. "The 'Arsenal of Democracy,'" writes Takaki, "was not democratic; defense jobs were not open to all regardless of race. The war against Nazi Germany was fought with a jim crow army."[138] As a result of such hypocrisy, blacks promoted the "Double Victory" campaign (against oppression abroad and at home), resulting in, among other things, Roosevelt's issuing important federal civil rights protections.[139]

The second movement influencing the civic-professional ideal was marked by shifting attitudes on the part of American intellectuals in conceptions of race. Historians such as R. Fred Wacker have demonstrated how the rise of a "new generation" of social scientists following World War I "thought it was unscientific as well as undemocratic to assume that hidden factors such as 'blood' or ambiguous concepts such as 'racial temperament' played a determinative role in the development of individuals."[140] Among those scholars were anthropologists such as Franz Boas, who began to question the existence of race as a biological fact as early as the late nineteenth century, and Boas's students, such as Ruth Benedict, whose 1934 work, *Patterns of Culture*, popularized the notion of cultural differences as having far greater significance than race in human development.[141] Other social scientists followed suit, discrediting the "science" of racial inferiority and leading liberal scholars to transfer their focus of study from races to individuals and from "race relations" to "intergroup relations."[142]

Gunnar Myrdal's *An American Dilemma*, published in 1944, epitomized these intellectual undertakings, and according to historian Walter A. Jackson, "played a key role in establishing a liberal orthodoxy on the race question that included advocacy of desegregation, equality of opportunity in the marketplace, social engineering to aid the black poor, and the assimilation of blacks into white American culture."[143] Describing *An American Dilemma* as a "definitive statement" of "assimilationist racial liberalism," historian Daniel Perlstein has similarly written that color-blind Myrdalian liberalism "fortified both Black aspirations that American institutions were open to fundamental change and White liberal hopes that racism could be eliminated without a fundamental reordering of American society."[144] Such an approach to the "Negro problem," as Myrdal termed it, was appealing to liberals in the United States and suggested the power they believed color-blind ideology might hold for the future of social relations in the United States.

The third movement contributing to the formation of the civic-professional ideal evolved out of educators' prewar conceptions of their profession. During the 1930s, teachers and administrators frequently applied the term "democratic" to their work, suggesting the effort many made to ignore class distinctions among students. In their study of public schools during the Great Depression, for example, David Tyack, Robert Lowe, and Elisabeth Hansot identified educators' class-blind approach to students as a "tenet" of teacher professional identity:

> School people preferred to think of their work as class-blind. In a sense they were right, despite the great disparities of schooling for children of different classes. What they meant by class-blindness was basically two things: that public schools took all comers, from every social group (in fact were required to do so by law); and that in classrooms teachers had an ideology of treating every child fairly. 'I treat all my children alike'—this norm of fairness was a tenet of professionalism supported by the expectations of parents and children.[145]

During World War II, educators extended this "norm of fairness" from class to race, a development represented by the growth of the "intercultural education" movement in the United States.[146] Although

Rachel Davis DuBois initially conceived of intercultural education as a pluralist approach to schooling that attended to students' racial, ethnic, and cultural differences, leaders in the liberal Progressive Education Association wrested control of the movement from DuBois in the 1930s and transformed intercultural education into a program predicated on color-blind ideology.[147] The wartime publication of the Seventeenth Yearbook of the California Elementary School Principals Association, entitled *Education for Cultural Unity*, reflected this approach to intercultural education in the state of California.

Helen Heffernan, chief of the Division of Elementary Education in the California State Department of Education, and Corinne Seeds, principal of the University Elementary School at the University of California, Los Angeles, provided an ideal illustration of the role of color-blind ideology in California's classrooms in "Intercultural Education in the Elementary School," a section of the principals' yearbook."[148] Addressing the importance of schooling in instilling racial, ethnic, and cultural tolerance among students, Heffernan and Seeds related the story of a black, five-year-old boy who arrived to a mostly white and economically privileged kindergarten classroom. When a white student described his new classmate as "Little Black Sambo," the kindergarten teacher immediately intervened, asking the class:

> "Does it really matter about the color of a person's skin?" The children agreed that color was of no great importance. To the teacher's question of, "What does matter to us?" The children gave the following replies:
> "It matters whether he is a good boy."
> "It matters whether he is a good American."
> "It matters whether he plays fair. . . . "
> "What are we going to do in the future when we see people whose skins differ from ours?" The children concluded that they were to make no comments but give every boy and girl a chance to become good members of the school.[149]

In addition to demonstrating the teacher's role in mediating explicit forms of racism, Heffernan and Seeds identified fairness and equal treatment of the individual as the hallmarks of mid-century racial liberalism in their justification for the end of school segregation. "Nothing but actual contact," Heffernan and Seeds wrote, "will make children understand that a wide range of individual traits and abilities exists in every group; that every culture has individuals capable of making important contributions; and that in a democracy an individual must be valued in terms of the quality of his contribution to the general welfare regardless of race, color, or creed."[150] By encouraging public school employees to hold such tolerant attitudes toward their students, the California State Department of Education provided an authoritative stamp of approval for liberal educators' views during the war years.

The convergence of the public's awakening to the hypocrisy of American domestic versus foreign policy, the evolution of liberal social scientists' anti-racist agenda, and the broadening of the educator's professional ideal to include race significantly influenced liberal teachers' and administrators' conceptions of their work. Although it would be easy to dismiss the civic-professional ideal that resulted from these developments as mostly rhetoric, we should not—for during a brief period practice at both the school and district levels reflected the language of civic-professionalism. Walter Helms, for instance, directed few district policies specifically toward ethnic and racial minority students throughout the war years. Although prewar systems of IQ testing and tracking would have been logistically difficult to maintain in Richmond given the exponential growth of student enrollments, Helms nevertheless might have employed such strategies to segregate students. Instead, he eliminated those tracking mechanisms as well as the district's eighth-grade achievement examination required for high school admission.[151] Helms also refused to relegate poorly performing migrant students, blacks in particular, to basic skills classes. Instead, he dispersed these pupils throughout classrooms so as to prevent any one teacher from having a disproportionate number.[152] Social promotion, the elimination of which might have served to "weed out" students from Richmond's overcrowded schools, continued throughout the war years. In 1940, 6 percent of Richmond's students were one or more years older than the average age for their grade; by 1944, this number had increased to only 7 percent.[153]

Both native and recently arrived residents of Richmond frequently opposed Helms's policies. Although racial mixing among elementary school students caused concern among many parents, particularly whites recently arrived from the South, mixing in the junior highs and high school led to public outcries against the school district. Detailed data on the number of students of color enrolled in the city's secondary schools during World War II is unavailable. Pictures in school yearbooks, student newspapers, and local newspaper reports, however, depict students of color participating in both the curricular and extracurricular secondary school program throughout the war years.[154] Indeed the strongest evidence for the existence of substantial racial, ethnic, and cultural mixing in Richmond's secondary schools during World War II comes from parent protests over policies that permitted such mixing.

When fights between black and white teenagers in the community led to a white student being wounded in a knife fight, many parents placed the blame for this and other conflicts at the feet of Richmond's school administrators.[155] Parents responded to the publicity surrounding the fights by boycotting the schools and demanding a meeting with district officials.[156] Although school administrators, led by Helms, explained that the fights in question occurred off school property and were therefore the responsibility of the Richmond Police Department, many parents rejected the claim. Instead, they insisted that school policies were the origin of such conflicts, with Richmond Assistant City Attorney John Pierce declaring, "The policy of the administration has been one of utter stupidity."[157] The journalist covering the meeting clarified Pierce's specific criticism, reporting, "Constantly during the course of the discussion it was proposed that segregation be ordered."[158] District officials refused the proposal, instead indicating the roles they believed local businesses, which sold knives to youngsters, and some parents who advocated violence, played in the conflicts. Principal C. V. Howell of Roosevelt Junior High School, for instance, described how one father told his student to "go to school and get a Negro."[159] "The boy," explained Howell, "was at a loss what to do when he was told that things were not run like that in California schools."[160]

As this meeting illustrates, school leaders other than Walter Helms demonstrated civic-professionalism in their work as educators during World War II. Indeed, color-blind ideology abounds in oral histories conducted with Richmond's administrators.[161] When asked whether migrant students struggled in adjusting to their new schools, for instance, one principal claimed:

> They took a lot of ribbing about being Okies. Kids are rough on other kids sometimes, more so than adults. They didn't hesitate to call the newcomers names, and the newcomers were a little shy. But there was no problem in the newcomers getting along with other kids. It was the adults who were fixed in their feelings, who had trouble adjusting, whose minds were set. The newcomers didn't change to be like the others. The kids here already took on the habits and experiences of the newcomers, and vice-versa. They mixed in together and you couldn't tell them apart.[162]

Teachers shared such sentiments. Alice Brimhall recalled that Nystrom Elementary School was severely overcrowded by students of varying ethnic and racial backgrounds. She did not remember this mixing as problematic, however. Instead, Brimhall emphasized the positive social relations that she developed with her students, and that her students, black and white, developed with each other:

> We had children from all walks of life. College professors that came out, and alot of the shipyard workers. I had some that could read and some that couldn't. . . . We had 60 children on our registers. . . . I still can't believe it. And yet we didn't have problems. . . . When I stop to think now—discipline became harder and harder as I went through teaching—but they [wartime students] got along fine. I remember— to me it was the most interesting thing . . . a lot of black children came, there were a lot of blacks that came, and some of the children had never seen blacks. . . . They took hands in this circle—they were playing a game—and this one little child had the hand of a black child, and he looked at his [the Black child's] hand, and I guess he thought it was chocolate or something because he looked close, and then he was perfectly happy.[163]

Evelyn Haag also exhibited the civic-professional ideal in remembering her classroom as consisting of students from "all different backgrounds" who "got along" with one another. However, Haag felt quite differently towards many of the parents of her students:

> Richmond changed very dramatically, very fast and they [migrant parents] were mostly in the shipyard industry because that's where the money was. One thing with the children coming from the south that I remember is . . . I would get notes from parents, white parents, saying quote, "Don't let my little boy sit next to that nigger." Unquote. I was just very upset by it. I couldn't understand. These little children would play together and have such fun together, and then their parents would step in and put this burden of discrimination on them.[164]

As with Haag, many of Richmond's wartime teachers claimed that migrant parents, black and white, were prejudiced, neglectful, and uninterested in their children's education. One teacher, for instance, believed that the "problem" regarding parents "was indifference." "They [migrant parents] just wouldn't be bothered," she claimed. "I tried to visit their homes. I couldn't raise anyone. They were either at work, or if they were sleeping they wouldn't bother to get up. I tried to make contact but I seldom could. . . . I can sum it up by saying that the newcomers had a total indifference towards the welfare of their kids."[165] This accusation is particularly striking considering that many migrants moved to Richmond to secure better financial futures for their families. Although paying relatively high wages, the Kaiser shipyards and Richmond's other defense industries frequently required employees to work ten- to twelve-hour shifts, often six days a week. Teachers' interpretations of such behavior as "indifference" suggests the lack of empathy many felt towards migrant parents and their efforts to recover from the financially devastating effects of the Great Depression.

Teachers, moreover, identified what they perceived to be migrant parents' lack of respect for schooling as being a significant obstacle to their students' success. One teacher, for instance, claimed:

> We had an influx of people from the Middle West with very little education. It was great mass of black people, all hoping to improve themselves, a worthy ambition. But some, white and black, had only a bare minimum of schooling. They didn't know what education was, and college was unheard of. . . . School to them was only a necessary evil, or just an evil. . . . They had no feeling of need for the schools. Many adults thought school was unnecessary, so why should they send their kids?[166]

The complexity of attitudes teachers held towards students and their parents suggests the limitations of the civic-professional ideal as implemented in Richmond during the war years. No greater contradiction existed, however, than teachers' silence on the sudden removal of Japanese and Japanese-American students from their classrooms. Beginning with the implementation of Executive Order 9066 in February 1942, these students and their families were interned in camps such as those in Manzanar, California, and Poston, Arizona.[167] Their absence from Richmond's schools during World War II stands in stark contrast to Lange's depiction of the city's racially mixed classrooms. The internment of classmates of Japanese descent undoubtedly taught students a lesson far more significant than any their teachers attempted to instruct. Chris Melgoza, a wartime junior high school student, for instance, remembered that his friend, Gilbert Sukihara, suddenly disappeared from school one day. Concerned, Melgoza asked his parents where his friend's family had gone. "They were Japanese," he was told. "They just disappeared."[168] Of course they had not, as the *Richmond Independent* made clear when it expressed support for Japanese internment. "We have learned the bitter lesson," the newspaper's editor declared, "that a race so steeped in its own prejudices and selfish racial solidarity as the Japanese, is a menace to all free peoples, and to all free government.... No other race in our midst had proved so unassimilable as the Japs."[169]

Conclusion

The civic-professional ideal permitted unprecedented racial mixing in Richmond's schools throughout the war years, revealing the potential of public education to counter the injustice of a racially fractured society. In this regard, Richmond's public schools were citadels of democracy during World War II. As practiced by the city's educators, however, civic-professionalism ignored the social and economic conditions confronting blacks in Richmond. Administrators and teachers did not identify the increasing diversity of their students as a problem to be solved; yet they also did not target that development as worthy of their professional attention and engagement. Considering, for instance, that the location of Richmond's war-worker housing created what historian Marilyn Johnson called a "migrant ghetto" consisting of white and black workers and their families, Walter Helms failed to equally distribute the impact of the city's school crisis throughout its districts.[170] Instead Helms maintained, as he did prior to the war, that all students should attend their neighborhood schools. As a result, schools nearest public housing developments, such as Nystrom Elementary, became severely overcrowded, while others in more affluent areas of the district, such as Kensington Elementary, remained comparably stable.

This profound overcrowding, along with teachers' passive acceptance of Japanese internment and their lack of empathy for migrant parents, demonstrated the degree to which Richmond's educators were either unaware of or uninterested in the consequences of race, ethnicity, and culture in American society. Inattention to these significant social markers ultimately undermined the civic-professional ideal in Richmond, particularly as black demands for social justice came to prominence in the postwar era. During the war years, Richmond officials estimated that with the close of hostilities the city's population would decline to approximately 50,000, twice the prewar level. Richmond's new residents, however, had other plans. The 1950 census indicated that the city's population was 99,545, a decline from peak war production years but still almost four times the number of residents in 1940.[171] Richmond was simply, as one postwar publication claimed, a "boomtown that didn't bust."[172]

In 1949, the NAACP indicated that blacks who moved to the San Francisco Bay Area were unlikely to return to the South even though the Bay Area's economic boom had slowed from its wartime peak. Relating the story of Willie Stokes, a black immigrant who worked in the Richmond shipyards during the war, the NAACP reported:

> Things are bad; they are very bad for Willie Stokes and his family out in California. But they will stay; there are good reasons. In California his children go to the same schools as other children. They go for nine months during the year. The buildings are new and warm and well lighted. He can ride on a bus without having to take a rear seat marked 'colored.' He can attend any movie and take any seat he likes. . . . He can walk down the street without having to move toward the curb when a white man passes."[173]

Yet as the story of Willie Stokes also indicated, "Negroes on the West Coast face a very uncertain future."[174] The extremes of boom town life magnified this uncertainty, especially as it related to employment and housing. As one commentator observed, "The social problem [in Richmond] was to make a campsite into a community."[175]

Although designated an "All-America City" in 1954 for the way it managed postwar readjustment, Richmond experienced increasing social conflict in the decades following World War II.[176] Defense housing, for instance, the most prevalent type of housing for Richmond's black residents following the war, was over 80 percent occupied in 1950. Nevertheless, the city's "Redevelopment Agency" moved that year to "clear blighted areas" consisting primarily of wartime public housing and replace them with "large privately constructed housing projects embodying the finest principles of modern living."[177] Such actions on the part of Richmond's civic and business organizations threatened the city's black residents, who responded by demanding fair treatment through organizations such as the NAACP.

Public schools, too, became arenas of racial and ethnic conflict in postwar Richmond. A "Master Plan" produced for the city's public schools and recreation programs in 1948 indicated that instead of achieving a degree of stability in providing services to children and youth following the war, Richmond continued to struggle. "The pressure upon facilities shows no sign of decreasing," noted the Richmond City Planning Commission, "School and playground space is used to capacity. Richmond, contrary to expectations, has not become a ghost town since the war."[178] Publicly admitting defeat in 1944, Walter Helms seemed aware of this reality. Having struggled for the previous four years to manage the severe disruption caused by homefront mobilization, Helms proclaimed, "Despite the best, all-out efforts of the Richmond schools . . . classroom shortages, teacher shortages, and dwindling finances have culminated in a permanent loss to the school children. Successful democracy requires the greatest possible number of enlightened future citizens. Here are twenty thousand future citizens who will have missed something in the way of adequate preparation to perpetuate what our armies are preserving.[179]

When Walter Helms retired from Richmond's school districts five years later, he was honored for his leadership of the public schools through the trying war years. Richmond's schools did, in fact, face unparalleled challenges during World War II. In response, school leaders implemented policies that would not have been considered prior to 1941, including 50-to-1 student teacher ratios and double and triple school sessions. Eventually, funding from the federal government, an increase in the city's tax rate, and two major bond issues allowed Richmond to spend over $7 million constructing new classrooms. Ironically, however, this expansion in physical capacity combined with increasingly segregated housing patterns to permit a previously impossible degree of *de facto* segregation to develop in the city's school districts.[180] Beginning in 1955, and for the next two decades, racial tension frequently erupted over school board proposals regarding the location of new school construction and district-wide enrollment policies.[181]

World War II presented a window of opportunity to bring the civic-professional ideal to fruition in Richmond's public schools. Although teachers and administrators ultimately failed to do so because of their inability or unwillingness to confront the association of race, ethnicity, and culture with oppression in the United States, they nevertheless demonstrated the capacity to transcend explicitly racist attitudes and beliefs firmly woven into the fabric of wartime society. The story of Richmond's public schools during World War II, then, illustrates the limitations of schools as mechanisms for social reform while also demonstrating the capacity of schoolteachers and administrators to promote civic-mindedness in a society frequently characterized by racism and intolerance. Understanding this historical complexity is a necessary prerequisite for developing strategies to implement the civic-professional ideal in ways that both attend to student difference and diversity and search for common ground among students in the present.

5

Wartime Nursery Schools in Richmond

> Long range guns which can shoot twenty years into the future are now firing on the United States in a war potentially as destructive as that being fought around the world today. No section of the country is out of their range.
>
> The victims are the youngest citizens of the United States, children who are being uprooted from their homes and family ties and orphaned every day in ever-increasing numbers by the industrial war effort their country is making.[1]
>
> —*The Saturday Evening Post*, 1942

Throughout the war years, many Americans believed that the social disruption resulting from homefront mobilization posed a serious threat to the "American way of life."[2] Nowhere was this instability deemed more pernicious than in its effect on the family. Children were portrayed as particularly vulnerable during wartime, as this chapter's opening quote from *The Saturday Evening Post* reveals. With fathers increasingly drafted into the military and mothers taking paid employment in ever-greater numbers in the nation's defense plants and shipyards, stories in the popular press reflected national concerns over child neglect and abandonment. American anxiety over "eight-hour orphans" and "latchkey children"—youngsters who wore door keys around their necks so as to let themselves into their homes while their parents worked—was compounded by reports of dramatically increasing rates of juvenile delinquency during the war years, also believed a result of social instability. As a consequence, many Americans proclaimed the need to protect the "traditional family," with its clearly delineated gender roles, from further erosion.

As a total war requiring the active engagement of both armed forces on the battlefront and civilian workers on the homefront, however, World War II demanded that millions of women work in the nation's defense industries. The female labor force expanded from 12 million to 18 million workers between 1940 and 1945, an increase that challenged traditional social norms and posed a significant societal dilemma—while Americans perceived the war as being fought to defend their way of life, winning the war entailed violating these popularly proclaimed ideals.[3]

For some, this dilemma was resolved by establishing federally endorsed centers of early childhood education for use by working mothers and their young children during World War II. As scholars have demonstrated, many Americans during the first three decades of the twentieth century considered publicly provided "day nurseries" to be low quality, charitable institutions designed to serve destitute families.[4] Especially in contrast to private "nursery schools," which catered to middle-class parents and claimed to provide constructive educational experiences for young children, day nurseries were perceived as a custodial welfare measure. Conceptions of the quality of publicly provided child care began to shift during the Great Depression, however, when the federal government sponsored "Emergency Nursery Schools" as a New Deal welfare program. Initially established to relieve the stresses of the national economic crisis by employing teachers and staff, the nursery schools' design and function were significantly influenced by the active involvement of leaders in the field of early childhood education. Yet not until World War II did federal and state governments, as well as cities and towns across the United States, take responsibility for establishing and subsidizing high-quality, low-cost preschool education for the young children of working mothers.[5]

The city of Richmond established and operated 12 of these wartime nursery schools as part of its public school system between 1942 and 1945. "Five O'Clock Mothers," as working women with children were frequently labeled, relied on the services of Richmond's nurseries, including one 24-hour "all-night" nursery, to care for their young children while they labored in the city's defense industries, especially the Kaiser shipyards.[6] Two of these schools are especially noteworthy. Frustrated at the federal government's slow pace in actively advancing child care for working mothers during World War II, shipbuilding magnate Henry Kaiser convinced the U.S. Maritime Commission to construct two buildings designed specifically to house nursery schools in Richmond.[7] The Maritime and Pullman Nursery Schools, developed in collaboration with experts in early childhood education, were hailed as innovations in both architectural design and curricular program. Although Henry Kaiser, through his son Edgar, was similarly responsible for establishing well-publicized nursery schools at his shipyards in Portland, Oregon, Richmond's Maritime Nursery School predated those in Portland. Moreover, unlike Kaiser's Portland centers, the Maritime and Pullman nurseries represented a unique nexus in the provision of early childhood education during World War II. The schools were catalyzed by private industry, constructed and subsidized by the federal government, administered by the Richmond City School District, and supported through parent fees.

Richmond's nursery schools were publicly credited with providing mothers of young children the support necessary to make a significant contribution to America's industrial capacity. Their success, however, should not be measured solely by the hundreds of thousands of "woman-hours" of labor they made available to the shipyards.[8] By implementing a curricular program strongly influenced by Progressive theories of education and emphasizing children's creative expression through the arts, the schools both legitimized the educational qualities of publicly provided nursery schooling and eroded the social stigma associated with working mothers' use of outside-the-home group care.[9] The curriculum, moreover, was meant to train the "little ones" in "good citizenship," an objective that nursery school educators defined as fostering civic-mindedness and democratic values while also instilling attitudes that prevented future juvenile delinquency and other antisocial behaviors.[10]

As a result of the importance that Richmond's nursery school teachers placed on providing educationally enriching experiences for children, the city's wartime nurseries came to resemble historically well-respected, private nursery schools. Administering the wartime nurseries as a downward extension of the public school system also contributed to their being thought of as a new layer of educational provision within the Richmond City School District rather than a program separate from public schooling.[11] Finally, thought of as citadels of democracy during a time of national crisis, Richmond's wartime nurseries illuminate Americans' enduring reliance on public education as an institutional response to the dilemmas associated with dramatic social, economic, and political dislocation in the United States.[12]

"This Absentee Wife and Mother Business"

On December 17, 1941, only ten days following the Japanese attack on Pearl Harbor, Katharine Lenroot, chief of the U.S. Children's Bureau, submitted to U.S. Secretary of Labor Frances Perkins the final report of the 1940 "White House Conference on Children in a Democracy." The conference, which was attended by more than 600 government officials, child welfare advocates, scholars, and bureaucrats, was the fourth sponsored by the White House since President Theodore Roosevelt called the initial meeting in 1909.[13] Discussions at the 1940 conference suggested that attendees were primarily concerned with Depression-era issues, including the impact of poverty on children in rural and urban areas, children's physical and emotional health, and the results of a decade's worth of experimentation with New Deal child welfare programs.[14] What was exceptional, however, was the conference's strong affirmation of the role of the "traditional" family, with its historically defined gender roles of the male breadwinner and the stay-at-home mother, in cultivating democratic values and behaviors in children. Labeling this "point of view" a central element in the conference's "Democratic Credo," the final report asserted:

> The pursuit of the democratic ideal in the ways of American life must go hand in hand with the democratic training of the child. . . . The most general and far-reaching institution in which democracy may be fostered is the family. The family may be, and therefore should be, for the child the threshold of democracy. Relations between parent and child, among all members of the family, and between family and world outside therefore offer the first materials in the school of democracy. In

this first school of democracy, the family, the child develops his first moral and ethical standards."[15]

Although conceptions of the family as a fundamental organ in the body of the democratic state were hardly new, historian Sonya Michel has identified the 1940 White House conference as the forum in which the "major themes" of what she calls the "discourse of the democratic family" were first articulated. According to Michel, with war fast approaching, "the family was regarded as a key link in the nation's defenses and women were deemed essential to the family's survival and stability. This discourse not only reinforced traditional views of women's role but also invested the family with political significance."[16] Indeed, as historian Robert Westbrook has shown, Americans' private interests, such as children and family life, intersected with perceived political and civic obligations during World War II to provide citizens with a compelling answer to the question, "Why should we fight?" "[S]uch obligations," Westbrook writes, "to family, to children, to parents, to friends, and generally, to an 'American Way of Life' defined as a rich (and richly commodified) private realm of experience—were tirelessly invoked in the campaign to mobilize Americans for World War II."[17]

The Roosevelt administration's efforts to put the nation on a war footing received a dramatic boost from Americans' beliefs that they were fighting for their families and the democratic way of life as much, or even more, than they were fighting for the nation-state.[18] Federal agencies, especially those that had historically privileged the traditional family in policy development, strongly endorsed this sentiment. In August 1941, for instance, participants in the U.S. Children's Bureau's "Conference on the Day Care of Children of Working Mothers" issued a statement of principle that inherently defended the traditional family, asserting, "We recognize the extreme importance of national defense and the necessity of maintaining the democratic way of life which makes successful defense imperative. Toward this end we believe that every effort should be made to safeguard home life, to strengthen family relationships, and to give parents a direct opportunity to participate in community planning."[19] Yet at that same conference, Mary Anderson, chief of the U.S. Department of Labor's Women's Bureau, reported preliminary figures from the 1940 census indicating that the traditional model of the American family was already in decline. A "larger proportion of the woman population was in the labor force in 1940 than had been gainfully employed in 1930," Anderson noted, with the most significant increase occurring among women ages 25 and 44, "the years when family responsibilities are normally the greatest."[20] Anderson also reported that in the 12 months between October 1939 and 1940 women's employment increased another 4 percent while the number of hours and variety of shifts worked, including the 3:00 p.m. to 11:00 p.m. "night shift," also rose.[21] Unconfirmed at the time, Anderson's data accurately identified a consistent increase in the number of mothers entering into paid labor in the United States, a trend that having begun earlier in the twentieth century accelerated during the Great Depression.[22]

Between 1929 and 1933, the worldwide economic collapse halved the United States' gross national product while raising the number of unemployed Americans from less than 3 million to more than 12 million, almost one-quarter of the nation's workforce.[23] In cities such as Cleveland and Toledo, Ohio, unemployment rates soared above 50 percent. Nationally, workers fortunate enough to retain jobs saw their wages slashed. Average family income declined from $2,300 to $1,500 annually and 9 million Americans lost their savings in bank closures.[24] During the worst two years of the Depression, 600,000 families were forced to abandon their homes due to foreclosure.[25] Unable to determine how long the decline would last and uncertain of the prospects for their families' survival, parents increasingly chose to entrust their children to more secure settings. The number of children placed in custodial institutions rose by 50 percent during the Depression—a figure that does not include those children relinquished to less formal arrangements such as distant family members.[26]

A significant number of women responded to this dramatic rise in fiscal and familial instability by seeking wage labor. In the Depression's early years, women lost their jobs at a much higher rate than men. By late 1932, however, because most women sought work in traditionally female occupational sectors that recovered more quickly from the crash, such as clerical, human services, and light industry, they began reentering the labor force at twice the rate of men.[27] As a result, many began to make important contributions to their family income and some became their family's primary breadwinner. As Alice Kessler-Harris writes in her study of wage-earning women in the United States, "Ideas that once had consigned women to inferior places in the labor force now preserved for them jobs that menfolk could not get. Their status as cheap workers and their marginal wages could, and did, keep whole families alive."[28]

As Women's Bureau Chief Mary Anderson reported, a large proportion of women who entered the workforce during the Depression were married and over 25 years of age.[29] In Berkeley, California, for instance, 40 percent of married women worked during the 1930s.[30] For women with young children, however, wage labor was only possible if adequate day care arrangements were available, and even then traditional social norms held white, middle-class mothers who worked outside the home guilty of child neglect.[31] Although the severely contracted labor market may have limited men's capacity to support their families, the "male breadwinner/female caretaker paradigm" remained a foundation of gender relations in the United States.[32] Its persistence offers a partial explanation for why federally subsidized "Emergency Nursery Schools" during the Depression era were primarily intended to employ out-of-work teachers, nutritionists, nurses, custodians, and maintenance workers rather than providing mothers with the flexibility needed to engage in wage labor.[33]

The origins of the Emergency Nursery Schools are evident in the social policies of the New Deal, through which President Roosevelt's initiatives frequently made public what had been historically conceived of as private affairs in American society, including charitable assistance, employment, financial security, old age dependency, and children's well-being. Established in 1933 as a jobs program under the Federal Emergency Relief Administration (later known as the Works Progress Administration), the Emergency Nursery Schools received funding from the federal government solely for teachers' salaries. State and local governments assumed responsibility for providing buildings, equipment, and children's meals, while public school districts administered the programs. Children between the ages of two and five whose parents were unemployed qualified for enrollment.

As a mechanism for employment and relief, the Emergency Nursery Schools might have been established as essentially custodial institutions. Indeed, until the late 1920s a distinction persisted in the United States between "day nurseries" (which were rooted in early twentieth century social reforms, reputed to serve a custodial function, and frequently sponsored by private, philanthropic associations as a charity for the destitute) and "nursery schools" (which were informed by the Progressive education reform movement, reputed to provide children with enriching educational experiences, and whose clients were primarily tuition-paying, middle-class families). That the Emergency Nursery Schools were not modeled on the day nurseries was a product of both the active involvement of professional early childhood educators in developing the schools' educational program and the hiring of unemployed teachers, many who had several years of classroom experience and understood their professional responsibilities as instructional rather than simply custodial.[34]

Members of the National Association of Nursery Educators, the Association of Childhood Education, and the National Council of Parent Education seized the opportunity to transform the Emergency Nursery Schools from a relief program into an educational one. "No one," early childhood educator Christine Heinig later recalled, "wanted [the schools] to be simply child-minding or babysitting centers."[35] Yet over the course of their ten-year existence, during which 3,000 nurseries enrolled almost 500,000 children in 43 states, the nation's capital, the Virgin Islands, and Puerto Rico, the nurseries struggled to maintain high educational standards.[36] Staff and student turnover was high (a result of the relief-oriented qualifications for employment and school attendance as well as the transience of the American people during the Depression years) and conflicting missions undermined the schools' sustainability. Moreover, as the American economy began to recover in the second half of the 1930s, support for the schools waned. By 1942, only 944 Emergency Nursery Schools remained in operation, serving fewer than 39,000 children—a striking increase over the approximately 300 private nursery schools existing in the United States prior to 1933, yet a decline that foretold of a rapidly approaching end to the federal program.[37]

However, as mobilization for war virtually eliminated unemployment in the United States and then created a nationwide labor shortage, a new need arose for government-sponsored nursery schools. Having established a clear precedent for federal involvement in early childhood education, the Emergency Nursery Schools served as a preliminary model for wartime nurseries that would provide high quality, affordable day care for children whose mothers labored in the nation's defense plants and shipyards.

In her study of wartime women shipyard workers, historian Amy Kesselman identified three solutions to what was considered the "problem" of day care for young children during World War II.[38] The first solution was to alter the "structure of industrial life" to provide women with more accommodating work schedules, making paid work and parenting more complementary than conflicting. This practice, as Kesselman writes, was "never taken seriously," even at Henry Kaiser's shipyards in Portland, Oregon—an absence worth noting given the national acclaim Kaiser received for his sensitivity to working women's child care needs during the war years. The second solution was to discourage the mothers of young children from engaging in paid labor at all. This option, although resting easily in the context of prewar conceptions of women's domesticity, became impractical as the draft drew greater and greater numbers of men into the armed forces and the nation's industrial capacity became increasingly reliant on working women. The third solution, which was considered a "last resort" by many, was to provide outside-of-the-home group care for preschool children between two and five years of age.[39]

As mobilization ended the nation's economic crisis and women entered the labor force in rising numbers, however, many Americans feared that expanding accessibility to nursery schools might have the unintended effect of encouraging mothers of young children to work outside the home.[40] In mid-1941, for instance, Mary Anderson, whose U.S. Women's Bureau was adamantly opposed to "barriers against the employment of mothers with young children," nevertheless announced, "We would not urge ... women with small children to go to work unless it was absolutely necessary."[41] U.S. Secretary of Labor Frances Perkins, the first woman in U.S. history to serve as a member of a presidential cabinet, echoed Anderson's sentiment:

> In this time of crisis, it is important to remember that mothers of young children can make no finer contribution to the strength of the Nation and its vitality and effectiveness in the future than to assure their children the security of home, individual care, and affection. Except as a last resort, the Nation should not recruit for industrial production the services of women with such home responsibilities.[42]

Groups such as the U.S. Children's Bureau, the War Manpower Commission, and the American Home Economics Association also initially opposed the employment of mothers of young children, even when such employment was touted as a patriotic act.[43] As a commentary in the *Journal of Home Economics* stated:

> Each day as the U.S. war effort gains in momentum there is an increase in the number of five o'clock wives and mothers—women who hastily prepare breakfast for their families and then leave for a day's work at the office and factory. Some, perhaps much, of this absentee wife and mother business is inevitable and necessary, as more men enter military service. Some of it may be carried out with no hurt to the children involved or to family life. Part of it, however, indicates a failure to realize the values to be achieved and preserved only through the wife and mother remaining at her post in the home.[44]

Such tenuous support for working mothers reflected both the ambivalence many Americans felt towards the entry of a growing number of mothers into the labor force and the heightened anxiety they experienced over the perceived widespread neglect of children by working mothers.[45]

Throughout the war era, images of children left to fend for themselves while their mothers labored in the nation's defense plants and shipyards captured Americans' attention, triggering strong emotional responses. The nation's most popular magazines and newspapers, including *The Saturday Evening Post*, *The Ladies' Home Journal*, *The Christian Science Monitor*, and the *New York Times*, ran stories featuring children as young as preschoolers who were neglected, abused, and abandoned by wage-earning parents.[46] In one report, nine children in southern California were found chained to trailers as their parents worked in factories. In another, investigators discovered that preschool age children in Connecticut were attending elementary school with an older child, having been instructed by parents to "wait outside until Johnny gets out of school."[47] *Washington Post* journalist Agnes Meyer contributed to these disturbing reports with her 1944 work, *Journey Through Chaos*. Having traveled the country in search of the effects of mobilization on the homefront, including visiting Richmond, California, Meyer reported on numerous instances of child neglect resulting from women's employment, writing:

In the San Fernando Valley, in the city limits of Los Angeles, where several war plants are located, a social worker counted 45 infants locked in the cars of a single parking [lot]. In Vallejo, the children sit in the movies, seeing the same film over and over again until mother comes off the swing shift and picks them up. Some children of working parents are locked in their homes, others locked out. . . .

I could pile horror upon horror of this sort, but there is no use in doing it again. I have done it before, and all the world knows that these crimes against childhood are taking place from one end of our country to another.[48]

As a result of such reporting, many Americans held working mothers in contempt. Indeed, historian William Tuttle has written that the "American latchkey child" was "one of the most pitied homefront figures of the Second World War" and that "his or her working mother was not only criticized but even reviled." As Tuttle also reminds us, however, most Americans exhibited this anxiety in relation to white children only. Rarely, if ever, was concern expressed for black children whose mothers had always worked outside of the home.[49]

Mothers who reportedly neglected their infants and young children by locking them in homes or parked cars in factory lots were scorned not only for their moral failings; they were also blamed for wider problems. Americans traced a perceived rise in rates of juvenile delinquency during World War II directly to an increase in the number of mothers who worked outside the home. Although children between the ages of two and five were obviously too young to engage in delinquent acts, Americans nevertheless believed that the seeds of such behavior were sown early in a child's life. They believed that wartime delinquency was caused, in part, by an increase in the number of mothers who participated in wage labor during the Depression, and that an even greater rise in the number of mothers of young children working outside the home during the war years would result in postwar social disaster.[50] "No one can blame the mothers who want to help in the war effort or make more money for their families," sympathized the author of a *Better Homes and Gardens* story, "*but the result has been neglected children and a sharp increase in child delinquency*" [emphasis original].[51] Even more concisely linking mothers' paid labor to the rise in juvenile delinquency, a 1942 *New York Times* headline read, "Plan Is Laid to Curb Delinquency; Mothers in War Jobs Create Problem."[52]

According to the U.S. Children's Bureau, the number of cases of juvenile delinquency in areas of 100,000 or more residents throughout the United States rose from approximately 64,000 in 1940 to 74,000 in 1942, an increase of almost 16 percent. By 1944, the Bureau estimated, the number had escalated to more than 105,000.[53] Cities across the United States confirmed the rise. Officials in Seattle claimed a 32 percent increase in the rate of delinquency between 1940 and 1943, while *Fortune* magazine indicated that by 1945 delinquency rates in boom towns such as Richmond, California, had reached 87 per 1,000 youth as compared to California's statewide rate of 25 per 1,000.[54] Summarizing trends around the nation, the *New York Times* reported, "Juvenile delinquency is on the increase and will continue to become a serious problem unless immediate measures are taken to combat it."[55] Prone to more soaring rhetoric, *The Saturday Evening Post* proclaimed, "All the elements of utter tragedy are in the making here. No informed American needs a psychologist to tell him that children separated from home ties and without competent care during their most impressionable age are the troublemakers, the neurotics."[56]

It is difficult to assess the accuracy of many of these claims. As a number of historians have observed, the term "juvenile delinquency" varied in meaning from community to community. In some cities, delinquent acts consisted of stealing or "being ungovernable" while in others youth were labeled delinquent if truant or caught engaging in "acts of carelessness or mischief."[57] The transience of the American people during the war years also undoubtedly contributed to the perception of a delinquency "crisis," as historian Richard Polenberg has suggested:

> Statistics that showed soaring juvenile crime rates must be taken with more than one grain of salt: particularly in towns which had an influx of war workers and their children, police were more likely to arrest juvenile offenders whom they did not know, and adults tended to be more stringent in defining permissible conduct. There was not only a change in adolescent behavior, then, but a change in what adults considered acceptable adolescent behavior.[58]

As overstated as the increase in rates of juvenile delinquency might have been, Americans during the war years nevertheless believed that the United States was losing its children to parental neglect and held the disruption of traditional gender roles and the dissolution of the family responsible.

"A Practical War Necessity"

By mid-1942, defense industries' increasingly strident labor demands made genuine opposition to employing the mothers of young children exceedingly difficult. In September, the U.S. Office of Education indicated that approximately 4.5 million women would be engaged in "direct war work" by the end of the year, with the number expected to climb to 6 million by the close of 1943. Similarly, the Census Bureau predicted that, given the increasing number of women taking non-war related jobs, it would "not be possible to meet labor shortages without drawing upon great numbers of women with children."[59]

In response to labor demands President Roosevelt established the Office of War Information (OWI), in part to lobby the magazine, advertising, and film industries to promote women's employment. Working with the War Advertising Council, which consisted of advertising industry executives and their staffers, the OWI made recruiting women into war production a central project. Historian Maureen Honey's examination of the OWI's efforts suggests the degree to which the federal government successfully collaborated with advertisers and the media to showcase women's defense work.[60] Advertisements ranging from Maxwell House coffee, to Smith Corona typewriters, to the Pennsylvania Railroad, glorified women's paid labor in magazines with millions of subscribers. At one point in the fall of 1943, the OWI successfully enlisted 146 magazines with a total circulation of more than 87 million to participate in a war worker recruitment campaign.[61] Indeed, that year that *The Saturday Evening Post* participated in the OWI's "Women in Necessary Services Campaign" by requesting that Norman Rockwell produce a cover illustration for its May 29 issue. Rockwell's resulting portrayal of "Rosie the Riveter"—a physically powerful, self-confident worker with her foot firmly planted on a copy of Hitler's *Mein Kampf*—popularized and solidified the image of the heroine-employee in the American mind.[62]

Confronted by economic, political, and cultural pressures, many opponents of women's employment, generally, and the employment of mothers of young children, specifically, began to acquiesce.[63] Rather than acknowledge mothers' right to paid labor, however, opponents framed the issue as a temporary departure from normal family relations necessitated by the war and emphasized the need to prevent child neglect by expanding accessibility to child care. Reflecting this shift in policy in early 1943, for instance, the U.S. Children's Bureau's "Commission on Children in Wartime" issued guidelines on legislation for the protection of children, asserting:

> To an increasing extent women not heretofore employed outside of their homes are being drawn into war production programs and other essential occupations. Many more will be required in the near future. Many of these women have children of preschool or school age and find it impossible to arrange for adequate care by relatives or friends. Day care for these children is a real and serious need.[64]

Similarly, the U.S. Office of Education signaled its advocacy of day care in a booklet entitled "Nursery Schools Vital to America's War Effort." Published at the height of the war, the booklet reflected the increasingly acceptable belief that nursery schools could resolve the dilemma of how to win the war without destroying the American way of life by serving as citadels of democracy. "Dare a nation at war allow the exploitation and neglect of young children?", the booklet queried. "What would it profit America to win the war if in the process the future of her children were sacrificed? Victory would mean little if, in the wake of war, children were left depleted and unable to carry on American democracy."[65] Yet federal officials also insisted that nursery schools for the young children of working mothers were "a matter of hard common sense, a practical war necessity."[66] The booklet concluded:

> The provision of nursery schools for young children of working mothers is no longer just a pleasant, kindly thing to do out of a sense of human decency, justice, and kindness to children; it is a grim, unsentimental necessity in a nation geared to the production of tanks and more tanks, bombs and more bombs, planes and more planes. . . . Nursery schools in America may mean victory in Europe, in Asia, in

Africa, and on the high seas. For the time being, at least, nursery schools have achieved the status of front-line defense.[67]

By underscoring the emergency character of wartime nursery schools as arsenals of democracy, several federal agencies, including the U.S. Office of Education, anticipated eliminating that support following the war. Indeed, as historian Susan Riley has pointed out, the wartime nurseries never received funding through direct congressional appropriation. Instead, the schools benefited from an amendment to the Lanham Act that permitted funding child care centers in "war-impact areas."[68] Because the process of amending the act circumvented the need for congressional debate on the issue of child care, no formal authorization of the wartime nursery schools was ever made.[69] The outcome, as Riley notes, was that "virtually no foundation was established for public support of child care outside of this emergency context."[70]

Meanwhile, the remaining Depression-era Emergency Nursery Schools were threatened with closure when federal officials announced that the Works Projects Administration would be dissolved in April 1943. Almost immediately, city and state officials overwhelmed the federal government with requests not only to maintain but expand the accessibility of nursery schools to working mothers.[71] In response, the War Public Services Bureau of the Federal Works Administration (FWA) assumed responsibility for the program.[72] FWA officials Florence Kerr (who served as assistant commissioner of the WPA and then head of the War Public Services Bureau) and Grace Langdon (who served as a WPA Emergency Nursery School specialist and then as chief of the wartime nursery school Child Care and Protection Program), informed directors of the WPA Emergency Nursery Schools that they were to request Lanham Act support if they intended to keep their schools open. Many did, becoming "Lanham Act Nursery Schools," as wartime nurseries were sometimes called.[73] More than 500 others closed, however, because they were not located in war-impact areas and thus did not qualify for Lanham Act funds.[74]

By the time the federal government began approving nursery school applications for Lanham funding, the demand for child care had become pronounced throughout the United States. By late 1942, for instance, 75,000 women were employed in Seattle yet only 7 Emergency Nursery Schools and 3 private nurseries were in operation, serving a total of 350 children. As a result, the Seattle Civilian War Commission amassed a backlog of 1,500 child care applications prior to establishing the city's first wartime nursery.[75] Similarly, in Baltimore, 145,000 working women relied on the services of 16 WPA nurseries. In Detroit, 17 centers served 350,000 women.[76] Moreover, use of even these centers was limited. In the San Francisco Bay Area, only 9 out of 25 nursery schools were open long enough to fully meet working mothers' child care needs.[77] At the San Francisco conference on "Children in Wartime" held in October 1943, U.S. War Manpower Commission officials confirmed that increasing labor demands in the Bay Area would easily exceed the region's child care capacity. In addition to the "womanpower" already employed, officials projected that 40,000 more women would need to be recruited for defense work in the region. Given that California received more defense contracts during World War II than any other state in the nation, officials noted that labor demands throughout the state, and in the Bay Area specifically, could not be met "by recruiting women without children."[78] Nationally, the War Manpower Commission estimated that the demand for child care centers in one-third of the war-impacted areas across the United States was so great "as to be a serious hindrance to the recruiting and retention of women in industry."[79]

In Richmond, California, too, the need for nursery schooling was urgent. A 1942 Kaiser Corporation study of 3,675 company families residing in the city indicated that 712 children under the age of five needed care either because both parents worked or because both would work if child care arrangements could be made.[80] Less than a year later, in January 1943, Kaiser company officials released another assessment claiming that 1,989 mothers working in the shipyards had 3,471 children, of which 1,300 were five years old or younger.[81] Combined with Kaiser Corporation claims that working mothers' high degree of absenteeism was primarily due to inadequate child care arrangements, these reports led Arthur Hall of the California State Employment Service to propose to the Richmond City Council that nursery schools be provided for the young children of working mothers.[82] School Superintendent Walter Helms, however, already reeling from dramatically overenrolled elementary and secondary schools, a severe shortage of classroom space, and a lack of funding for Richmond's public schools, initially resisted what he perceived as yet another wartime burden on the Richmond City School District.[83] Helms had reacted similarly to proposals to sponsor an Emergency Nursery School in Richmond during the Depression, although his opposition to the nursery's founding faded when he learned that WPA funds would finance the school's teacher salaries.[84] In turn, the city of Richmond established the Peres Nursery School in 1937. Located in a temporary building on the grounds of the Peres Elementary School site, the nursery served between 50 and 60 children per day.[85] When the WPA informed Helms that financial support would be cut back in the early 1940s, however, requiring school districts to supplement the loss, Helms argued that it was not legal for the Richmond City School District to expend funds to operate nursery schools and proposed eliminating the program.[86] By late 1942, however, Hope Cahill, the state's nursery school administrator for northern California, informed Helms that Lanham Act funding awaited an application from city officials to support the development of wartime nursery schools in Richmond.[87] Under increasing pressure from Kaiser company executives, the California State Department of Education, and the Richmond City Health Department, Chamber of Commerce, and City Council, Helms agreed to form a committee consisting of representatives from local organizations to investigate the possibility of establishing wartime nursery schools in Richmond.[88] In January 1943, the committee submitted applications for Lanham Act funding to support ten nurseries, with Walter Helms agreeing that the Richmond City School District would administer the schools.[89] Three months later, the city established its first wartime nursery.

"It Was an Educational Program ... It Was a Cadillac Program"

On April 23, 1943, the Richmond City School District announced the opening of the Terrace Nursery School. "Working Mothers See Tots Safely in Modern School" was the headline in the *Richmond War Homes Weekly* on the nursery's first day in session, in a story that reported that "the Richmond Terrace Nursery School is humming with activity and some forty-five working mothers are breathing easier."[90] The bulletin then announced that a second nursery, "Canal Nursery School," would begin enrolling children two to three weeks later, followed by the opening of eight more nurseries in the coming months.[91]

Located in one of Richmond's many defense housing projects, Terrace Nursery School served children between the ages of two and about four and a half whose mothers were employed by one of the city's approximately 50 defense plants and shipyards.[92] As with the Terrace Nursery, all of Richmond's wartime nursery schools were open at least 12 hours a day, from 6:00 a.m. to 6:00 p.m., six days a week and maintained a student-teacher ratio of six to one. Parent fees, which purchased a mid-morning snack, dinner at noon, and a mid-afternoon snack, were 50 cents per day for one child and 25 cents each for the second and third child. A fourth child was free.[93] For an additional ten cents, a child was provided with breakfast. All of the children who attended the schools received daily physical examinations by a nurse and weekly ones by a pediatrician.[94]

The nurseries' typical day began with "quiet activities" from 6:15 a.m. until 7:30 a.m., including table games, reading, drawing, and preparing for breakfast. Breakfast was held from 7:30 a.m. to 8:00 a.m. and usually consisted of juice, cereal, toast, milk, and a daily serving of cod liver oil.[95] Following breakfast, children divided into various age groups to begin their first "creative activities" of the day. These lasted from 8:15 a.m. until 9:15 a.m. and included painting, picture study, clay work, music appreciation and drama, and scrapbooking. Children then went outdoors or played "organized games" indoors, coming back together at 10:00 a.m. to begin a "special activity." Teachers reserved a different activity for each day of the week, including stories on Monday, music on Tuesday, wood craft and sewing on Wednesday, folk dancing and singing on Thursday, and nature study on Friday. On Saturdays, children chose their own special activity.[96]

At 11:00 a.m. students began cleaning up and prepared for "dinner," a full, hot meal consisting of main courses such as meat loaf, scalloped potatoes, beef stew, and cheese soufflé.[97] Following dinner, the children rested in the "sleep room." Beginning at 2:15 p.m., the children were awakened and at 3:00 p.m. they began "nutrition," which usually involved a 30-minute lesson on personal hygiene, diet, and good health. At 3:30 p.m. the children returned to their special activity, and one hour later, began their second creative activity of the day. From 5:30 p.m. until 6:00 p.m., the school completed its day as it had begun, with children engaged in quiet activities until they were picked up from the center by a parent.[98]

Two weeks following the Terrace Nursery's opening, the Kaiser Corporation's public relations newsletter, the *Fore 'n' Aft*, publicized the school's success in meeting the needs of Richmond's working mothers. "FOUND—at last—a home for Richmond's eight hour orphans!" declared the newsletter. "Since Pearl Harbor America has been preparing to meet every kind of emergency—except one. That one, failure to provide adequate care for the children of working mothers, is probably the gravest home problem we face. For it would be folly to win the war—and find that we had lost our children."[99] The *Fore 'n' Aft* regularly reported on Richmond's nursery schools over the following two years, offering insight into what Kaiser officials thought mothers would find most appealing about the schools. These stories frequently emphasized the virtues of the nurseries' educational programs. Coverage of the Terrace Nursery School's opening, for instance, included a photographic essay depicting its classrooms and playground. A photograph portraying children seated at a table working piles of clay into figures of various shapes and sizes suggested the degree to which students were provided numerous opportunities for artistic expression. "Only subjects which interest the pupil are taught," the photo's caption read, "as witness the undivided attention of a group learning to model birds, bunnies, or whatever they can conjure up from clay."[100] In the caption to another photo, which depicted two small boys eagerly engaged in construction, the *Fore 'n' Aft* observed, "These busy little fellows are laying new-type keel blocks, maybe, or conducting their own experiments in Liberty Ship prefabrication. Free play is encouraged, each child being allowed to pursue his own interests."[101]

Wartime nursery school teacher Ruth Powers later recalled that many of the children who attended Richmond's nurseries were from across the country. "Most of these children were from other states," Powers remembered. "They traveled here. They felt very much confused. . . . They had a lot of adjusting to do. But once they were adjusted, had been in their room a few weeks, it was home. They loved it." Powers also recalled that positive relations developed between the students and their teachers, "There was a great feeling between the children and the teacher—that this is my home and I'm going to stay here until my Mommy comes. They were very comfortable."[102]

Mary Hall Prout, who began working in Richmond's wartime nurseries in 1944, recalled the emphasis that school leaders in Richmond placed on developing an educationally based program designed to dispel conceptions of nursery schools as custodial institutions serving impoverished families. "We just didn't want to be labeled as a welfare program," Prout remembered, "It was an educational program. The teachers were not simply aides; they knew a lot about child-development. Our first director was a real educator. She didn't want any part of welfare. She just didn't want the program to have that stigma. It was really wonderful, she hired only credentialed teachers. They knew about early childhood [education]."[103]

After graduating from San Jose State University with degrees in psychology and education, Prout had sought an opportunity to become involved in early childhood education in the Bay Area. Hearing that Erla Boucher, director of Richmond's wartime nursery schools, was interviewing candidates for jobs in the district, Prout applied and was hired on the spot.[104] Her career in Richmond lasted 41 years. After serving as a nursery school teacher for 8 months and head teacher for 20 years, she directed the nursery school program from 1964 to 1985. Prout recalled that during the nurseries' early years, in addition to the schools' educational focus, teachers paid significant attention to children's health. "We had a fine medical program," she remembered, "We did a lot health-wise." Prout continued:

> We kept track of all the immunizations, which some of the parents didn't. By the time the children got to kindergarten, we had the whole record so we could just turn it over to the schools. . . . We had a psychiatrist that we could refer the parents to if we had a child that had really deep problems. We had a dental hygienist and a full-time nurse at each site. . . . We had nurses observing the children at all times and when they became ill at school we had an isolation room. And it was right next to our desk, and usually there was someone working in there so the child wouldn't be by himself.[105]

The nurseries' emphasis on children's health, according to Prout, was also reflected in the importance that the schools placed on children's daily nutrition. Prout remembered "a lovely nutrition program" in the schools, intentionally designed to counter the poor nutrition many students seemed to be receiving at home. She recalled:

> Breakfast was served at 7:30 and it was brought from the kitchen on carts into the classroom. They would set up a little cluster of tables, and the teacher would sit down and eat with them. It was lovely. . . . I think that a lot of kids got an awful lot out of it. So many parents were working so hard that I don't think that they ever sat down and had a nice meal. I just don't think that they had the time. That worked out well. We also had a well-balanced dinner that was served in the various classrooms from 11:00–12:30. That was set up the same way. Then the little ones had a nap for about two hours. We would bring the beds in and put them down. Each child had his own bed. Nice clean sheets on it all the time. And then in the afternoon we would get up and have a little snack. We would have milk, and there would be fruit wedges and sandwiches- so they would have a little bit more to eat before they went home.[106]

Prout's recollections indicate that the Richmond nursery schools blended high-quality caretaking with a substantive educational program. Her memories also reveal the degree to which the nursery school curriculum reflected the importance that teachers assigned to both academic preparation and creative expression.[107] "We had all kinds of educational activities," Prout recalled, "science, art, music— everything that a preschool child should have. [We had] all of the equipment that taught them how to read, eventually, how to write, eventually—it was a regular early childhood curriculum. . . . We felt a real responsibility towards the children and the parents. We wanted to give them the best."[108] As Prout remembered, the Richmond City School District did, indeed, hold the wartime nursery schools to the same institutional standards as the city's elementary school program. Many of the city's nursery school teachers held college degrees, they were required to prepare daily lesson plans, and their work was frequently and formally evaluated, in part, based on the following program objectives:

> To afford the opportunity for the release and development of creative abilities by presenting to the child materials adequate for this development, such as easel painting, clay work, cutouts, murals, crayon and pencil work, and finger painting.
> To teach co-operative play by means of games inside and outdoors which require organization and group participation.
> To stimulate knowledge of the outside world through story material and library contact and nature study.
> To develop the child's interest and understanding of music, rhythm and song.[109]

The emphasis on creative arts indicated by these program goals was a central part of the nursery school curriculum, which was developed by Monica Haley. Hired in 1943 as a teacher in the Canal Nursery School, Haley was quickly promoted to the position of arts and crafts supervisor in Richmond, requiring that she visit the city's nurseries weekly to participate in and evaluate the implementation of the schools' arts and crafts programs.[110] Haley argued that "creative activities" should contain a significant portion of the nursery school curriculum because of children's need for the "success experience," which she stated was "developed through the release of creative energies."[111] Asserting that student creativity could be expressed through a number of different mediums, such as clay work, block printing, weaving, and easel painting, Haley convinced Erla Boucher to invest in the necessary equipment and materials (see Figure 5.1).

Richmond's nursery schools became best known for their display of students' easel paintings. Haley maintained an extensive collection of child art, which today is preserved at the Richmond Museum of History. In contrast with contemporary forms of art instruction encouraging students to replicate already existing subjects, Haley believed that easel painting provided children ages two and above with an ideal medium for "spontaneous creative expression." She wrote:

> These paintings give striking evidence of a dominant aesthetic potential, and amply document the child's innate capacity to convert the art materials into paintings of considerable artistic force and vitality. These paintings indicate his intuitive spontaneous interest in participating in creative experiences. The lyrical linear rhythms, the balance of color combinations within the easel paintings of children of all

Figure 5.1 USMC nursery school, c. 1943
Courtesy, The Bancroft Library, University of California, Berkeley

these recorded age groups are indicative of sensibilities that are aroused by the opportunity to work with creative materials.[112]

As evidence of students' interest in the creative process, Haley noted the children's extended attention span, an "eagerness to take part" in the painting, an "unwillingness to stop," and the "desire for possession of the finished painting usually to give to his mother."[113] She also believed that the creative experience fostered children's social development. "In this school situation," she wrote, "the child is learning to pursue his interests without losing a sense of group cooperation. He becomes aware of necessary restrictions and conforms where situations require it. He is learning of the rights of others in relation with his own drive for self-expression."[114]

Haley observed that many of the easel paintings completed by two- and three-year-olds reflected children's experimentation with art materials. Figure 5.2, painted in 1945, provides an example from this age group.[115] Although the work is presented here in black and white, the two-year-old artist who composed this painting chose a variety of colors. Haley identified using many different colors "in hurried succession" as characteristic of this age group, with children frequently choosing 15 colors or more.[116] In Figure 5.3, a painting by a four-year-old girl depicts the beginning of distinct shapes and forms, including the mushroom-looking shape just right of the paper's center, which the child identified as a tree, and the oval figure with a black dot towards its bottom located further to the right, which the child identified as an owl.[117]

After the young children completed their paintings, Haley frequently questioned them about their finished work. Haley's notes are, unfortunately, not matched to specific paintings in her collection. In these brief interviews, however, children often described the subject of their paintings. One five-year-old, for example, informed Haley that his painting depicted "a picture about a boat." "The red is water," he told her, "Boats have to have water to sail on. I used red water because it looks a little gooder to me."[118] In contrast, a four-year-old observed of her work, "I don't know what it looks like. I like it, but I

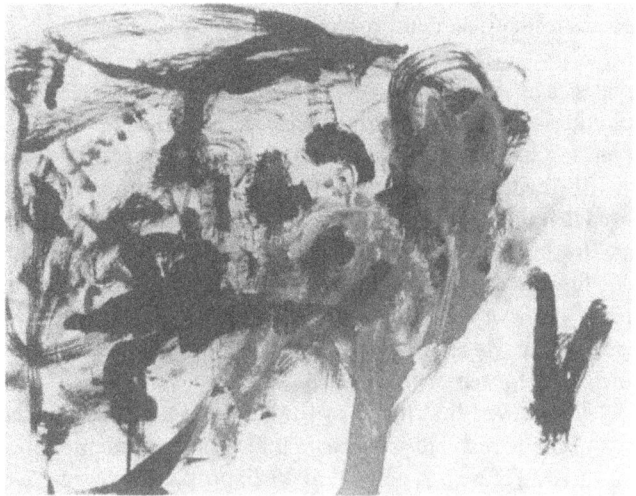

Figure 5.2 Two-year-old student art
Courtesy, The Richmond Museum of History Collection

Figure 5.3 Four-year-old student art
Courtesy, The Richmond Museum of History Collection

don't know what it is."[119] In other instances, children commented on the materials they were using. "This paint is too thin," insisted one five-year-old. "Red—look it's leaking. I'll take black, that's my favorite color."[120] Children also explained what they planned to do with their paintings once they had dried. One three-year-old who had just completed painting a house, which Haley noted "in no way resembled a recognizable object," declared, "See my house. Come look at it. When I get home my mama's going to say it's pretty. My daddy, too. They both say, 'It's pretty.' This is for my mama. I'm going to put this picture up there when I get through. When it's dry, I'll take it with me."[121]

Haley occasionally exhibited her students' work, leading the paintings to receive a good deal of attention from the surrounding communities. The *Oakland Post-Enquirer*, for instance, reported in 1944 that there was a "new development" occurring "out at the Richmond shipyards, close to the clang and clatter of round-the-clock building of ships."[122] This new development was, noted the newspaper, "the making of a bunch of up and coming artists from a crew of just average and often rowdy cross-section kids. Every state in the union is represented by the young artists who have opened the first exhibition of their work at the old Washington School in Point Richmond."[123] Regarding a display of the children's art held at the University of California, Berkeley, immediately following the war, the *Richmond Independent* reported, "Considered by authorities to be the best exhibit of child art in the United States is the display of work of Child Care Center children. . . . Collected during the war years, the art exhibit represents the work of children . . . from all over the United States who were in Richmond while their parents worked in the shipyards."[124]

As strikingly creative as Haley's curriculum was, her work was not unique. Private nursery schools had been engaging students in artistic forms of creative expression for decades. With programs rooted in the educational theories of Germany's Friedrich Froebel, Switzerland's Johann Pestalozzi, and America's John Dewey, as well as the practices of educators such as Caroline Pratt at her Greenwich Village City and Country School and Marietta Johnson at the Organic School in Fairhope, Alabama, many private nursery schools by the 1920s encouraged free play and artistic expression.[125] Publications from the period also endorsed these pedagogical practices. The National Society for the Study of Education's Twenty-Eighth Yearbook on Preschool and Parental Education, for instance, included more than a hundred studies on "art experiences" with children.[126] In her books *Two to Six* (published in 1933) and *Children's Centers* (published in 1942), Rose Alschuler, who served as head of the National Commission for Young Children during World War II, also advocated the use of "raw materials" such as paint, clay, crayons, and blocks with children, providing an opportunity for creative expression.[127] "Children should have frequent opportunities to play with dirt, mud, sand, clay, water, paint, sticks, and stones as they get keen pleasure from handling, manipulating, and seeing what can be done with these materials," wrote Alschuer. "The feel and smell and color of them give satisfaction to children's developing senses. The child should do what he wants at his own speed, learning, in so far as possible, through trial and error. He will usually learn more through experimenting in his own way than if a teacher or some other adult shows him a 'better way to do it.'"[128]

Although Haley acknowledged these earlier approaches as influential on her work, she also perceived an important distinction between them. "In the early twenties," she claimed, "the progressive education movement introduced . . . what one might call self-expression theory of art education. Actually it has little to do with art. It gives the child the paraphernalia of art production, then leaves him severely alone, not granting him much guidance even when he seriously asks for it."[129] In contrast, Haley claimed that, although the teacher should never dictate what children paint, she was responsible for guidance in handling materials and providing assistance when requested.[130] "A chaotic uncontrolled use of creative materials," Haley wrote, "is not to be confused with the child's creative use of art materials, nor is it to be tolerated. Spontaneous creative expression is not to be confused with permissiveness which usually inhibits the creative process."[131]

Haley's criticisms corresponded with a broader wartime assault on the "permissiveness" of Progressive education. Existing for decades in the United States, the attack on Progressive pedagogy intensified in the militaristic climate of the war and Cold War eras, leading to a conservative backlash and the general decline of the movement. Nevertheless, the curriculum Haley designed for Richmond's wartime nursery schools clearly reflected the educational programs implemented in well-respected Progressive, private preschools prior to, during, and following World War II. In that regard, Haley's work contributed to the shifting of Americans' perceptions of day care from that of a welfare measure for the poor to an educationally beneficial form of care for all children.

Progressive, child-centered principles infused not only Richmond's nursery school curriculum but also the architectural design of two of the city's most well-publicized nurseries. Kaiser company officials, dismayed by both Walter Helms's initial resistance to establishing nursery schools in Richmond and the slow pace with which the federal government processed Lanham Act applications, appealed directly to the U.S. Maritime Commission in 1943 to construct two new nursery schools.[132] Although the Maritime Commission was under no legal obligation to build the schools, Kaiser's Richmond shipyards produced the Commission's Liberty Ships and Maritime Commission officials therefore had a vested interest in shipyard employees' productivity. Moreover, Kaiser intended the schools to serve two separate and extremely large U.S. Maritime Commission defense housing projects.[133] In response to Kaiser's request, the U.S. Maritime Commission agreed to undertake the construction of the "Maritime" and "Pullman" Nursery Schools, designed to care for 180 children each.[134]

In the architectural design of the Maritime and Pullman nurseries, Kaiser Corporation sought the expertise of Catherine Landreth, professor of home economics and director of the nursery school of the Institute of Child Welfare at the University of California, Berkeley.[135] Landreth, who during the war published *Education of the Young Child: A Nursery School Manual*, was a well-respected figure in the field of early childhood education with a growing reputation as an expert in child-centered architectural design.[136] Like Monica Haley, Landreth believed in encouraging children's freedom of expression.[137] This philosophy evidenced itself in architectural plans consisting of open space, with abundant opportunities for children to be physically active, such as on the jungle gym, rings, and swings. Moreover, Landreth wanted the facilities to be aesthetically pleasing, and she thus included such nonessentials as a fountain and bird baths in her plans. Indoors, Landreth's designs included spaces for children to express themselves through the use of blocks, art, and a piano for sing-alongs. She also insisted that nursery school "equipment," including chairs, toilets, desks, coat racks, and handrails, be designed to meet the needs of a small child.[138]

Landreth's designs were reflected in Ruth Powers's memories of the Pullman Nursery School classrooms. Powers recalled:

> The set up of the room was that one side was left clear for play. All the activities were over there. And we had little tables here that they could use, too, for puzzles or whatever table games they did, and this is where they had their food. There were tables of various heights in rooms with chairs of various heights—it was very important that the child could have his feet on the floor and that his table and chair fit him—it was very important for his growth and for his comfort. . . . There was a little slide . . . for the indoor play for the children, and all the blocks and things. . . . Beds were canvas cots that were scrubbed every week. Each child had his own cot with his name on it. . . . There was a little sheet that went on the bed and had a little hook that just went over the bottom, and each had his own blanket.[139]

Believing that the direction learning took in a nursery school setting was necessarily influenced by the "social philosophy of those who teach nursery school children," Landreth felt that nursery school teachers should be highly trained and that university students who planned to teach observe children before interacting with them.[140] As a result, Landreth taught "Techniques with Young Children," a course offered at UC Berkeley that required students to record observations of children at the university's nursery school.[141] As a result of this course and the training offered, approximately 40 of Landreth's advanced students provided assistance in staffing Richmond's wartime nurseries throughout the war years.[142]

Mary Hall Prout recalled that both the Maritime and Pullman Nurseries were highly regarded, with people coming by bus "from all over California and all over the United States" to see them. "They were the first early childhood centers that were really developed on a large scale," she remembered. "They had the classrooms and they had the little bathrooms attached to them and lots of windows to look out of. It was a beautiful setup. . . . The federal government financed the program, and the school district administered it. . . . It was a Cadillac program."[143] By making no reference to the Kaiser Corporation in her discussion of the Maritime and Pullman Nursery Schools, Prout indicated the extremely limited role the company played in the nurseries' actual operation after they were constructed. Nevertheless, Henry Kaiser's efforts to provide high-quality, low-cost preschool for the children of mothers working in his Richmond shipyards initially received a great deal of attention. *Business Week* provided national coverage of the opening of the Maritime Nursery in May 1943 (the school officially opened on June 1) and the *Richmond War Homes Weekly* reported in November that the school "has been a showplace for parents and distinguished visitors ever since its opening."[144]

Ultimately, the Kaiser Corporation's establishment of Swan Island and Oregonship "Child Service Centers" in its Portland, Oregon, shipyards combined with Eleanor Roosevelt's high-profile role in founding those centers to overshadow the unique qualities of the Maritime and Pullman Nursery Schools.[145] Indeed, by the end of the war, Henry Kaiser had garnered a reputation for providing privately owned and operated nursery schooling as part of his industrial undertakings. In contrast, the Maritime and Pullman nurseries represented an unusual collaboration between private industry, the federal government, the Richmond City School District, and fee-paying parents. The resulting nursery school program was, by all accounts, highly successful in achieving its central aims. The nurseries afforded mothers of young children the opportunity to work in defense industries while nursery school teachers provided their students with both high-quality child care, including preventative health care and nutritious meals, and a Progressive educational program rivaling those in private nursery schools catering to the middle class. Thus, by the end of the wartime nurseries' first calendar year of operation, the *Richmond War Homes Weekly* could report:

> We have here a child care program that has served as guide and inspiration to the entire nation. These 12 centers are more than just roofs over the heads of small children, more than the serving of well cooked balanced meals. For the little ones who come under the program supervised by Mrs. Boucher are already being trained in good citizenship. They are learning to fraternize with other tots of their own age, learning to give-and-take, to share with others and become harmonious members of a group.[146]

Conclusion

By June 1944, women constituted approximately 28 percent of all employees in the Richmond shipyards, including 70 percent of all laborers, 41 percent of all welders, and 33 percent of all burners (workers who used torches to eliminate excess metal and cut holes during ship construction).[147] To serve the mothers of young children among these and other war workers, the Richmond City School District eventually operated 12 nursery schools, including the "Washington Nursery," which was open 24 hours a day to provide care for the young children of parents working the day shift (7:00 a.m. to 3:00 p.m.), the swing shift (3:00 p.m. to 11:00 p.m.), and the graveyard shift (11:00 p.m. to 7:00 a.m.).[148] Between April 1943 and June 1945, just over $1,244,000 was spent in constructing, operating, and maintaining Richmond's nursery schools, with parent fees and state and local agencies providing almost half of that support and the federal government supplying the remainder.[149] By 1945, the Federal Works Agency through the Lanham Act had allocated more than $50 million nationally for the development and operation of more than 3,000 nursery schools. At their height, the Lanham nurseries enrolled 130,000 children throughout the United States. Over the course of their existence, they served an estimated 550,000–600,000 children.[150] At their peak in California, 536 centers served more than 25,500 children and was the largest program in the country.[151]

Richmond's nursery schools were important contributors to the city's wartime industrial capacity.[152] Between May 1943 and 1944, for instance, the Maritime Nursery School alone made 303,620 "woman-hours" of labor available to the Kaiser shipyards—enough to produce an entire Liberty Ship.[153] Yet demand for nurseries across the nation, and in Richmond specifically, was never great enough to stir dramatic expansion.[154] Although the city's wartime nurseries were occasionally filled to capacity, openings were frequently reported.[155] In April 1944, for instance, *The Richmond War Homes Weekly* announced vacancies at several schools, at one point asking, "Is it possible that working mothers of Canal [public housing development] are not aware of the advantages offered by the Nursery . . . ? There are at the present time vacancies for 15 children, ages 2 to 5."[156] The *Fore 'n' Aft* also reported on available openings. Seemingly confused by the schools' underenrollment, one commentator suggested that the nurseries were full and then proceeded to list available spots, "To date, perhaps the only community in the East Bay where the available nursery school facilities are being fully used is Richmond. . . . And even here, in this jammed area, the Peres Nursery School in North Richmond lacks 25 children of being full. Even in the Terrace School there is room for five more youngsters. El Cerrito's Fairmont School reports there is room there for 35 more."[157]

Observers ascribed low enrollment to parents' attitudes towards the schools, including the belief that children's participation indicated "an inability to care for one's own," that nursery care had "a vague incompatibility with the traditional idea of the American home," and a feeling on the part of some parents that nursery schools were laced with socialism.[158] Scholars have attributed low nursery school enrollment in Kaiser's Oregon facilities to poor publicity and inconvenient locations. Moreover, as Amy Kesselman notes, "parents were reluctant to leave their children with people they didn't know, lacked confidence in the quality of care the centers provided, and feared the spread of contagious disease in large groups of children."[159]

In addition to these explanations, race provided an important reason for the under-utilization of wartime nursery schools. In contrast to Richmond's elementary and secondary school classrooms, where students of varying racial, ethnic, and cultural backgrounds mixed in proportion to their numbers in the population, black Richmondites frequently did not enroll their children in the city's nurseries.[160] Although there were no legal restrictions on black families using the nurseries, historian Shirley Ann Wilson Moore discovered in oral histories conducted with Richmond's wartime residents that some black women remembered the nursery schools as closed to their children.[161] Black women, instead, relied on family networks, with grandmothers, older siblings, and other relatives caring for young children while mothers worked.[162] Black mothers' unwillingness to enroll their children in Richmond's wartime nurseries suggests the extent to which city officials failed to convince a racial and ethnic cross section of Richmond's residents that the nurseries were open to the young children of all working mothers.

Underutilization, while not necessarily indicating the success or failure of the wartime nursery schools, suggests the limitations of employing public schools as an institutional response to social and economic changes in the United States. Although women's increased participation in the workforce predated America's declaration of war, homefront mobilization accelerated this trend, leading to a rise in the number of mothers with young children engaged in paid labor. As the nation became increasingly reliant on working mothers to maintain its industrial capacity, the federal government was compelled to provide a "practical" solution to the "problem" of day care. Public schools were chosen as the appropriate site for resolving this dilemma. Yet the schools, too, operated within the context of broad social values and beliefs regarding women's role in American society. The results of a Gallup poll conducted in 1943, for instance, which surveyed women as to whether or not they would accept paid work in a defense industry if they received free care for their children, indicated that 29 percent would accept such work while 56 percent would not.[163] Moreover, as historian D'Ann Campbell has shown, the labor force participation rate of mothers with children under six years of age ultimately only increased from 9 to 12 percent during World War II.[164] Ambivalence towards working outside the home undoubtedly contributed to an inability to fill vacant spaces in nursery schools across the nation.[165]

Nevertheless, as historians such as Elizabeth Rose have argued, establishing federally funded nurseries during World War II "furthered the dawning perception" that the schools might provide "a public service for ordinary families, not a charity for those who had nowhere else to turn."[166] Certainly the high-quality educational nature of nursery school programs such as those in Richmond contributed to this transformation. Moreover, by conceiving of nursery schools as embodying a civic purpose, wartime nursery school educators developed and implemented a curriculum that provided democratically enriching educational experiences for children by fostering student creativity and self-expression, leading the authors of a 1949 report on child care centers administered and operated by California school districts to conclude, "The Child Care Center program was originally conceived by the California State Legislature to provide custodial care for children of working parents. The operation of this program has not only provided this care but has also supplied the needs of young children, and is designed to develop socially healthy, well-adjusted junior citizens."[167]

James L. Hymes Jr., who assisted in developing and administering Kaiser's Swan Island and Oregonship Child Service Centers during the war years, affirmed the importance of the nursery's role as a citadel of democracy in late 1942, writing:

> [T]his is not just war. It is a revolution against all the meanness, large and small, that impoverishes and embitters living—against the meanness of prejudice and unkindness, against cruelty and against the isolation that does not care what happens to the other fellow. This is a fight to create a new world of new values. In this context the good growth of young children takes on its full meaning; it is here that their education truly becomes a mission. . . . The roots of democratic adult behavior or of later-day fascist behavior (at home, in the club, the factory or in Congress), the roots of the isolationism that ignores or of the interventionism that cares (in the city block, the community or the world) all go down to a very considerable extent to these

early attitudes. . . . Collective security can be analyzed in high school and college seminars and in adult forums but the will to have it in the first place must be built in the nursery room."[168]

Like Hymes, nursery school educators in Richmond such as Mary Hall Prout, Ruth Powers, and Monica Haley frequently identified their desire to foster "early attitudes" in their young students, including cooperation, responsibility, and self-expression. Indeed, throughout California, this program objective was articulated as a central rationale for the need to expand access to nursery schooling following World War II. "Advocates for Child Care Centers," writes scholar Emilie Stoltzfus, asserted that the centers "both curbed juvenile delinquency and reduced its potential by training young children in the duties and values of democratic citizenship."[169]

By early 1945, with the end of the war in sight, the emergency justification for the wartime nurseries began to evaporate, along with the dilemma of how to win the war without destroying the American family and democratic way of life. Although generally praised by parents who enrolled their children in wartime nurseries, the schools nevertheless failed to develop a national constituency strong enough to secure their continued operation into the postwar era. In response to outspoken calls for the schools' dissolution, the Federal Works Administration announced that Lanham Act funding for the schools would be terminated on September 30.[170] When federal officials attempted to implement this decision, they were strongly criticized, with many communities claiming that women whose husbands had yet to return from overseas service were still reliant upon the schools.[171] An extension was granted until the end of February 1946, when most of the Lanham nurseries throughout the United States closed.[172]

One important exception was in California, where the state legislature passed an emergency measure to continue funding the nurseries on the grounds that wartime conditions still existed in many California communities. According to Stoltzfus, nursery school advocates framed their demands for continued funding in terms of education and citizenship rather than welfare, and emphasized the benefits that society reaped from young children's attendance.[173] Mothers who petitioned state and federal officials, for instance, described the nursery schools as "an essential builder of strong citizens" and asserted that the schools gave young children a "head start towards becoming good, useful citizens."[174] The State of California responded to these entreaties with stop-gap funding measures for almost 11 years until, in 1957, nursery schools advocates finally won permanent status for their programs.[175]

In Richmond, however, nursery schools began to be eliminated as the city tore down the facilities that housed the programs along with temporary war-worker housing. By 1953, only five wartime facilities continued to provide nursery schooling to the children of families in Richmond. By 1986, this number had declined to two, the Maritime and Pullman facilities.[176] During the postwar period, moreover, state officials introduced a means test to determine eligibility for program participation and a sliding-scale fee schedule based on family income.[177] Although both of these revisions were made in a good faith effort to support California's most economically disadvantaged families following the war, the result in Richmond, as throughout California, was a reaffirmation of publicly funded preschool as a social service for the poor.[178] By implementing class-sensitive criteria, the state circumvented equally important issues regarding the legitimacy and acceptability of women's paid labor. By avoiding this politically charged issue, the state government fostered conditions for the development of a disjointed array of preschool programs in California that neither met the needs of all women who chose to work outside the home nor provided an innovative educational experience for all of their children—it is a legacy that remains with California's working mothers today.

6

Education in a Time of War

On the afternoon of August 24, 1946, a plane carrying the ten-member "United States Education Mission to Germany" landed in the war-torn city of Berlin. The education mission was chaired by George Zook, president of the American Council on Education, and consisted of such prominent educators as theologian Reinhold Niebuhr; Bess Goodykoontz, an official in the U.S. Office of Education; and Henry H. Hill, president of the George Peabody College for Teachers. The education mission had been invited by the State Department to "observe and evaluate" the U.S. Military Government's program for reconstructing educational institutions in a defeated Germany. Education mission members spent almost four weeks visiting elementary, secondary and vocational schools, and universities in the American zone of occupation. They interviewed U.S. military officials as well as German teachers, students, and professors; toured the burned-out remains of Germany's school buildings; and produced a 50-page report on the challenges and dilemmas the U.S. Military Government confronted in rebuilding Germany's educational system in the postwar era.[1]

Even prior to the fall of Berlin in May 1945, the U.S. State Department assigned reconstructing Germany's educational system a high priority. The Allied failure to secure a lasting peace in Europe following World War I had convinced many Americans, including government officials, that military victory in World War II was only the first phase in establishing postwar international stability. "Winning of the peace," claimed U.S. Assistant Secretary of State William Benton, necessitated reeducating the German people away from "Nazism and militarism toward the acceptance of peace-loving, democratic ideals and ways of life."[2] Allied leaders gave formal approval to this strategy at the Potsdam Conference in the summer of 1945, when Harry S. Truman, Josef Stalin, and Clement Attlee agreed that German educational institutions "shall be so controlled as completely to eliminate Nazi and militaristic doctrines and to make possible the successful development of democratic ideas."[3] General Lucius Clay, who served as deputy governor and then governor of the American zone of occupation between 1945 and 1949, and whose job it was to implement elements of the Potsdam accord, later affirmed the importance that the Allies attributed to education by describing the U.S. Military Government's policies during the immediate postwar era as an "appeal to the German mind."[4]

Members of the education mission used their final report to voice strong approval for U.S. occupation policies that both "denazified" German schools and universities (referring to the removal of Nazi Party members from positions in these institutions) and explicitly promoted democratic ideals. The mission reserved the bulk of its report, however, to issue a harsh criticism of the philosophical underpinnings and organizational structure of Germany's traditional educational system.

Historically, Germany's schools and curricula were differentiated into academic and vocational tracks. By World War II, most children attended some preschool, or *Kindergarten*, and beginning at age five or six lower elementary school, or *Grundschule*. This common elementary school experience lasted only four years. At the age of nine or ten, children underwent examination for admission to secondary school. Ten percent of students gained entrance to institutions intended to prepare them for higher education, including the *Gymnasium*, which offered a classical curriculum, and the *Oberrealschule*, which offered a curriculum emphasizing sciences and modern languages. The *Aufbauschule*, a school designed to provide students who had fallen slightly behind their higher-achieving peers a chance to advance, also allowed access to higher education. The other 90 percent of students proceeded to the upper grades of elementary school, known as the *Volksschule*, or to the *Realschule* for eventual business, technical, or other vocational training. When these students turned

14 or 15, they began four or more years of full-time vocational education (divided between classroom and practical training) in the *Berufsschule*, or full- or part-time vocational training through the *Fachschule*. The outcome of this organizational structure was a system of education that determined, to a significant degree, students' educational and career opportunities at a strikingly early age.

Perceiving the school as "a primary agency for the democratization of Germany," education mission members determined that German education had "cultivated attitudes of superiority in one small group and inferiority in the majority of the members of German society, making possible the submission and lack of self-determination upon which authoritarian leadership has thrived." "Nowhere," the education mission declared, "is there the possibility of a common school life, nor in fact any place for that broad base of general education which in many other countries provides a common cultural and social experience.... It is clear that the educational system of a country may reenforce the foundations of a 'class society,' or it may build a common culture for all citizens. For a democratic society, the second is the only possible choice."[5]

Instead of Germany's prewar educational system, the education mission proposed establishing American-style elementary and secondary schools to better foster democratic values among German children and adolescents, with the "most important" component of this reform involving instruction in democratic citizenship.[6] At the level of higher education, education mission members similarly noted that denazifying university faculty and staff was a necessary but not adequate condition for developing democracy in Germany. "Instruction must be provided which will inform students about domestic and international affairs and teach them the habits and techniques of democratic living," the members wrote. "It is recommended that all universities and higher schools include within each curriculum the essential elements of general education for responsible world citizenship."[7] Concluding the report by restating their essential belief in the power of education to catalyze and sustain a movement towards German democracy, the mission members further wrote, "For this process of attaining democracy in Germany in this generation, education is the one best instrument to employ.... Hence, so long as the United States continues as an occupying power in Germany, it should encourage and use the instruments of education to attain its major purpose, namely the attainment both of a democratic spirit and form of government."[8]

By encouraging the U.S. Military Government to reconstruct Germany's educational system in the image of America's, education mission members demonstrated their faith in the capacity of U.S. schools, colleges, and universities to strengthen democracy by educating a competent citizenry. Indeed, the education mission's report can and should be read as an affirmation of the belief that educational institutions in the United States had successfully served as citadels of democracy during World War II, defending democratic ideals against the challenges posed by fascist militarism. Yet education's democratic civic function did not go unchallenged during the war era. The demands of home front mobilization also led Americans to believe that educational institutions should radically restrict, if not eliminate, their historic mission of educating for civic mindedness. Instead, many argued, schools, colleges, and universities should serve as arsenals of democracy by dedicating their resources towards meeting the more immediate needs of a nation at war.

Those who called for the conversion of educational institutions into wartime arsenals were responding in part to the acceleration of a series of educational trends in the United States that had begun prior to the war. At the level of higher education, for instance, historian Roger Geiger has demonstrated how select colleges and universities began conducting applied research for industry and the federal government early in the twentieth century.[9] As U.S. research universities such as Harvard University and the Massachusetts Institute of Technology evolved, they rapidly increased their national and international reputations. World War II sped this development at a remarkable rate. Quickly sidelined were concerns, such as those voiced by Stanford University President Ray Lyman Wilbur, that universities would become obligated to the demands of government and business leaders through contracted research. With the draft drawing down male student enrollments across the nation, colleges and universities such as Stanford lobbied for research contracts with alacrity. Moreover, Stanford's ability to claim that such research directly advanced the national interest by contributing to the war effort—a claim that was explicitly acknowledged as beneficial to the university's institutional prestige—provided a formidable rationale, if not motivation, for further transforming Stanford's research agenda.

Higher education leaders during World War II also sought government and military contracts to justify maintaining personnel at their institutions and to fill the classrooms and laboratory facilities left vacant by draftees. When the U.S. Office of Education instituted the Engineering Science Management War Training program (ESMWT), many colleges and universities, including Stanford, eagerly participated. Although regarded as a strictly wartime measure, Stanford's adoption of ESMWT dramatically expanded the previously established practice of offering "extension" courses to members of the surrounding community. These classes were financially beneficial to the university and heightened Stanford's presence in the region, especially in relation to its nearby competitor, the University of California, Berkeley.

As with ESMWT, Stanford University administrators, again desperate to locate a substitute for declining enrollments and tuition dollars, urged the armed forces to capitalize on their institution's expertise in providing technical training and instruction in areas of study such as engineering and foreign languages. The Army Specialized Training Program (ASTP) compensated Stanford University for making its personnel and facilities accessible to an outside agency. One outcome, however, was the militarization of the university's collegiate environment. World War II was not the first time Stanford had been overtaken by soldiers in its classrooms and on its athletic fields. During World War I, the campus underwent a similar experience, albeit with fewer numbers of recruits and for a shorter period of time. As in 1918, the armed forces mostly withdrew from Stanford at the end of World War II. Nevertheless, the university solidified and expanded its relationship with the military between 1940 and 1945, a relationship that students later enthusiastically and sometime violently challenged during the Vietnam War era.

The demands of homefront mobilization accelerated prewar institutional trends in the nation's public schools as well, especially in the area of vocational education. Between 1880 and 1930, as historian Harvey Kantor has shown, vocational education became firmly established in many of California's school districts.[10] During the 1930s, programs such as the National Youth Authority and the Civilian

Conservation Corps further advanced vocational education opportunities for secondary school students across the United States. Following the attack on Pearl Harbor, however, vocational education offerings expanded even more swiftly. Through the development of Vocational Education for National Defense (VEND), even emerging suburban districts serving predominantly college-bound student populations, such as Palo Alto's, adopted vocational education as an important component of the school program.

Prior to World War II, although vocational courses were available through Palo Alto's Evening High School, school officials did not take advantage of federal funding to develop a vocational education program at their high school. Following the outbreak of war, however, district leaders proclaimed the importance of vocational opportunities for secondary students in preparing for a place on the homefront or the battlefront. Combined with the urging of state officials and the financial opportunity that the VEND program afforded, Palo Alto school leaders established a vocational day school, the Peninsula Defense Training Center. The center offered instruction to students and adults in such war-related skills as welding, riveting, and mechanics. As a result of this program, Palo Alto's expenditures for vocational education rose from $5,913 in 1940/41 to $127,577 just two years later.

Although Palo Alto residents rejected school officials' efforts to extend the life of the district's vocational day school by developing a junior college, the tension between vocational and academic courses of study continued into the postwar era. According to historian Herbert Kliebard, two significant wartime reports on postwar education, *Education for ALL American Youth* and *General Education in a Free Society*, represented a return to the national debate over "vocational preparation" versus "academic subject matter" in the school curriculum.[11] Kliebard observes that a central postwar curricular reform, which reflected the logic of vocationalism, had a "semi-official" birthday on June 1, 1945, when Charles A. Prosser delivered an address proclaiming the need to provide 60 percent of secondary school students with "life adjustment training." Known as the "Prosser Resolution," this proposal gave birth to "Life Adjustment Education" in the United States, the most prevalent and probably most highly criticized school reform movement in the years immediately following World War II.[12]

Between 1940 and 1945, the acceleration of previously existing social trends in the nation at large, such as women's entrance into the paid workforce, also resulted in changes to the nation's elementary and secondary schools. During the Great Depression, the decline in family income resulting from male unemployment led to an increasing number of women entering the job market. At the end of the 1930s, as military mobilization increased the demand for workers in the nation's defense industries and the draft eventually removed millions of men from the labor supply, women rapidly increased their rates of participation in the labor force, especially in manufacturing. By 1944, women had become an essential element in maintaining the nation's industrial capacity.

As a result, thousands of female teachers resigned their positions, leaving classrooms for better pay as unskilled workers in the nation's defense industries. Richmond's teacher shortage was a product of both the numerous employment opportunities opened to women during World War II and the comparatively low level of compensation teachers received. And although the teacher shortage ultimately led to increased salaries for Richmond's teachers (more a product of supply and demand than an increase in the public's esteem of teaching), working conditions declined dramatically.

Simultaneously, an increasing number of mothers entering the workforce accelerated the provision of federally supported child care. In the 1930s, the federal government established nursery schools through the Works Projects Administration to employ teachers, nurses, and custodians and to care for the young children of working mothers. Less than a year after America's declaration of war, federal officials expanded this program both because of an increase in the number of working women requiring care for their children and because they feared a rise in the rate of child neglect resulting from mothers' employment. These nursery schools for two- to five-year-olds created an almost entirely new layer of educational provision in public school districts throughout the nation.

Prewar demographic shifts in the nation's population also accelerated between 1940 and 1945. Although the movement of Americans from the country to the city began long before World War II, the sudden opening of employment opportunities in the nation's defense plants, most of which were located in or near major metropolitan areas, increased the migration of Americans of varying races and ethnicities from rural to urban areas. As these families moved to more densely populated areas of the United States, cities and towns were obliged to provide migrant children a place in the local public schools. When these families moved to boomtowns in record numbers, local school districts struggled to fulfill this responsibility.

Although referring to public schools during the war years as the nation's "first line of defense" against fascism and totalitarianism, the federal government assigned them a low priority, making it difficult for districts such as Richmond's to receive the financial support and building material approval required to construct new classrooms. Lack of federal support led to severe overcrowding in Richmond's elementary and secondary schools that lasted more than a decade. Schools operated on double sessions in Richmond well into the 1950s, resulting in a publicly acknowledged decline in the quality of education provided to the city's children and youth.

Acceleration, then, of previously existing trends both in education and in American society more broadly resulted in important wartime changes to the nation's schools, colleges, and universities. Yet, to varying degrees, these institutions resisted calls to reorient their operations solely to support the war effort. How? Institutions at all three levels of educational provision examined in this study engaged in a "conservationist" approach to the challenges of wartime mobilization, providing colleges and universities, elementary and secondary schools, and nursery schools with a strategy for fulfilling many of the war-related obligations that Americans ascribed to them while simultaneously maintaining their previously established civic purposes. Such conservationism, frequently condemned as foot-dragging in times of peace and stability, may have been a virtue in a time of national crisis.

Respected educational and political authorities during World War II issued a series of proclamations urging that America's educational institutions be placed directly in service to the nation's war machine. The Educational Policies Commission's insistence that the nation's public elementary and secondary schools had but "one dominant purpose" after 1941—"complete, intelligent, and enthusiastic cooperation in the war effort"—provides just one instance of this supposed singularity of purpose. Undermining the transformative intent of these proposals, educational institutions demonstrated a conservationist tendency that both fostered constancy and permitted change between 1940 and 1945. The degree to which schools, colleges, and universities sustained their commitment to serving as citadels of democracy, however, was wholly dependent upon the challenges each level of provision confronted.

After vigorously, but unsuccessfully, lobbying against the lowering of the draft age from 21 to 18, Stanford President Ray Lyman Wilbur had little choice but to seek financial assistance from outside the university to ensure his institution's survival. Uncomfortable with developing relationships with the federal government and industry, Wilbur nevertheless accepted the need to transform the university's research agenda to reap the financial benefits of contract-driven research. Moreover, Wilbur acknowledged Stanford's reliance on the federal government and the armed forces to substitute recruits for students drafted away from campus. Wilbur also, however, provided the institutional support necessary to establish Stanford's School of the Humanities. Counter to the prevailing trends in higher education, the School of the Humanities reaffirmed Stanford's founding mission to "promote the public welfare" by rounding out an educational program in which "any person" could "find instruction in any study," not simply that relating to the war. The employment of Lewis Mumford as one of the school's first faculty members demonstrated the university's commitment to a civic purpose that transcended the provision of an education solely dedicated to preparing soldiers for the battlefront or workers for the homefront.

The founding of the School of Humanities reflected a more general concern that by the end of the 1930s colleges and universities in the United States and Europe had lost "a sense of direction and purpose in education."[13] The pressure that the international emergency brought to bear on these institutions led to debates over the role of the humanities in higher education that were characterized by a heightened sense of immediacy. Stanford's humanities conferences provided an important forum for these discussions during and after

World War II, and according to I.L. Kandel, resulted in reemphasizing "the urgent need of the guidance of values if education was to make its contribution to the preservation of the democratic ideal."[14]

Unlike Stanford's leaders between 1941 and 1945, Palo Alto Unified School District officials and administrators never believed that wartime events threatened their schools' continued operation. Although enrollment in the district's secondary schools declined, school officials' greatest challenge was in formulating a response to demands that they reorient school programs to directly support the war effort. Changes to the schools' extracurriculum, modification of courses peripheral to the academic program such as physical education, the implementation of new elective courses such as aeronautics, and the establishment of the Peninsula Defense Training Center were all undertaken to meet the perceived needs of a nation at war. Throughout World War II, however, the central part of the Palo Alto High School program—the academic core curriculum—remained virtually unchanged. Reflecting a conservationist approach, district officials and administrators declared their willingness to adjust the school program as a result of the pressures of mobilization while permitting a large majority of students' classes to remain generally unaltered.

In Richmond, it was inevitable that wartime developments would significantly alter the operation of the city's public schools. Yet even in a boomtown such as Richmond, school administrators strove to conserve their schools' prewar qualities. Superintendent Walter Helms permitted students of varying racial, ethnic, and cultural backgrounds to mix in neighborhood schools as they had prior to the war. Although the number of these students increased dramatically between 1940 and 1945, Helms responded to a radical transformation in the demographic characteristics of the city's student population with civic-professionalism. By doing so, Helms ensured that in the midst of social turmoil Richmond's students would not be further harmed by discriminatory policies similar to those present in the city's public housing and defense industries. When, at the end of the war, he publicly admitted the schools' failure to maintain prewar educational standards, Helms's language underscored the civic-professional ideal. The defining principle on which Helms based his judgment regarding students' educational "loss" during World War II had little to do with migrant students' status as newcomers, their lack of academic preparation, or their racial, ethnic, and cultural backgrounds. Helms noted, instead, Richmond schools' failure to fulfill their civic responsibility in preparing students to be "enlightened future citizens."

As the number of students in Richmond's classrooms doubled and even tripled during the war years, teachers also engaged in conservationism by striving to maintain order in their overcrowded classrooms and by teaching the prewar curriculum as best they could. Although many fulfilled what they perceived as a professional duty to educate students regardless of race, ethnicity, or culture, they were not as generous to migrant parents who they held accountable for neglecting their children in general and their children's education, specifically. Teachers' conservationist efforts to stand their ground in the face of social upheaval also led them to ignore students' individual needs during the war years. Having been suddenly uprooted from their homes and communities, transported across the state or nation, and thrust into an area of overwhelming instability, children and youth suffered the trauma of homefront mobilization in ways not easy to overstate. Richmond teachers' civic-professionalism may have mediated the harshest elements of this instability for their students, but it did not encourage sensitivity to the racial, ethnic, and cultural challenges that many of them faced in their new home.

By implementing educationally innovative programs prior to 1942, Works Projects Administration nursery schools began to shift Americans' perceptions of child care from that of a social service to an educationally enriching experience for young children. During World War II, when the Lanham Act greatly expanded federal support for child care in the United States, wartime nursery schools maintained these pedagogical qualities. Developing and implementing curricular programs that emphasized children's creative self-expression, wartime nursery school educators described their work in the language of democracy's citadel rather than its arsenal. Dedicated to fostering "good citizenship" among their young students, wartime nurseries also demonstrated a conservationist approach to education throughout the war years. Although government officials conceived of the wartime nurseries as a pragmatic response to the perceived increase in child neglect and juvenile delinquency resulting from the employment of mothers with young children, Richmond Nursery School Director Erla Boucher insisted that the nurseries serve more than simply a "welfare" function. The California State Department of Education acknowledged the nurseries' success in achieving this objective when it concluded after the war that although the schools were initially intended "to provide custodial care for children of working parents," they developed "socially healthy, well-adjusted junior citizens."[15]

Why did American educational institutions employ a conservationist response to wartime mobilization? As early as 1942, progressive educator Horace M. Kallen suggested a viable explanation. Americans' surprise at their sudden involvement in a war against Japan, Kallen observed, mirrored their reaction to the United States' declaration of war against Germany just 24 years earlier.[16] Attributing this development to a unique quality in American democracy rather than citizens' amnesia, Kallen concluded that "Americans are disposed to identify aristocracy and war, democracy and peace."[17] Although the history of the United States was rooted in a frontier tradition involving almost continuous warfare, Kallen argued, Americans adhered to a democratic tradition in direct opposition to the totalitarian practice of employing schools to prepare future generations for war. "The American spirit," he noted, "has remained unshakably set toward peace and indefeasibly amateur in war."[18] Although Kallen went on to suggest that the events of World War II provided ample justification for "rethinking our entire conception of the education of free men with respect to the theory and practice of war," he insisted that it was counterintuitive for American education to abandon its historic function of educating for civic competence, even in wartime.[19] "The American school," Kallen wrote, "is unique of its kind, the carrier of the democratic culture, and the insurance of the democratic faith."[20]

That institutions at all three levels of educational provision in the United States demonstrated conservationist tendencies in response to World War II does not imply that each experienced the same degree of change. Indeed, vulnerability to wartime pressures correlated with the changes that nursery schools, elementary and secondary schools, and colleges and universities underwent during the war years. As a result, between 1940 and 1945 institutions at the upper and lower levels of the educational hierarchy experienced significant alterations, while those in the middle made relatively minor modifications.

As with many institutions of higher education during the war years, Stanford University responded to the loss of tuition-paying male students by accommodating defense industries, the federal government, and the armed forces. Although the implementation of the G.I. Bill returned draftees to campus after the war in even greater numbers than might otherwise have enrolled, wartime adjustments resulted in the eventual evolution of Stanford from a predominantly undergraduate, student-focused institution respected in the western United States into an internationally renown research university. As Rebecca Lowen has demonstrated, the Cold War played a significant role in this transformation. The changes that Stanford experienced during World War II, however, assured the presence of the institutional characteristics and relationships necessary for this development in the postwar era. Moreover, although the School of the Humanities assured the place of the liberal arts in Stanford's academic program, the university became heavily supported by outside sources of funding during World War II, sources that frequently originated in contracts reliant upon predominantly technical disciplines.

World War II's effect on early childhood education was precisely the opposite of the one it had on higher education in the United States, with enrollments in wartime nursery schools consistently expanding rather than declining. The development of wartime nurseries in cities such as Richmond was a direct result of homefront mobilization, with women's increasing participation in the labor force providing a justification for the growth of federally supported child care between 1940 and 1945. As the war drew to a close, however, prevailing social norms called into question the need for these institutions in American society. That the federal government announced terminating financial support for nursery schools even prior to the return of a majority of fathers from overseas service indicates the extent to which many Americans, especially government officials, assumed mothers would abandon paid employment immediately after the war. Indeed, eliminating the nursery schools ensured that some did just that. However, even after wartime nurseries across the nation closed their doors in 1946, many working mothers chose to remain engaged in paid labor. An exception to developments nationally, California's state and local governments continued to fund child care programs well into the postwar era. Like those in Richmond, however, most were transformed from institutions serving families from a range of socioeconomic backgrounds to ones providing a social service to the disadvantaged.

In comparison to institutions of higher education and early childhood education, elementary and secondary schooling in the United States experienced little lasting change during World War II. The decline in secondary student enrollments, although of concern early in the war, began to reverse as early as 1944. In Palo Alto, little readjustment of the school program was necessary after 1945, especially given the relative constancy of wartime academic curricular patterns. As the nation demobilized, so did schools' extracurricular activities. And although schools in boomtown cities such as Richmond continued to struggle with overcrowding in the postwar period, the teacher shortage was eliminated with the return of veterans into the labor force. Moreover, with the dissolution of VEND in 1945, federal expenditures in support of secondary school vocational programs plummeted.

World War II led to fear, anxiety, and concern on the part of many Americans, not only over the course of the conflict but in response to the political, social, and economic forces it had unleashed on the nation's homefront. Higher education, public elementary and secondary schooling, and early childhood education, as much as any of the country's other axial institutions, bore the brunt of these forces. Educational institutions in the United States all responded to the acceleration of prewar developments within and outside of their purview in a conservationist fashion throughout the war years, adjusting to the demands of mobilization yet remaining strongly dedicated to previously conceived educational and civic purposes. American education during World War II was truly a citadel of democracy.

Education at all levels continues to be one of the greatest commitments the United States makes in terms of financial and human resources. Although clearly influenced by political, social, and economic changes such as those experienced on the American homefront during World War II, education also directs the development of American values and beliefs. In the words of historian Bernard Bailyn, "[E]ducation not only reflects and adjusts to society; once formed, it turns back upon it and acts upon it."[21] The ways education will serve as an agent of change in the twenty-first century are rooted in twentieth century developments. Similarly, whether or not the civic purposes of the nation's educational institutions are advanced in this new century or slowly dissolve over the course of time is partially a product of their historical trajectory. It is my hope that this book has heralded contemporary issues in education in a particularly vivid way by highlighting enduring tensions in the development and practice of liberal democratic education in the United States.

Notes

Chapter 1

1. Thomas H. Briggs and Will French, eds., "Education for Democracy" (Proceedings of the Congress on Education on Democracy, Teachers College, Columbia University, 1939), 1.
2. "To Define Hold of Democracy," *New York Times*, August 13, 1939, p. D5.
3. Briggs and French, eds., "Education for Democracy," ii.
4. William O'Neill, *A Democracy at War: America's Fight at Home and Abroad in World War II* (New York: Free Press, 1993), 106.
5. "A War Policy for American Schools," (Washington, DC: Educational Policies Commission of the National Education Association and the American Association of School Administrators, 1942), 3.
6. On educator George Stoddard's use of the term "citadel" to describe American high schools at the end of World War II, see Robert L. Hampel, *The Last Little Citadel: American High Schools Since 1940* (Boston: Houghton Mifflin, 1986).
7. David M. Kennedy, *Freedom from Fear: The American People in Depression and War, 1929–1945* (New York: Oxford University Press, 1999), 857.
8. On the conservationist ideal, see David Tyack, *Seeking Common Ground: Public Schools in a Diverse Society* (Cambridge, MA: Harvard University Press, 2003).
9. Briggs and French, eds., "Education for Democracy," ii.
10. See Carl F. Kaestle, *Pillars of the Republic: Common Schools and American Society, 1780–1860* (New York: Hill and Wang, 1983); Diane Ravitch, "Education and Democracy," in *Making Good Citizens: Education and Civil Society*, ed. Diane Ravitch and Joseph P. Viteritti (New Haven, CT: Yale University Press, 2001); David Tyack, "Forming the National Character: Paradox in the Educational Thought of the Revolutionary Generation," *Harvard Educational Review* 36, no. 1 (1966): 29–41; David Tyack, "School for Citizens: The Politics of Civic Education from 1790 to 1990," in *E Pluribus Unum? Contemporary and Historical Perspectives on Immigrant Political Incorporation*, ed. Gary Gerstle and John Mollenkopf (New York: Russell Sage Foundation, 2001); William J. Reese, *America's Public Schools: From the Common School to No Child Left Behind* (Baltimore: Johns Hopkins University Press, 2005); Julie Reuben, "Patriotic Purposes: Public Schools and the Education of Citizens,"

in *The Public Schools*, ed. Susan Fuhrman and Marvin Lazerson (Oxford: Oxford University Press, 2005), 1–24, among others.
11. Quoted in Lorraine Smith Pangle and Thomas L. Pangle, *The Learning of Liberty: The Educational Ideas of the American Founders* (Lawrence: University of Kansas Press, 1993), 107–8.
12. Quoted in ibid., 96.
13. Their failure was not complete, of course. Jefferson's advocacy, for instance, led to establishing the University of Virginia, in part to provide civic leaders for public service.
14. Quoted in Reese, *America's Public Schools*, 22.
15. Ibid., 24.
16. Kaestle, *Pillars of the Republic*, 97.
17. Quoted in Ibid., 98.
18. David Labaree, "Public Goods, Private Goods: The American Struggle over Educational Goals," *American Educational Research Journal* 34, no. 1 (1997): 67.
19. Ibid., 46–50.
20. Ibid., 50–58.
21. Ibid., 58.
22. Ibid., 67.
23. Tyack, *Seeking Common Ground*, 12. Similarly, political scientist Robert Reich observes that "public purposes are less clear" during times of peace and stability than during periods of social crises such as wars and depression. Robert B. Reich, ed., *The Power of Public Ideas* (Cambridge, MA: Ballinger, 1988), 10.
24. Mark J. Harris, Franklin D. Mitchell, and Steven J. Schechter, *The Homefront: America During World War II* (New York: G. P. Putnam, 1984), 46.
25. Kenneth Paul O'Brien and Lynn Hudson Parsons, eds., *The Home-Front War: World War II and American Society* (London: Greenwood Press, 1995), 3.
26. Karen Anderson, *Wartime Women: Sex Roles, Family Relations, and the Status of Women During World War II* (Westport, CT: Greenwood Press, 1981), 6.
27. Ibid., 6.
28. O'Brien and Parsons, eds., *The Home-Front War*, 107.
29. Ibid., 107.
30. Susan M. Hartmann, *The Home Front and Beyond: American Women in the 1940s* (Boston: Twayne Publishers, 1982), 31–51.
31. Anderson, *Wartime Women*, 23–74. Also see William M. Tuttle, *Daddy's Gone to War: The Second World War in the Lives of America's Children* (New York: Oxford University Press, 1993), 30–48.
32. Anderson, *Wartime Women*, 95.
33. Harris, Mitchell, and Schechter, *The Homefront*, 30–31.
34. Ibid., 38.
35. O'Brien and Parsons, eds., *The Home-Front War*, 120; Kennedy, *Freedom from Fear*, 768.
36. Ronald Takaki, *Double Victory: A Multicultural History of America in World War II* (Boston: Little, Brown, 2000), 43; Gretchen Lemke-Santangelo, *Abiding Courage: African-American Migrant Women and the East Bay Community* (Raleigh: University of North Carolina Press, 1996), 107–31.
37. Marilyn S. Johnson, *The Second Gold Rush: Oakland and the East Bay in World War II* (Berkeley: University of California Press, 1993), 113–42.

38. Richard Lingeman, *Don't You Know There's a War On? The American Home Front, 1941–1945* (New York: G. P. Putnam, 1970), 77.
39. Takaki, *Double Victory*.
40. Ibid., 24; Susan E. Hirsch, "No Victory at the Workplace: Women and Minorities at Pullman During World War II," in *The War in American Culture: Society and Consciousness During World War II*, ed. Lewis A. Erenberg and Susan E. Hirsch (Chicago: University of Chicago Press, 1996), 241–62.
41. Edward J. Escobar, "Zoot-Suiters and Cops: Chicano Youth and the Los Angeles Police Department During World War II," in *The War in American Culture: Society and Consciousness During World War II*, ed. Lewis A. Erenberg and Susan E. Hirsch (Chicago: University of Chicago Press, 1996), 284–309.
42. Takaki, *Double Victory*, 144–65.
43. Philips, Charles. Interview by author. Palo Alto, CA, July 21, 2002.
44. Martin, Henry. Interview by author. Palo Alto, CA, August 7, 2000.
45. Edmondson, Peter and Sally (Allen). Interview by author. Palo Alto, CA, September 23, 2000.
46. Haag, Evelyn. Interview by author. Walnut Creek, CA, July 12, 2000.
47. Prout, Mary Hall. An oral history conducted in 2002 by Ben Bicais, Regional Oral History Office, Bancroft Library, University of California–Berkeley.
48. I. L. Kandel, *The Impact of the War upon American Education* (Chapel Hill: University of North Carolina Press, 1948), 160.
49. Oakley Furney and C. Kenneth Beach, "Vocational Education for National Defense," in *The Forty-Second Yearbook of the National Society for the Study of Education: Part I- Vocational Education*, ed. Nelson B. Henry (Chicago: Department of Education, University of Chicago, 1943), 186–87; Arthur F. McClure, James Riley Chrisman, and Perry Mock, *Education for Work: The Historical Evolution of Vocational and Distributive Education in America* (London: Associated University Press, 1985), 92–93; Layton S. Hawkins, Charles A. Prosser, and John C. Wright, *Development of Vocational Education* (Chicago: American Technical Society, 1951), 476–502.
50. Thomas D. Snyder, "120 Years of American Education: A Statistical Portrait," (Washington, DC: U.S. Department of Education National Center for Education Statistics, 1993), 37.
51. O'Neill, *A Democracy at War*, 249.
52. Hartmann, *The Home Front and Beyond*, 59; Susan E. Riley, "Caring for Rosie's Children: Federal Child Care Policies in the World War II Era," *Polity* 26, no. 4 (1994): 669; Anderson, *Wartime Women*, 146; Tuttle, *Daddy's Gone to War*, 82.
53. "School's Open—for War," *Time*, September 14, 1942, p. 86.
54. Kandel, *The Impact of the War*, 10.
55. Lingeman, *Don't You Know There's a War On?*; Geoffrey Perrett, *Days of Sadness, Years of Triumph: The American People, 1939–1945* (New York: Coward, McCann & Geoghegan, 1973); John Morton Blum, *V Was for Victory: Politics and American Culture During World War II* (New York: Harcourt Brace Jovanovich, 1976); Anderson, *Wartime Women*; Studs Terkel, *"The Good War:" An Oral History of World War II* (New York: Pantheon, 1984).
56. Kennedy, *Freedom from Fear*; Doris Kearns Goodwin, *No Ordinary Time: Franklin and Eleanor Roosevelt, the Homefront in World War II* (New York: Simon and Schuster, 1994).

57. O'Neill, *A Democracy at War*; Tuttle, *Daddy's Gone to War.*
58. O. L. Davis, "The American School Curriculum Goes to War, 1941–1945: Oversight, Neglect, and Discovery," *Journal of Curriculum and Supervision* 8, no. 2 (1993): 126.
59. Diane Ravitch, *The Troubled Crusade: American Education, 1945–1980* (New York: Basic Books, 1983); Henry J. Perkinson, *The Imperfect Panacea: American Faith in Education, 1865–1976*, 2nd ed. (New York: Random House, 1977); Joel Spring, *The American School, 1642–1985* (New York: Longman, 1986); Lawrence Cremin, *American Education: The Metropolitan Experience, 1876–1980* (New York: Harper and Row, 1988).
60. Ronald D. Cohen, "World War II and the Travail of Progressive Schooling: Gary, Indiana, 1940–1946," in *Schools in Cities: Consensus and Conflict in American Educational History*, ed. Ronald K. Goodenow and Diane Ravitch (New York: Holmes and Meier, 1983), 263.
61. Alan W. Garrett, "Planning for Peace: Visions of Postwar American Education During World War II," *Journal of Curriculum & Supervision* 11, no. 1 (1995): 6.
62. Roger L. Geiger, *To Advance Knowledge: The Growth of America's Research Universities, 1900–1940* (New York: Oxford University Press, 1986); Roger L. Geiger, *Research and Relevant Knowledge: American Research Universities since World War II* (New York: Oxford University Press, 1993); Stuart W. Leslie, *The Cold War and American Science: The Military-Industrial-Academic Complex at MIT and Stanford* (New York: Columbia University Press, 1993); Rebecca S. Lowen, *Creating the Cold War University: The Transformation of Stanford* (Berkeley: University of California Press, 1997).
63. Louis E. Keefer, *Scholars in Foxholes: The Story of the Army Specialized Training Program in World War II* (Jefferson, NC: McFarland, 1988); V. R. Cardozier, *Colleges and Universities in World War II* (Westport, CT: Praeger, 1993).
64. John R. Thelin, *A History of American Higher Education* (Baltimore: Johns Hopkins University Press, 2004).
65. Christopher P. Loss, "'The Most Wonderful Thing Has Happened to Me in the Army': Psychology, Citizenship, and American Higher Education in World War I," *The Journal of American History* 92, no. 3 (2005): 867.
66. Perrett, *Days of Sadness, Years of Triumph*, 374.
67. Gerard Giordano, *Wartime Schools: How World War II Changed American Education*, ed. Alan R. Sadovnik and Susan F. Semel, vol. 34 of *History of Schools & Schooling* (New York: Peter Lang, 2004), xxi.
68. Ibid., xix.
69. Andrew Spaull, "World War II and the Secondary School Curriculum: A Comparative Study of the USA and Australia," in *Education and the Second World War: Studies in Schooling and Social Change*, ed. Roy Lowe (Bristol: Falmer Press, 1992), 160.
70. Ibid., 161.
71. Davis, "The American School Curriculum," 126.
72. Sonya Michel, *Children's Interests/Mothers' Rights: The Shaping of America's Child Care Policy* (New Haven, CT: Yale University Press, 1999).
73. Barbara Beatty, "The Politics of Preschool Advocacy: Lessons from Three Pioneering Organizations," in *Who Speaks for America's Children? The Role of Child Advocates in Public Policy*, ed. Carol J. De Vita and Rachel

Mosher-Williams (Washington, DC: Urban Institute Press, 2001), 165–90. Also see Barbara Beatty, *Preschool Education in America: The Culture of Young Children from the Colonial Era to the Present* (New Haven, CT: Yale University Press, 1995).
74. Elizabeth Rose, *A Mother's Job: The History of Day Care, 1890–1960* (New York: Oxford University Press, 1999), 153.
75. Emilie Stoltzfus, *Citizen, Mother, Worker: Debating Public Responsibility for Child Care after the Second World War* (Chapel Hill: University of North Carolina Press, 2003), 151.
76. Division of Public School Administration Child Care Center Staff, "Report of Child Care Centers Administered and Operated by California School Districts," (Sacramento: California State Department of Education, 1949), i.
77. Between 1940 and 1946, federal investment accounted for 45 percent of California residents' personal income. See Johnson, *The Second Gold Rush*, 8, 30; Gerald D. Nash, *The American West Transformed: The Impact of the Second World War* (Lincoln: University of Nebraska Press, 1985), 25–26.
78. Nash, *The American West Transformed*, 25–26.
79. Ibid., 26.
80. Johnson, *The Second Gold Rush*, 8.
81. Nash, *The American West Transformed*, 38–39; Johnson, *The Second Gold Rush*, 41–45.
82. United States Department of Commerce, Bureau of the Census, Sixteenth Census of the United States: 1940, Population, Volume II, Part I, 599, 601.
83. Johnson, *The Second Gold Rush*, 27; Sixteenth Census of the United States: 1940, Population, Volume II, Part I, 601.
84. Ibid., 10. Referring to a medal given to a soldier wounded in battle, the term "Purple Heart" was also applied to cities suffering the greatest effects of mobilization during World War II.
85. Nash, *The American West Transformed*, 69.
86. William J. Reese, "Public Schools and the Elusive Search for the Common Good," in *Reconstructing the Common Good in Education*, ed. Larry Cuban and Dorothy Shipps (Stanford, CA: Stanford University Press, 2000), 31.

Chapter 2

1. Quoted in "Freedom Must Be Learned," *Time*, January 25, 1943, p. 43.
2. Stanford University Archives, Ray Lyman Wilbur Presidential Papers, 1914–51, Old Box 115, Fiftieth Anniversary Celebration Program.
3. Edgar Eugene Robinson and Paul Carroll Edwards, eds., *The Memoirs of Ray Lyman Wilbur* (Stanford, CA: Stanford University Press, 1960), 584–88.
4. John Aubrey Douglass, *The California Idea and American Higher Education* (Stanford, CA: Stanford University Press, 2000), 92–100. Leland and Jane Stanford established their university as a private institution with a public purpose. Like Cornell University, the private, land-grant institution that Stanford was modeled on, the university was tuition-free (making it more affordable to working-class students than the nearby University of California, Berkeley). It regularly admitted students who had not attended prestigious college preparatory schools (a practice which led part of the student body to be known as the "Stanford Roughs" for their working-class background and

appearance), and admitted both women and men (although in disproportionate numbers). On Stanford's history, see John Swett, *Public Education in California: Its Origin and Development, with Personal Reminiscences of Half a Century* (New York: American Book, 1911); David Starr Jordan, *The Days of a Man*, 2 vols. (New York: World Book, 1922), vol. 1; Orrin Leslie Elliott, *Stanford University: The First Twenty-Five Years* (Stanford, CA: Stanford University Press, 1937); Alice Windsor Kimball, *The First Year at Stanford: Sketches of Pioneer Days at Leland Stanford Junior University* (San Francisco: Stanley-Taylor, 1905).

5. Jared Stallones, "Hanna and Stanford: Saving the University by Throwing It to the Wolves," *Midwest History of Education Journal* 26, no. 1 (1999): 151.
6. Quoted in ibid., 152.
7. *Stanford University Bulletin*, vol. 38, *Annual Register, 1929* (Stanford, CA: Stanford University Press, 1929), 595; *Stanford University Bulletin*, vol. 42, *Annual Register, 1933* (Stanford, CA: Stanford University Press, 1933), 615; Stallones, "Hanna and Stanford," 151.
8. See Stanford University Archives, Registrars Office Records, 1891–1928, Box 1, "Minutes of the Committee on Admission and Advanced Standing." In an effort to boost enrollments, in 1933 university officials also eliminated the 500-female student limit established by Jane Stanford in 1899. See J. Pearce Mitchell, *Stanford University, 1916–1941* (Stanford, CA: Board of Trustees of the Leland Stanford Junior University, 1958), 48–51.
9. Quoted in Edwin Kiester, *Donald B. Tresidder: Stanford's Overlooked Treasure* (Stanford, CA: Stanford Historical Society, 1992), 39.
10. Stallones, "Hanna and Stanford," 151–56.
11. Rebecca S. Lowen, *Creating the Cold War University: The Transformation of Stanford* (Berkeley: University of California Press, 1997), 70; Kiester, *Donald B. Tresidder*, 38–39.
12. I. L. Kandel, *The Impact of the War Upon American Education* (Chapel Hill: University of North Carolina Press, 1948), 160–61. Although initially offering college and university students a one-year deferment, the draft had an immediate effect on graduate student enrollment. V. R. Cardozier, *Colleges and Universities in World War II* (Westport: Praeger, 1993), 2. For the wartime decline in Stanford's graduate student enrollment, see Figure 2.1.
13. Although Wilbur had set August 1941 as his retirement date, the Board of Trustees asked him to remain in the Office of the President until they appointed his successor. Wilbur assumed the title of Chancellor in 1941 but continued to serve as president until Tresidder's inauguration in September 1943. See J. Pearce Mitchell, *Stanford University, 1916–1941* (Stanford, CA: Board of Trustees of the Leland Stanford Junior University, 1958), 41.
14. "Stanford Goes Humanist," *Time*, March 23, 1942, p. 60.
15. Wilbur demonstrated his anxiety regarding a potential wartime decline in student enrollments as early as 1940, when he formed the Stanford National Emergency Committee. Stanford University Archives, Ray Lyman Wilbur Presidential Papers, 1914–51, Old Box 116, "National Emergency 1941," "Stanford National Emergency Committee."
16. Stanford University Archives, Stanford War Records, 1917–45, Box #22, Folder 185, "World War II Misc. S.U. Printed Matter 1941–45," "Letter from Ray Lyman Wilbur to the Members of the Faculty of Stanford University,

dated March 10, 1941." See also "Annual Report of the President of Stanford University, 1941" (Stanford, CA: Stanford University, 1941), 8–11.
17. "Letter from Ray Lyman Wilbur to the Members of the Faculty of Stanford University, dated March 10, 1941." Also, see Mike Kresge, "Stanford Revises Curriculum to Meet Demands of War," *The Stanford Daily*, January 12, 1942, p. 1; "Farm to Run Full Blast This Summer; 2000 Expected in Expanded Courses," *The Stanford Daily*, May 14, 1942, p. 12.
18. "Annual Report of the President of Stanford University, 1942," (Stanford, CA: Stanford University, 1942), 25.
19. Wilbur was outspoken in his criticism of lowering the draft age, calling the proposal to do so a "national disgrace." "Wilbur Hits 18-Year-Old Draft Bill," *The Stanford Daily*, November 4, 1942, p. 1.
20. *Higher Education and the War: The Report of a National Conference of College and University Presidents, Held in Baltimore, Md., January 3–4, 1942*, vol. 6, *Reports of Committees of the Council* (Washington, DC: American Council on Education, 1942).
21. Kandel, *The Impact of the War Upon American Education*, 6–8; Louis E. Keefer, *Scholars in Foxholes: The Story of the Army Specialized Training Program in World War II* (Jefferson, NC: McFarland, 1988), 13–16.
22. See *Organizing Higher Education for National Defense: The Report of a Conference Called by the National Committee on Education and Defense Held in Washington, D.C., February 6, 1941*, vol. 4, *Reports of Committees of the Council* (Washington, DC: American Council on Education, 1941).
23. "Western Educators Plan Commission for Co-Operation in National Defense," *Stanford Daily*, June 26, 1941, p. 1. See also Stanford University Archives, Ray Lyman Wilbur Presidential Papers, 1914–51, Old Box 115, "Conference on Higher Education."
24. See *Higher Education Cooperates in National Defense: The Report of a Conference of Government Representatives and College and University Administrators, Held in Washington, D.C., July 30–31, 1941*, vol. 5, *Reports of Committees of the Council* (Washington, DC: American Council on Education, 1941).
25. "Annual Report of the President of Stanford University, 1942," 20–21.
26. Ibid., 21.
27. At Stanford, other solutions, such as admitting qualified high school seniors prior to graduation, were also implemented although they were not expected to have as positive a financial impact. "Stanford Steps Ahead," *Stanford Today*, January 18, 1943, p. 1.
28. Lowen, *Creating the Cold War University*, 99–102.
29. Ibid., 95–119.
30. Stanford University Archives, Ray Lyman Wilbur Presidential Papers, 1914–51, Old Box 125, "Planning and Development," "Letter from Paul Davis to Dr. Donald B. Tresidder, dated November 20, 1942"; "Stanford University: The Founding Grant with Amendments, Legislation and Court Decrees," (Stanford, CA: Stanford University Press, 1971), 1–2.
31. Lowen, *Creating the Cold War University*, 72.
32. Stanford University Archives, Ray Lyman Wilbur Presidential Papers, 1914–51, Old Box 112, "Education, School of (Sept. to Feb.)," "Letter from Paul Hanna to Chancellor Ray Lyman Wilbur, dated February 11, 1942."
33. Ibid.

34. Ibid.
35. Stanford University Archives, Stanford War Records, 1917–45, Box #22, Folder 182, "Committee on University Services," "Stanford University–Committee on University Services–A Statement of Principle."
36. Stanford University Archives, Stanford War Records, 1917–45, Box #22, Folder 182, "Committee on University Services," "Stanford University–Committee on University Services–The Organization of The Resources of Stanford University for Greater Public Service."
37. Lowen, *Creating the Cold War University*, 57, 99; Stuart W. Leslie, *The Cold War and American Science: The Military-Industrial-Academic Complex at MIT and Stanford* (New York: Columbia University Press, 1993), 1–13.
38. Cardozier, *Colleges and Universities in World War II*, 168–69; Keefer, *Scholars in Foxholes*, 30–31.
39. On the mechanized nature of World War II and the corresponding need for technical knowledge, see David M. Kennedy, *Freedom from Fear: The American People in Depression and War, 1929–1945* (New York: Oxford University Press, 1999), 615–68.
40. Cardozier, *Colleges and Universities in World War II*, 169.
41. Ibid., 168–169; Keefer, *Scholars in Foxholes*, 30–31.
42. Henry H. Horsby, *Engineering, Science, and Management War Training: Final Report* (Washington, DC: U.S. Office of Education, 1946).
43. "Annual Report of the President of Stanford University, 1942," 32.
44. Horsby, *Engineering, Science, and Management War Training*, 3.
45. Stanford University Archives, Stanford War Records, 1917–45, Box #22, Folder 183, "E.S.M.W.T. Courses," "ESMWT–A Brief Description of Engineering Science and Management War Training as offered by Stanford University." While these courses were not initially open to regular university students, in January 1942 the U.S. Office of Education began allowing them to enroll on the condition that the course not be taken for credit and that the students enter into defense employment soon after completing the course. See "War Industry Courses Are Thrown Open," *The Stanford Daily*, January 29, 1942, p. 2.
46. "ESMWT–A Brief Description of Engineering Science and Management War Training as offered by Stanford University"; "Annual Report of the President of Stanford University, 1944," (Stanford, CA: Stanford University, 1944), 158–59.
47. "ESMWT–A Brief Description of Engineering Science and Management War Training as offered by Stanford University."
48. Stanford University Archives, Ray Lyman Wilbur Presidential Papers, 1914–51, Old Box 130, "ESMWT Courses–Mar. April May"; Mitchell, *Stanford University, 1916–1941*, 145, "Annual Report of the President of Stanford University, 1942," 255; "Annual Report of the President of Stanford University, 1944," 158–59.
49. Stanford University Archives, Stanford War Records, 1917–45, Box #22, Folder 183, "E.S.M.W.T. Courses," "War Production Training–Fall 1942."
50. "ESMWT–A Brief Description of Engineering Science and Management War Training as offered by Stanford University"; "Annual Report of the President of Stanford University, 1944," 158–59.

51. "ESMWT–A Brief Description of Engineering Science and Management War Training as offered by Stanford University."
52. Stanford University Archives, Ray Lyman Wilbur Presidential Papers, 1914–51, Old Box 131, "ESMWT–Correspondence–Sept. Oct. Nov.," "Letter from Eugene L. Grant, Institutional Representative, ESMWT, to Dr. Donald B. Tresidder, dated November 3, 1943"; Stanford University Archives, Stanford War Records, 1917–45, Box #22, Folder 183, "E.S.M.W.T. Courses," "Memo to Donald B. Tresidder from Eugene L. Grant, Institutional Representative for ESMWT, dated June 24, 1944."
53. "Annual Report of the President of Stanford University, 1942," 255.
54. Stanford University Archives, Stanford War Records, 1917–45, Box #22, Folder 183, "E.S.M.W.T. Courses," "Fall 1943–Fundamentals of Marine Drafting and Chemical Analyst Training for Women" and "Summer 1943–Fundamentals of Industrial Management for Women." Nationally, women's enrollment in the program increased from less than 1 percent in 1940/41 to more than 20 percent in 1942/43. By 1945, women's total enrollment was 282,235. See Stanford University Archives, Ray Lyman Wilbur Presidential Papers, 1914–51, Old Box 131, "ESMWT–Correspondence–Sept. Oct. Nov.," "Progress Report–ESMWT by George W. Case, Director, Engineering, Science, and Management War Training Program. Address presented at the 57th Annual Conference of the Association of Land Grant Colleges and Universities, Chicago, Illinois, October 26, 1943"; Horsby, *Engineering, Science, and Management War Training: Final Report*, 45.
55. Stanford University Archives, Stanford War Records, 1917–45, Box #22, Folder 183, "E.S.M.W.T. Courses," "Letter dated May 5, 1945, Subject: Termination of ESMWT;" "Memo to Donald B. Tresidder from Eugene L. Grant, Institutional Representative for ESMWT, dated June 24, 1944."
56. Ibid.
57. Ibid.
58. Stanford University Archives, Ray Lyman Wilbur Presidential Papers, 1914–51, Old Box 131, "ESMWT–Correspondence–Sept. Oct. Nov.," "Letter from Eugene L. Grant, Institutional Representative, ESMWT, to Dr. Donald B. Tresidder, dated September 24, 1943."
59. Ibid. To put Stanford's participation in context, the 1942/43 ESMWT program received a congressional appropriation of $30 million, of which $27 million was spent. During the year, the government approved 223 colleges for participation in the program, with 216 actually offering courses. These institutions employed 37,000 instructors on a part-time basis (for an approximate total of 7,500 full-time instructors) and 6,500 administrative personnel. Seventy-five percent of the courses were designed to meet the shortage of engineers, 5 percent for chemists and physicists, and 20 percent for non-engineering production supervisors. "Progress Report–ESMWT by George W. Case, Director, Engineering, Science, and Management War Training Program." (address presented at the 57th Annual Conference of the Association of Land Grant Colleges and Universities, Chicago, Illinois, October 26, 1943).
60. "Memo to Donald B. Tresidder from Eugene L. Grant, Institutional Representative for ESMWT, dated June 24, 1944."
61. Stanford University Archives, Ray Lyman Wilbur Presidential Papers, 1914–51, Old Box 131, "ESMWT—Correspondence—Sept. Oct. Nov.,"

"Letter from J. Hugh Jackson, Dean, Graduate School of Business, to Dr. Donald B. Tressider, dated October 20, 1943."
62. Horsby, *Engineering, Science, and Management War Training*, 64.
63. Carol S. Gruber, *Mars and Minerva: World War I and the Uses of Higher Learning in America* (Baton Rouge: Louisiana State University Press, 1975), 213–19.
64. Cardozier, *Colleges and Universities in World War II*, 41.
65. Stanford University Archives, Ray Lyman Wilbur Presidential Papers, 1914–51, Old Box 130, "Old File– Dec. 1942–June 1943– ASTP," "Letter from Colonel Herman Beukema, Director, Army Specialized Training Division, to University and College Heads, dated January 5, 1943."
66. Stanford University Archives, Ray Lyman Wilbur Presidential Papers, 1914–51, Old Box 130, "Old File– Dec. 1942–June 1943– ASTP," "Memorandum from Paul R. Hanna to Dr. Ray Lyman Wilbur dated January 5, 1943."
67. Stanford University Archives, Ray Lyman Wilbur Presidential Papers, 1914–51, Old Box 130, "Old File– Dec. 1942–June 1943– ASTP," "The Army Specialized Training Division, Agenda, Meeting of the Advisory Committee on the Army Specialized Training Program February 2–3, 1943."
68. Stanford University Archives, Ray Lyman Wilbur Presidential Papers, 1914–51, Old Box 130, "Old File– Dec. 1942–June 1943– ASTP," "Letter from Colonel W. H. Root, Director, Army Specialized Training Program, to Dr. Ray Lyman Wilbur, dated February 25, 1943." The Army Specialized program, although by far the largest military program adopted by Stanford during the war and considered "the principal military activity of the University," was only one of several. Other programs included a Navy V-12 program, a physical therapy training program for the Women's Army Corps, a Specialized Training and Reassignment Unit, a Civil Affairs Training School, a school of Naval Administration, and a Civil Communications Intelligence school. See "Annual Report of the President of Stanford University, 1943," (Stanford, CA: Stanford University, 1943), 3; "Annual Report of the President of Stanford University, 1944," 163–65.
69. Stanford University Archives, Ray Lyman Wilbur Presidential Papers, 1914–51, Old Box 131, "ASTP Curriculum, Tests, Etc.–Sept. Oct. Nov.," "Letter To Members of the Stanford Faculty from Ray Lyman Wilbur, Chancellor, dated March 12, 1943."
70. "Army Instead of Navy to Train Men Here," *Stanford Today*, January 18, 1943, p. 1.
71. Stanford University Archives, Ray Lyman Wilbur Presidential Papers, 1914–51, Old Box 130, "Old File– Dec. 1942–June 1943– ASTP," "Memorandum from Paul Hanna to Chancellor Ray Lyman Wilbur, Subject: Army Specialist Training Program, dated April 2, 1943."
72. Benjamin Fine, "Army's College Program Is Reported Bogged Down," *New York Times*, May 22, 1943, p. 1.
73. Stanford University Archives, Ray Lyman Wilbur Presidential Papers, 1914–51, Old Box 130, "Old File– Dec. 1942–June 1943– ASTP," "Letter from Major A. W. Nordwell, Corps of Engineers Contracting Officer, Hq. Ninth Service Command, to The Board of Trustees of the Leland Stanford Junior University, dated April 22, 1943."

74. In general, ASTP courses were offered separately from civilian courses, leading to a marked increase in faculty course loads. See "Annual Report of the President of Stanford University, 1943," 209.
75. Army Service Forces Manual, "Catalog of Curricula and Courses, Army Specialized Training Program," Headquarters, Army Service Forces. March 1945, U.S. Government Printing Office, Washington, DC, 1945.
76. The military's ever-changing wartime needs led the Army to frequently reassign ASTP recruits in the midst of their training. For those who completed the entire program, however, several paths were typical. Trainees might continue in the ASTP and receive advanced training, be assigned to Officer Candidate School (as many ASTP recruits expected), be chosen for further advanced technical training in an Army Service School, or return to other military duty. *Fifty Questions and Answers on Army Specialized Training Program*, (Washington, DC: War Department, 1943), 13.
77. Stanford University Archives, Ray Lyman Wilbur Presidential Papers, 1914–51, Old Box 131, "ASTP Curriculum, Tests, Etc.–Sept. Oct. Nov.," "Army Specialized Training Program, Advanced Phase, Curriculum No. 0-2, Term 9L, Linguistics Fields."
78. Stanford University Archives, Ray Lyman Wilbur Presidential Papers, 1914–51, Old Box 131, "ASTP Medical School & School of Health September, October, November," "Letter from Frank F. Walker, Financial Vice-President To the Honorable Board of Trustees of The Leland Stanford Junior University, dated September 8, 1943." The Stanford School of Medicine was located in San Francisco during the war years and was not a noticeable part of student life on the Palo Alto campus.
79. Army Service Forces Manual, "Catalog of Curricula and Courses, Army Specialized Training Program." Also, see Stanford University Archives, Ray Lyman Wilbur Presidential Papers, 1914–51, Old Box 131, "ASTP Curriculum, Tests, Etc.–Sept. Oct. Nov.," "Letter from Paul Hanna to Dr. Donald B. Tresidder, dated September 21, 1943."
80. This total reflects all of the Army's military programs implemented at Stanford, with the ASTP by far the largest in number and presence. See "Annual Report of the President of Stanford University, 1945," (Stanford, CA: Stanford University, 1945), 155.
81. Stanford University Archives, Ray Lyman Wilbur Presidential Papers, 1914–51, Old Box 131, "ASTP Press Day," "Press Release– HX38 By Nick Bourne, United Press Staff Correspondent."
82. "Annual Report of the President of Stanford University, 1944," 3.
83. "Annual Report of the President of Stanford University, 1943," 5; Kiester, *Donald B. Tresidder*, 51.
84. Philips, Charles. Interview by author. Palo Alto, CA, July 21, 2002.
85. Ibid.
86. Considering the size of the ASTP nationally, involving approximately 219,000 trainees over the course of the war, individual experiences varied widely. Philips's recollections, however, correlate with the interviews and letters received from over 250 ASTP trainees on which Louis Keefer based his history of the ASTP. See Keefer, *Scholars in Foxholes*.
87. Interview with Charles Philips.
88. Marshall, Clyde. Interview by author. Palo Alto, CA, June 11, 2002.

89. Ibid.
90. Ibid.
91. Although colleges and universities were not meant to "profit" from the ASTP, Stanford reaped significant financial rewards from its involvement. For the U.S. Army's "Principles of Contract" regulating financial gain, see "Army Service Forces Manual, Training Unit Contract Instructions for University and College Authorities Offering Training Facilities for Army Trainees, Army Specialized Training Program," Headquarters, Army Service Forces, December 1, 1943, pp. 5–12.
92. Stanford University Archives, Ray Lyman Wilbur Presidential Papers, 1914–51, Old Box 130, "Army Contracts Binder," "Training Unit Contract–War Department dated May 3, 1943"; "ASTP Contract No. W-59-AST-(SC IX)-11."
93. Stanford University Archives, Ray Lyman Wilbur Presidential Papers, 1914–51, Old Box 131, "ASTP Directors and Assistant Directors," "Memorandum of Meeting of the AST Directors, with the President and Financial Vice President on Thursday, December 30, 1943."
94. Paul Hanna, writing first to Wilbur and then to Tresidder from the University's Washington, DC, office consistently noted the "significant" part Stanford played in the ASTP, the "leadership position" it might assume in the program, and how "for the record" the military was "having great difficulty getting anything going at the University of California." Stanford University Archives, Ray Lyman Wilbur Presidential Papers, 1914–51, Old Box 130, "Old File– Dec.1942–June 1943– ASTP," "Memoranda from Paul Hanna to Chancellor Ray Lyman Wilbur, dated May 28, 1943." Also, see Stanford University Archives, Ray Lyman Wilbur Presidential Papers, 1914–51, Old Box 130, "Old File– Dec.1942–June 1943– ASTP," "Memorandum from Paul Hanna to Chancellor Ray Lyman Wilbur, dated June 1, 1943."
95. Cardozier, *Colleges and Universities in World War II*, 31.
96. Stanford University Archives, Ray Lyman Wilbur Presidential Papers, 1914–51, Old Box 131, "ASTP Curriculum, Tests, Etc.–Sept. Oct. Nov.," "Memo from Colonel John R. Eden, Commandant to The President, Stanford University, California, 1 December 1943."
97. Stanford University Archives, Ray Lyman Wilbur Presidential Papers, 1914–51, Old Box 131, "ASTP Curriculum, Tests, Etc.–Sept. Oct. Nov.," "Memorandum on the proposed Contracts from the War Department for Test Construction and Standardization for Army Specialized Training Program."
98. Stanford University Archives, Ray Lyman Wilbur Presidential Papers, 1914–51, Old Box 131, "ASTP Curriculum, Tests, Etc.–Dec., Jan., Feb.," "Memo from Paul Hanna to Dr. Donald B. Tresidder, Subject: Conference with Dr. Rubin of the ASTP, dated January 27, 1944."
99. Ibid.
100. Mitchell, *Stanford University, 1916–1941*, 143.
101. In making this claim, Leland and Jane Stanford again borrowed from Ezra Cornell, who issued a similar statement defining the mission of his institution. Kimball, *The First Year at Stanford*, 29–47.
102. Stanford University Archives, Ray Lyman Wilbur Presidential Papers, 1914–51, Old Box 118, "School of Humanities," "Letter from Ray Lyman

Wilbur to President Raymond B. Fosdick of the Rockefeller Foundation, dated November 29, 1941"; Old Box 123, "Humanities, School of," "Draft of letter from Ray Lyman Wilbur to newly appointed faculty."
103. C. S. Lewis, *The Weight of Glory and Other Addresses* (New York: Macmillan, 1949), 43–54.
104. Ibid., 43–54.
105. Mark Van Doren, *Liberal Education* (New York: Henry Holt, 1943), vii.
106. Sidney M. Shalett, "New Plan Suspends Liberal Education," *New York Times*, December 18, 1942, p. 1.
107. "Professors at Work," *Time*, June 14, 1943, p. 56.
108. Benjamin Fine, "Liberal Arts Eclipsed by Vocational Courses," *New York Times*, January 24, 1943, p. E7.
109. Student interest, in turn, was undoubtedly influenced by the government's policy of limited draft deferments for students in curricular programs associated with "national survival," such as engineering and mathematics. See Cardozier, *Colleges and Universities in World War II*, 131.
110. "Class of '45," *Time*, September 29, 1941, p. 38.
111. Fine, "Liberal Arts Eclipsed by Vocational Courses," p. E7.
112. Ibid.,
113. Cardozier, *Colleges and Universities in World War II*, 121–22. One exception relating to the issue of relevance was the proposal that women increase their course taking in the liberal arts in an effort to balance the expected loss of liberally educated men in the postwar era. At Stanford University, women were encouraged to both maintain a commitment to the study of the liberal arts so as to be "broadly educated for a lifetime" and to complete a "wartime minor," including coursework that would lead to becoming an "Engineering Aide," "Junior Chemist," "Nurses Aide," and "Secretary." See American Council on Education Studies, *Organizing Education for National Defense* (Washington, DC, 1941); American Council on Education, *Higher Education and National Defense*, Bulletin No. 53, May 6, 1943; "Wartime Program for Stanford Women," Stanford University, Stanford, CA, March 1943.
114. See, for instance, Kandel, *The Impact of the War*, 174–75.
115. Gruber, *Mars and Minerva*, 110.
116. George T. Blakey, *Historians on the Homefront: American Propagandists for the Great War* (Lexington: University of Kentucky Press, 1970); Gruber, *Mars and Minerva*, 118–62.
117. C. Hartley Grattan, "The Historians Cut Loose," *The American Mercury* 11, no. 44 (1927): 413–30; Harry Elmer Barnes, *A History of Historical Writing*, 2nd ed. (New York: Dover, 1963), 277–90.
118. Laurence R. Veysey, *The Emergence of the American University* (Chicago: University of Chicago Press, 1965), 207–8.
119. Gilbert Allardyce, "The Rise and Fall of the Western Civilization Course," *The American Historical Review* 87, no. 3 (1982): 695.
120. Allardyce locates the actual development of the course in a "strange marriage between war propaganda and the liberal arts. . . . " Ibid., 706.
121. Ibid., 721.
122. Stanford University Archives, Ray Lyman Wilbur Presidential Papers, 1914–51, Old Box 116, "Defense– Stanford National Emergency Committee," "Harold Chapman Brown to Samuel B. Morris, Dec. 12, 1941."

123. Stanford University Archives, Ray Lyman Wilbur Presidential Papers, 1914–51, Old Box 123, "Humanities, School of," "Draft of letter from Ray Lyman Wilbur to newly appointed faculty."
124. Gruber, *Mars and Minerva*, 159.
125. Quoted in ibid., 159.
126. Stanford University Archives, Ray Lyman Wilbur Presidential Papers, 1914–51, Old Box 118, "School of Humanities," "Organization of the School of the Humanities."
127. "Stanford Goes Humanist," 60.
128. Theodore M. Greene et al., *Liberal Education Re-Examined: Its Role in a Democracy* (New York: Harper and Brothers, 1943), vii.
129. Ibid., 115.
130. Kandel, *The Impact of the War Upon American Education*, 172.
131. In defining the "humanities," the committee reported that it did not "restrict itself" to the "narrower meaning" as suggested by "the academic disciplines and modes of activity which that term connotes" but rather understood the "true nature and value of the humanities" to exist only in the "wider context" of liberal education. Greene et al., *Liberal Education Re-Examined*, vii, x.
132. Ibid., viii. Theodore M. Greene, who served as professor of philosophy at Princeton University, chairman of the committee appointed by the American Council of Learned Societies in 1936 to "reexamine" liberal education, and primary author of the committee's report, also served as a visiting professor in the Humanities at Stanford during World War II.
133. Ibid., 115. One of the well-publicized examples of this concern is found in Robert Maynard Hutchins' series of lectures delivered in 1936 and compiled into *The Higher Learning in America*. Robert Maynard Hutchins, *The Higher Learning in America* (New Haven, CT: Yale University Press, 1936).
134. Greene et al., *Liberal Education Re-Examined*, 115, 118.
135. Patricia Beesley, *The Revival of the Humanities in American Education* (New York: Columbia University Press, 1940), 7, 71.
136. In the spring of 1941, for instance, when faculty members responded to a questionnaire distributed by the school's organizational committee, none raised concerns relating to the war. Instead, faculty identified, among other issues demanding attention, the integration of the school into the university's previously existing departmental structure. Stanford University Archives, John W. Dodds papers, Box 1, Folder 19, "Some Questions for the Executive Committee of the School of the Humanities."
137. "Organization of the School of the Humanities."
138. "Annual Report of the President of Stanford University, 1941," 3.
139. "Stanford Goes Humanist," 60.
140. "Annual Report of the President of Stanford University, 1942," 20–21.
141. "Freedom Must Be Learned," 43; Wendell L. Willkie, "Freedom and the Liberal Arts," in *The Humanities after the War*, ed. Norman Foerster (Princeton: Princeton University Press, 1944), 5.
142. "Warren Warns against Change in Educating." *Contra Costa Gazette*, May 24, 1943.
143. James Bryant Conant, "No Retreat for the Liberal Arts," *New York Times Magazine*, February 21, 1943, pp. 5, 37.

144. Omar N. Bradley, "What You Owe Your Country," *Collier's*, February 26, 1949, p. 38. Thanks to Jeffrey Mirel for alerting me to this source.
145. Cardozier, *Colleges and Universities in World War II*, 122.
146. Kandel, *The Impact of the War*, 172.
147. James P. Baxter, "Commission on Liberal Education Report," *Association of American Colleges Bulletin* 29, no. 2 (1943): 269–99.
148. Fred B. Millett, *The Rebirth of Liberal Education* (New York: Harcourt, Brace, 1945).
149. *General Education in a Free Society* (Cambridge, MA: Harvard University Press, 1945), xv.
150. *The Humanities Look Ahead*, (Stanford, CA: Stanford University Press, 1943), v.
151. Ibid., vi.
152. David Mitrany, "The Humanities Look Ahead," *Nature* 154, no. 3917 (1944): 254.
153. Ibid., 254.
154. Kandel, *The Impact of the War Upon American Education*, 200–201.
155. See "Committee on Humanities Education in the South," *Higher Education* 1, no. 6 (1945): 7.
156. *Stanford University Bulletin*, vol. 38, *Announcement of Courses: 1942–43* (Stanford, CA: Stanford University, 1942), 164.
157. Ibid.
158. Ibid., 166. For its second year, the school modified these introductory courses, although the course objectives remained the same. Grouped under the theme "The Nature of Man," the three revised courses were entitled, "Ancient Times," "Middle Ages and the Renaissance," and "Modern Times." *Stanford University Bulletin*, vol. 63, *Announcement of Courses: 1943–44* (Stanford, CA: Stanford University, 1943), 163.
159. "Annual Report of the President of Stanford University, 1942," 308.
160. "Humanities Head," *Time*, June 8, 1942, p. 62.
161. "The School of the Humanities: A Description." (Stanford, CA: Stanford University, 1942), 3–6.
162. "Annual Report of the President of Stanford University, 1942," 37.
163. "Letter from Ray Lyman Wilbur to President Raymond B. Fosdick of the Rockefeller Foundation, dated November 29, 1941."
164. "Annual Report of the President of Stanford University, 1943," 246.
165. "Full-Time Japanese Class Now Being Given," *Stanford Today*, January 18, 1943, p. 4.
166. "A Report for the Rockefeller Foundation on the Activities of the School of Humanities, Stanford University, September, 1942—September 1943," 14.
167. Stanford University Archives, Ray Lyman Wilbur Presidential Papers, 1914–51, Old Box 123, "Humanities, School of," "Memorandum from John Dodds to Humanities Faculty, dated November 1942."
168. Ibid.
169. Stanford University Archives, Ray Lyman Wilbur Presidential Papers, 1914–51, Old Box 123, "Humanities, School of," "Letter from John Dodds to Raymond B. Fosdick, President, Rockefeller Foundation, dated November 18, 1942."
170. *Stanford University Bulletin*, 161.

171. "Annual Report of the President of Stanford University, 1943," 244.
172. "Annual Report of the President of Stanford University, 1941," 3; "Annual Report of the President of Stanford University, 1943," 244.
173. "Annual Report of the President of Stanford University, 1944," 1.
174. *Stanford University Bulletin*, vol. 108, *Announcement of Courses: 1945–46* (Stanford, CA: Stanford University, 1945), 128.
175. Stanford University Archives, Stanford War Records, 1917–45, Box #22, Folder 185, "World War II Misc. S.U. Printed Matter 1941–45," "Stanford and the War."
176. Ibid.
177. Ibid.
178. Ibid.
179. To the shock of many, Tresidder himself did not live to see the results of this process. Struck down by a heart attack in 1948, Tresidder died in New York City while touring to promote the value of the university's resources. Kiester, *Donald B. Tresidder*, 109–11.
180. Lowen, *Creating the Cold War University*, 148.

Chapter 3

1. "A War Policy for American Schools," (Washington, DC: Educational Policies Commission of the National Education Association and the American Association of School Administrators, 1942), 3.
2. See, for instance, "What the Schools Should Teach in Wartime," (Washington, DC: Educational Policies Commission of the National Education Association and the American Association of School Administrators, 1943); "Handbook on Education and the War" (National Institute on Education and the War: Sponsored by the U.S. Office of Education Wartime Commission, Washington, DC, August 28–31, 1942); John W. Studebaker, "The American Schools and Colleges in the War," *The American School Board Journal* 105, no. 2 (1942): 35–36.
3. "Education and the Defense of American Democracy," (Washington, DC: Educational Policies Commission of the National Education Association and the American Association of School Administrators, 1940), 21.
4. On changes to the school curriculum during World War II, see Ronald D. Cohen, "World War II and the Travail of Progressive Schooling: Gary, Indiana, 1940–1946," in *Schools in Cities: Consensus and Conflict in American Educational History*, ed. Ronald K. Goodenow and Diane Ravitch (New York: Holmes and Meier, 1983), 263–86; Gordon C. Lee, "Government Pressures on the Schools During World War II," *History of Education Journal* 2, no. 3 (1951): 65–74; S. L. Field, "Doing Their Bit for Victory: Elementary School Social Studies During World War II" (Ph.D. diss., University of Texas, Austin, 1991); Andrew Spaull, "World War II and the Secondary School Curriculum: A Comparative Study of the USA and Australia," in *Education and the Second World War: Studies in Schooling and Social Change*, ed. Roy Lowe (Bristol: Falmer Press, 1992), 159–76; K. M. Filkins, "American Secondary School Science Coursework Curriculum for "the Duration", 1939–1945" (Ph.D. diss., University of Texas–Austin, 1996); David E. Hanson, "Home-Front Casualties of War Mobilization: Portland Public Schools, 1941–1945," *Oregon Historical*

Quarterly 96, no. 2–3 (1996): 192–225; and especially, O. L. Davis, "The American School Curriculum Goes to War, 1941–1945: Oversight, Neglect, and Discovery," *Journal of Curriculum and Supervision* 8, no. 2 (1993): 112-127.
5. Ward Winslow, *Palo Alto: A Centennial History* (Palo Alto, CA: Palo Alto Historical Association, 1993), 15.
6. Orrin Leslie Elliott, *Stanford University: The First Twenty-Five Years* (Stanford, CA: Stanford University Press, 1937), 109–13.
7. U. S. Department of Commerce, Bureau of the Census, Sixteenth Census of the United States: 1940, Population, Volume II, Part I, 542, 599, 601, 680.
8. Guy C. Miller, ed., *Palo Alto Community Book* (Palo Alto, CA: Arthur H. Cawston Publisher, 1952), 122–124; J. R. Overturf, "Report of the Superintendent of Schools of the Palo Alto Unified School District," (Palo Alto, CA: Palo Alto Unified School District, 1941).
9. C. R. Holbrook, "Palo Alto Unified School District Financial Report for 1943–1944," (Palo Alto, CA: Palo Alto Unified School District, 1944), 3.
10. Carol Blitzer, "The 1940s: On the Home Front," Palo Alto On-Line, Publication Date: April 15, 1994, url: http://www.paloaltoonline.com/news_features/centennial/1940SA.php
11. Edmondson (Allen), Sally. Interview by author. Palo Alto, CA. September 23, 2000.
12. Paulin (Manning), Joan. Interview by author. Palo Alto, CA. September 15, 2000.
13. Berka (Minard), Paula. Interview by author. Palo Alto, CA. September 25, 2000.
14. "School Head to Emphasize Fundamentals," *Daily Palo Alto Times*, December 2, 1941.
15. "C. W. Lockwood Assumes Control," *Daily Palo Alto Times*, January 3, 1942.
16. Quoted in Benjamin Fine, "War Status Held Vital at Schools," *New York Times*, February 13, 1942, p. 19.
17. William G. Bruce, "Schools—but Not as Usual," *The American School Board Journal* 105, no. 4 (1942): p. 11.
18. "What the Schools Should Teach in Wartime," 7.
19. Results were drawn from 1,426 survey responses from school districts across the country. Henry Harap, "Front Lines in Education," *Educational Leadership* 1, no. 1 (1943): 43.
20. Ibid., 43.
21. In the Stanford report, questionnaires were sent to all California secondary schools. Of 201 responses, the 182 selected for inclusion in the study were claimed to represent a "wide sampling of the communities of the State," providing data from "small towns, rural areas, and great metropolitan centers." Charlotte D. Elmott, "Survey of High School Wartime Practices," *California Journal of Secondary Education* 17, no. 7 (1942): 395–409.
22. Ibid., 399. In addition to this study, graduate students in the Stanford School of Education completed a number of wartime master's theses investigating the impact of World War II on a range of elementary and secondary school areas. The theses included those of Marjorie Hastings and Rosemary Bell (examining secondary school English), Dolores Lucille Hintze (examining secondary school mathematics), Irma Jean Hannibal (examining "courses on

the war and postwar world"), and Helen Elizabeth Hart (examining the effect of the war on physical education).
23. "Curriculum Changes Disclosed to Seniors; Four Classifications Offered to Students," *The Campanile*, January 15, 1943, p. 1.
24. Kay Zubal, "Senior High School Slants Curriculum Towards War," *Daily Palo Alto Times*, January 27, 1943, p. 10.
25. "Curriculum Changes Disclosed to Seniors; Four Classifications Offered to Students," 1.
26. "New Semester Courses Prepare for War," *The Campanile*, January 22, 1943, p. 1; "Superintendent Lockwood Explains," *Daily Palo Alto Times*, April 13, 1943.
27. Palo Alto High School, like secondary schools throughout the nation, experienced a decline in student enrollment during the war years, predominantly a product of male students leaving school for employment prior to enlisting in the armed forces or being drafted. Average daily attendance at Palo Alto High School dropped from a prewar high of 810 students during the 1940/41 academic year to a low of 634 students in 1943/44 before again increasing to 703 students in 1944/45. This decline and the subsequent rise in student attendance influenced both the courses that comprised the school program and the number of class periods offered for each course. It should also be remembered that the war's impact on the curriculum did not occur at any one single moment but developed over time. I have therefore chosen to compare the courses and number of class periods offered prior to America's declaration of war (October 1939–October 1941) with those offered following (October 1942–October 1945).
28. "Students Take Math Courses as Aid to War," *The Campanile*, April 2, 1943, p. 4; Betty Maycock, "Students Swamp War-Important Classes," *Daily Palo Alto Times*, September 22, 1943.
29. See, for instance, Henry Grattan Doyle, "Americans, Awake to Language Needs," *The American School Board Journal* 102, no. 3 (1941): 19–21, 98.
30. Jean Hutton, "Many of the Seniors at Palo Alto High School Already Have College or Career Plans Made," *Daily Palo Alto Times*, March 14, 1942.
31. Ibid.
32. "World Affairs: Students to Study Peace Plans," *The Campanile*, March 12, 1943, p. 4.
33. Given the limited number of courses offered in this field even prior to the war, Palo Alto's School Board voted to close the departments of art and instrumental music in 1943. Community support led the board to rescind the decision weeks later. See "Superintendent Lockwood Explains."
34. Ivan Linder, "Strengthening Palo Alto's Nonacademic Work," *California Journal of Secondary Education* 17, no. 4 (1942): 215–17.
35. See, for instance, G. M. Gloss, "Aviation and Physical Education," *The American School Board Journal* 105, no. 1 (1942): 23–25.
36. "Handbook on Education and the War," 286–94.
37. Cover Art, *The American School Board Journal* 105, no. 3 (1942): 17.
38. "High Schools, Air-Conditioned," *Time*, October 12, 1942, p. 74.
39. On the implementation of aviation instruction in California, see Frank B. Lindsay, "Preflight Aeronautics in California Schools," *California Journal of Secondary Education* 18, no. 1 (1943): 9–12; and B. C. Winegar, "The

Aeronautics Curriculum Gains Momentum," in *Integration of the War Effort and of the Long-Term Program in California Secondary Schools*, ed. Aubrey A. Douglass, *California Society of Secondary Education Monograph Series* (Berkeley: California Society of Secondary Education, 1942), 27–30.
40. Martin, Henry. Interview by author. Palo Alto, CA. August 7, 2000.
41. I. L. Kandel, *The Impact of the War Upon American Education* (Chapel Hill: University of North Carolina Press, 1948), 67.
42. See, for instance, Frederick Rand Rogers, "The Amazing Failure of Physical Education," *The American School Board Journal* 109, no. 6 (1944): 17–19; William P. Uhler, "Military Training in Secondary Schools," *The American School Board Journal* 102, no. 2 (1941): 28–29.
43. The program's official title remained "California High School Cadets" until 1947, when the state legislature adopted the popular name "Cadet Corps." For a detailed curriculum of the wartime Cadet Corps program, see *California High School Cadets: A Manual for Period Instruction* (Sacramento: Adjutant General, State of California, 1944). Also see *California Cadet Corps: The Cadet Manual*, (Sacramento: California State Printing Office, 1953), 3–5.
44. "No High School Cadet Corps," *Daily Palo Alto Times*, September 13, 1940; "Education Board Suggests Course to 'Harden' Boys," *Daily Palo Alto Times*, October 11, 1940.
45. "Toughen Up: Ray to Enlarge, Improve Program of Physical Fitness at High School," *Daily Palo Alto Times*, July 10, 1942, p. 5; Howard C. Ray, "School Adapts 'Physical Ed' to Wartime," *Daily Palo Alto Times*, October 1, 1942.
46. Palo Alto Unified School District School Board Minutes, 25 Churchill Blvd., Palo Alto, CA (September 9, 1943) and (August 24, 1944).
47. Mary Katherine Hays and Frank Greenfield, "Uniforms Appear in Paly Halls as Cadet Corps Gets Started," *Daily Palo Alto Times*, October 5, 1944 ; "Cadet Corps to Be Part of Paly Life," *The Campanile*, September 28, 1944.
48. "Cadet Corps to Be Part of P.A. High School Life," *Daily Palo Alto Times*, September 6, 1944.
49. Interview with Sally Edmondson. Historian O. L. Davis reports a similar development in Texas during the war years, writing, "The world history course offered during the 1943–44 school year at Lometa (Texas) High School did not venture beyond the confines of the state-adopted textbook. The course's invariantly dull routine held steady against the news of fierce battles in Italy between Allied armies and Wehrmacht legions, the costly preparatory buildup to Operation Overlord, the bitterly contested struggles between Americans and Japanese on Pacific Islands largely unknown before the war, and the continuing shortages and dislocations at home. Not only did events of the war not seep into that course, they never made a welcomed visit." Davis, "The American School Curriculum Goes to War, 1941–1945," 112–27.
50. Herbert Kliebard, *Schooled to Work: Vocationalism and the American Curriculum, 1876–1946* (New York: Teachers College Press, 1999), 204.
51. Edwin A. Lee, "Vocational Education and the War Offensive," *The American School Board Journal* 104, no. 4 (1942): 25.
52. Ibid., 26.
53. David M. Kennedy, *Freedom from Fear: The American People in Depression and War, 1929–1945* (New York: Oxford University Press, 1999), 618.

54. For an informative description of vocational developments prior to and during World War II, see Andre Roger O'Coin, "Vocational Education During the Great Depression and World War II: Challenge, Innovation and Continuity" (Ph.D. diss., University of Maryland–College Park, 1988).
55. Layton S. Hawkins, Charles A. Prosser, and John C. Wright, *Development of Vocational Education* (Chicago: American Technical Society, 1951), 475.
56. On the detailed steps involved in this rapid approval, see Ibid., 472–76.
57. John W. Studebaker, "Annual Report of the United States Commissioner of Education: For the Fiscal Year Ended June 30, 1941," (Washington, DC: U.S. Office of Education, 1941), 2.
58. "Vocational and Technical Wartime Training," *Education for Victory* 1, no. 2 (1942): 7.
59. When the VEND program was first instituted, only training of "less than college grade" qualified for funding. Later, appropriations were included for courses of college grade as well as agricultural occupations, leading to a change in the program name to indicate two distinct yet jointly funded programs, "Vocational Training for War Production Workers" and "Food Production War Training Program." These later appropriations included funding for the Engineering, Science, and Management War Training (ESMWT) program discussed in Chapter 2. See Oakley Furney and C. Kenneth Beach, "Vocational Education for National Defense," in *The Forty-Second Yearbook of the National Society for the Study of Education: Part I- Vocational Education*, ed. Nelson B. Henry (Chicago: Department of Education, University of Chicago, 1943), 186–87; Arthur F. McClure, James Riley Chrisman, and Perry Mock, *Education for Work: The Historical Evolution of Vocational and Distributive Education in America* (London: Associated University Press, 1985), 92–93; Hawkins, Prosser, and Wright, *Development of Vocational Education*, 476–502.
60. On the history of prewar vocational developments in California specifically, see Harvey Kantor, *Learning to Earn: School, Work and Vocational Reform in California, 1880–1930* (Madison: University of Wisconsin Press, 1988). For historical perspectives on vocational education as it relates to schooling and youth, see Harvey Kantor and David B. Tyack, eds., *Work, Youth, and Schooling: Historical Perspectives on Vocationalism in American Education* (Stanford, CA: Stanford University Press, 1982). A good general overview of the Smith-Hughes and George-Deen Acts can be found in McClure, Chrisman, and Mock, *Education for Work: The Historical Evolution of Vocational and Distributive Education in America*. For a documentary history of vocational education, see Marvin Lazerson and W. Norton Grubb, eds., *American Education and Vocationalism: A Documentary History, 1870–1970* (New York: Teachers College Press, 1974).
61. "War Production Workers Training Program," *Education for Victory* 1, no. 14 (1942): 15–18.
62. For a description of the VEND programs as implemented statewide in California, see California State Archives, Dept. of Education and State Board of Education Records, Records of the Department of Education, War Production Training, 1941–47. F3752:2105, "Department of Education—Vocational Education," Bureau of Industrial Education, State Plans, 1941–44. "California Plan for Vocational Training for War Production Workers."

California State Department of Education, Commission for Vocational Education, Bureau of Trade and Industrial Education, Vocational Education of Defense Workers, Sacramento, November, 1941, p. 9.
63. John W. Studebaker, "Annual Report of the United States Commissioner of Education: For the Fiscal Year Ended June 30, 1940," (Washington, DC: U.S. Office of Education, 1940), 35–38.
64. California State Archives, Dept. of Education and State Board of Education Records, Records of the Department of Education, Walter Dexter (1937–45), Subject Files, 1937–45. F3752: 574, "Dept. of Education- S.P.I.- Walter Dexter," Subject Files–School Districts B-S. "Letter from Charles W. Lockwood to Walter F. Dexter, California Superintendent of Public Instruction, dated March 13, 1944." Palo Alto High School did offer courses considered to have "vocational aspects" in their content, such as "home arts," but the district never conceived of these courses as qualifying for federal funding. See Overturf, "Report of the Superintendent of Schools of the Palo Alto Unified School District," 15. Also, see Winslow, *Palo Alto: A Centennial History*, 138. Palo Alto's establishment of an Evening High School was not unusual. In California, the history of what was called "night school" was rooted in providing English and citizenship instruction to immigrants. State authorization permitted public school districts to "establish and maintain in connection with any high school under its jurisdiction special day and evening classes for the purpose of giving instruction to such minors or adults as in the judgment of the governing board of such district, may profit by such instruction." California State Archives, F:3752:580 Dept. of Education-S.P.I.-Walter Dexter, Subject Files-State Board of Education, 1943–44. "State Board of Education, report for the 1942–43, 1943–44 Biennium, Sacramento, CA, January 12, 1945."
65. Overturf, "Report of the Superintendent of Schools of the Palo Alto Unified School District," 26; California State Archives, Dept. of Education, Bureau of School Apportionments and Reports Records, October Reports, 1915–21, 1924–52. F:3601:1143, Education–School Apportionments and Reports, J-35, P-Q, 1939. "October Report of Secondary School Principal, October 13, 1939-Part Two, Palo Alto Evening High."
66. California State Archives, Dept. of Education. Bureau of School Apportionments and Reports Records, October Reports, 1915–21, 1924–52. F:3601:1143, Education–School Apportionments and Reports, J-35, P-Q, 1939. "October Report of Secondary School Principal, October 13, 1939-Part Two, Palo Alto Evening High"; F:3601:1160, Education– School Apportionments and Reports, J-35, High Schools, P, 1940, "October Report of Secondary School Principal, October 18, 1940–Part Two, Palo Alto Evening High."
67. Palo Alto Unified School District School Board Minutes, 25 Churchill Blvd., Palo Alto, CA (April 2, 1941).
68. "Letter from Charles W. Lockwood to Walter F. Dexter, California Superintendent of Public Instruction, dated March 13, 1944."
69. As with districts across the nation, Palo Alto also took advantage of VEND funding to create a work-experience program at the senior high school level. Students who remained enrolled in school were permitted to engage in supervised work off campus, as long as the work experience "definitely

related to the in-school training of the pupil." Students received credit toward graduation as a result of their participation. On this program's implementation in Palo Alto, see Palo Alto Unified School District School Board Minutes, 25 Churchill Blvd., Palo Alto, CA (December 10, 1942); "Palo Alto High School to Continue Student Work Experience Program," *Daily Palo Alto Times*, September 2, 1943; "Work Program and Tutoring on Curriculum," *The Campanile*, March 31, 1944, p. 7. For wartime guidelines regarding work-experience programs in California, see California State Archives, Department of Education and State Board of Education Records, Records of the Department of Education, War Production Training, 1941–47. F3752:2105, "Department of Education –Vocational Education," Bureau of Industrial Education, State Plans, 1941–44. "California Plan for Vocational Training for War Production Workers." California State Department of Education, Commission for Vocational Education, Bureau of Trade and Industrial Education, Vocational Education of Defense Workers, Sacramento, November, 1941, p. 19.
70. Palo Alto Unified School District School Board Minutes, 25 Churchill Blvd., Palo Alto, CA (August 28, 1941).
71. C. R. Holbrook, "Palo Alto Unified School District Financial Report for 1944–1945," (Palo Alto: Palo Alto Unified School District, 1945), 19. By the 1944/45 school year, expenditures had declined to $7,606.60.
72. Bill Mead, "Senior Classes Making Tours of Defense Center," *The Campanile*, October 1, 1942, pp. 1, 4.
73. Holbrook, "Palo Alto Unified School District Financial Report for 1944–1945," 4. Increasing enrollment at the Peninsula Defense Training Center and the accompanying decrease in high school enrollment occurred as the overall population of the city of Palo Alto rose. A special census held in 1944 indicated Palo Alto's population increased 8.9 percent between 1940 and 1944, from 16,774 to 18,261 residents. U.S. Department of Commerce, Bureau of the Census, Series P-SC, No. 40, Special Census of Palo Alto, California, May 20, 1944.
74. "War Work Conference Sets Vocational Education Goals," *Education for Victory* 1, no. 21 (1943): 1.
75. Grayson N. Kefauver, "Relation of Vocational Education to National Defense," in *The Forty-Second Yearbook of the National Society for the Study of Education: Part I- Vocational Education*, ed. Nelson B. Henry (Chicago: Department of Education, University of Chicago, 1943), 33.
76. Kandel, *The Impact of the War Upon American Education*, 84–88. Nationally, high school enrollments declined from a high of 6.7 million in 1940/41 to 5.5 million in 1943/44. See Herbert M. Kliebard, *The Struggle for the American Curriculum, 1893–1958*, 2nd ed. (New York: Routledge, 1995), 205–8.
77. "War Work Conference Sets Vocational Education Goals," 20. There was, of course, opposition to such claims during and following the war. See, for instance, Robert D. Baldwin, "The Impact of War on American Education," *Educational Administration and Supervision* 31, no. 4 (1945): 412–13.
78. "Vocational College May Be Set Up to Use War Shop Equipment," *Daily Palo Alto Times*, January 14, 1944.
79. Albert M. Davis, "Proposal for the Reorganization of the Secondary Schools and the Establishment of a Four-Year Junior College within the Palo Alto

Unified School District," (Palo Alto: Palo Alto Unified School District, 1944), 14.
80. Ibid. Palo Alto reflected a national trend in its desire to establish a junior college. Between 1920 and 1940, the number of junior colleges in the United States increased from 52 to 456, with a corresponding increase in enrollment from 8,102 to 149,954. On the history of the Junior College movement, see Steven Brint and Jerome Karabel, *The Diverted Dream: Community Colleges and the Promise of Educational Opportunity in America, 1900–1985* (New York: Oxford University Press, 1989); David O. Levine, *The American College and the Culture of Aspiration, 1915–1940* (Ithaca, NY: Cornell University Press, 1986), 162–84; Thomas Diener, *Growth of an American Invention: A Documentary History of the Junior and Community College Movement* (New York: Greenwood Press, 1986).
81. Davis, "Proposal for the Reorganization of the Secondary Schools and the Establishment of a Four-Year Junior College within the Palo Alto Unified School District," 1–2. The data that the school board offered to support this claim and others like it can be found in Lucille Lyon McParland, "Vocations and the Vocational Training Program" (M.A. thesis, Stanford University, 1944).
82. Palo Alto Unified School District School Board Minutes, 25 Churchill Blvd., Palo Alto, CA (November 30, 1944). Charles Prosser proposed what came to be known as the "Prosser Resolution" on June 1, 1945, at a conference held to discuss the findings of a U.S. Office of Education study entitled "Vocational Education in the Years Ahead." See Kliebard, *The Struggle for the American Curriculum, 1893–1958*, 212. On the inaccuracy of Prosser's assessment, see Robert L. Hampel, *The Last Little Citadel: American High Schools since 1940* (Boston: Houghton Mifflin Company, 1986), 43–45.
83. Palo Alto Unified School District School Board Minutes (November 30, 1944).
84. "Vocational College May Be Set Up to Use War Shop Equipment."
85. "Letter from Charles W. Lockwood to Walter F. Dexter, California Superintendent of Public Instruction, dated March 13, 1944."
86. Winslow, *Palo Alto: A Centennial History*, 138.
87. Davis, "Proposal for the Reorganization of the Secondary Schools and the Establishment of a Four-Year Junior College within the Palo Alto Unified School District," 4–6.
88. Ibid., 1.
89. Albert M. Davis replaced Lockwood as Superintendent. "Letter from Charles W. Lockwood to Walter F. Dexter, California Superintendent of Public Instruction, dated March 13, 1944."
90. California State Archives, Department of Education and State Board of Education Records, Records of the Department of Education, Walter Dexter (1937–45), Subject Files, 1937–45. F3752: 574, "Dept. of Education–S.P.I.–Walter Dexter," Subject Files–School Districts B-S. "Letter from Walter F. Dexter, California Superintendent of Public Instruction, to Charles W. Lockwood, dated March 17, 1944."
91. California State Archives, F3752:1997, Department of Education-Vocational Education, Commission for Vocational Education, 1944–48, "Minutes of a Meeting of the Commission for Vocational Education, March 21, 1944."

92. "Discussion of Junior College Project Is Lively," *Daily Palo Alto Times*, February 2, 1945; "Jr. College Expansion Held Unjustified," *Daily Palo Alto Times*, March 8, 1945; "Forum: Writer Doesn't Favor Junior College Here," *Daily Palo Alto Times*, February 6, 1945; "Forum: Alternative Advised to Junior College," *Daily Palo Alto Times*, March 9, 1945.
93. "Junior College Straw Poll Is Heavily Against Project," *Daily Palo Alto Times*, March 21, 1945.
94. Palo Alto Unified School District School Board Minutes, 25 Churchill Blvd., Palo Alto, CA (March 22, 1945).
95. Palo Alto Unified School District School Board Minutes (March 22, 1945).
96. Palo Alto Unified School District School Board Minutes (March 22, 1945); "School Board Defers Junior College Project," *Daily Palo Alto Times*, March 23, 1945. A decade later, the Palo Alto Unified School District, in a joint proposal with nearby Mountain View and Fremont Union high school districts, succeeded in obtaining approval for the creation of a junior college to serve their communities. The result was Foothill College, now a part of the Foothill-De Anza Community College District. See Winslow, *Palo Alto: A Centennial History*, 138–40.
97. Studebaker, "The American Schools and Colleges in the War," 35.
98. Jean Hutton, "War Reflected in Classrooms and Activities," *Daily Palo Alto Times*, March 2, 1942.
99. "High School Girls Make Dressings for Red Cross," *Daily Palo Alto Times*, January 15, 1943.
100. "Red Cross Collections Go Over the Top," *The Campanile*, November 19, 1943, p. 1.
101. "Girls' League War Projects Successful," *The Campanile*, October 29, 1943, p. 1.
102. Sally Maycock, "Join the Junior Red Cross," *The Campanile*, November 10, 1942, p. 4.
103. "Trooper Reeves: 'It's Rugged'; Field Enlists in Nurse Corps," *The Campanile*, October 15, 1943, p. 4.
104. Richard M. Ugland, "'Education for Victory': The High School Victory Corps and Curricular Adaptation During World War II," *History of Education Quarterly* 19, no. 4 (1979): 435.
105. Quoted in Phillip W. Perdew, "The Secondary School Program in World War II," *History of Education Journal* 3, no. 2 (1952): 44.
106. Ugland, "Education for Victory," 438.
107. Hanson, "Home-Front Casualties of War Mobilization," 197.
108. Ugland, "Education for Victory," 438.
109. Kandel, *The Impact of the War Upon American Education*, 92.
110. Fred Loomis, "All Out for Victory," *The Campanile*, January 15, 1943, p. 3.
111. Perdew, "The Secondary School Program in World War II," 44; Cohen, "Schooling Uncle Sam's Children," 50; Spaull, "World War II and the Secondary School Curriculum,"164.
112. Cohen, "Schooling Uncle Sam's Children," 50.
113. Perdew, "The Secondary School Program in World War II," 44–45.
114. Interview with Henry Martin.
115. "Martin Teaches Morse Code," *The Campanile*, April 2, 1943, p. 1.

116. "Aviation Club Formed; International Writes Letters," *The Campanile*, December 10, 1943, p. 4.
117. Richard Lingeman, *Don't You Know There's a War On? The American Home Front, 1941–1945* (New York: G. P. Putnam, 1970), 265–66.
118. B. Stever, "Man Behind the Man Behind the Gun," *The Campanile*, April 2, 1943, p. 2.
119. Edmondson, Peter. Interview with author. Palo Alto, CA, September 23, 2000.
120. "Many Students Aid Labor Trouble by Working in Local Business," *The Campanile*, April 2, 1943, p. 1.
121. In May 1943, the school board agreed to postpone approving the 1943/44 school program until more specific information was available on agricultural labor demands for the coming months. The board eventually permitted students to register late for the academic year if they were involved in the work. See "Board Asked Not to Set School Program 'Til Harvest Situation Crystalizes," *Daily Palo Alto Times*, May 31, 1943, p. 8; Palo Alto Unified School District School Board Minutes, 25 Churchill Blvd., Palo Alto, CA (August 12, 1943).
122. Interview with Sally (Allen) Edmondson.
123. Interview with Peter Edmondson.
124. Interview with Paula Berka.
125. "Local Farmers Hit by Labor Shortage; Depend on Students," *The Campanile*, September 24, 1942, p. 1.
126. Jean Hutton, "Palo Alto High School Students Are Busy Harvesting Valley Crops," *Daily Palo Alto Times*, October 7, 1942.
127. Charles W. Lockwood, "Palo Alto's Students Work in the Harvests," *California Journal of Secondary Education* 18, no. 4 (1943): 236. These high school students earned a total of $15,961 for their labor. The 233 junior high school students who worked earned $10,579. "High School Harvesters Earn $26,540," *Daily Palo Alto Times*, January 26, 1943.
128. B. Allen, "No Gym for War-Working Students?" *The Campanile*, April 9, 1943, p. 2.
129. Cover Art, *The American School Board Journal* 106, no. 5 (1943), p. 15.
130. William O'Neill, *A Democracy at War: America's Fight at Home and Abroad in World War II* (New York: Free Press, 1993), 79–80; Robert W. Kirk, *Earning Their Stripes: The Mobilization of American Children in the Second World War* (New York: Peter Lang, 1994), 79.
131. Kirk, *Earning Their Stripes*, 81–83.
132. For a program announcement, see Stanford University, Hoover Institution on War, Revolution and Peace, Hoover Library Archives, Microfilm NX4165, Pamphlet #12, U.S. Treasury Department and the U.S. Office of Education, "Sharing America: A Defense Savings Program for Schools," U.S. Government Printing Office, 1941.
133. Jean Hutton, "War Stamp Contest Launched," *Daily Palo Alto Times*, October 27, 1942.
134. "Sequoia High Accepts Paly's Challenge; War Stamp Purchasing Duel Underway," *The Campanile*, October 29, 1942, p. 1.
135. Interview with Joan Paulin.
136. Interview with Peter Edmondson.
137. Interview with Paula Berka.

138. "Pursuit Plane: First Day of School Drive Nets $14,750," *Daily Palo Alto Times*, April 8, 1943.
139. "Picture of Paly's B-25 Bomber Here," *The Campanile*, October 15, 1943, p. 1; "School Can Buy Medium Bomber," *Daily Palo Alto Times*, May 13, 1943.
140. Cover Art, *The American School Board Journal* 109, no. 3 (1944).
141. "Berkeley High Students Go to Work," *Berkeley Jacket*, May 15, 1942, p. 3.
142. See William M. Tuttle, *Daddy's Gone to War: The Second World War in the Lives of America's Children* (New York: Oxford University Press, 1993), esp. 112–33.
143. Bruce, "Schools–but Not as Usual," 11.

Chapter 4

1. Sauer, Marian. An oral history conducted by Jon Plutte for the Rosie the Riveter/World War II Home Front National Historical Park on December 14, 2000, at the Richmond Public Library, Richmond, CA. National Park Service, Golden Gate National Recreation Area.
2. J. A. McVittie, "An Avalanche Hits Richmond," (Richmond: City of Richmond, California, 1944), 77. Although City Manager J. A. McVittie compiled this report, Part V, Section I, which addressed the city's schools, was written by Superintendent Walter Helms. Also, see U.S. Department of Commerce, Bureau of the Census, Sixteenth Census of the United States: 1940, Population, Volume II, Part I, 601 and U.S. Department of Commerce, Bureau of the Census, Special Census of Richmond, California: September 14, 1943, ser. P-SC, no. 6; Hubert O. Brown, "The Impact of War Worker Migration on the Public School System of Richmond, California, from 1940 to 1945" (Ph.D. diss., Stanford University, 1973), 2. Throughout this chapter I draw on the work of Hubert Brown and Donald Woodington, whose doctoral dissertations were invaluable resources. In particular, Brown's heavy reliance on Richmond's local newspaper, the *Richmond Independent*, permitted me to utilize his dissertation as an index to articles addressing the city's schools. Brown, "The Impact of War Worker Migration on the Public School System of Richmond, California, from 1940 to 1945"; Donald DeVine Woodington, "Federal Public War Housing in Relation to Certain Needs and the Financial Ability of the Richmond School District" (Ph.D. diss., University of California–Berkeley, 1954).
3. Robert Wenkert, *An Historical Digest of Negro-White Relations in Richmond, California* (Berkeley: Survey Research Center, University of California–Berkeley, 1967), 18.
4. McVittie, "An Avalanche Hits Richmond," 2.
5. On the effects of wartime mobilization on California and its cities, specifically, see Lotchin, Roger, *The Bad City in the Good War: San Francisco, Los Angeles, Oakland, and San Diego* (Bloomington: Indiana University Press, 2003); Roger W. Lotchin, *Fortress California: 1910–1961* (New York: Oxford University Press, 1992).
6. It is my contention that wartime developments resulted in a significantly different conception of the educational profession in Richmond than had existed prior to the war, particularly as it related to students' race, ethnicity,

and culture. I labeled this conception "civic-professionalism" because of the democratic principles with which this professional ideal was bound up. It is important to note, however, that during and after the war historically defined gender roles in public school teaching and administration were solidified, leading to, among other things, men "taking control" of school and district administration. See Marjorie Murphy, *Blackboard Unions: The AFT and the NEA, 1900–1980* (Ithaca, NY: Cornell University Press, 1990); Kathleen Weiler, *Country Schoolwomen: Teaching in Rural California, 1850–1950* (Stanford, CA: Stanford University Press, 1998); Jackie Blount, *Destined to Rule the Schools: Women and the Superintendency, 1873–1995* (New York: State University of New York Press, 1998).
7. David M. Kennedy, *Freedom from Fear: The American People in Depression and War, 1929–1945* (New York: Oxford University Press, 1999), 760–63.
8. Daniel Perlstein, "American Dilemmas: Education, Social Science, and the Limits of Liberalism," *Research in Politics and Society* 6 (1999): 357–79.
9. Gunnar Myrdal, *An American Dilemma: The Negro Problem and Modern Democracy* (New York: Harper, 1944); Ruth Benedict, "Transmitting Our Democratic Heritage in the Schools," *The American Journal of Sociology* 48, no. 6 (1943): 722–27.
10. David B. Tyack, "Constructing Difference: Historical Reflections on Schooling and Social Diversity," *Teachers College Record* 95, no. 1 (1993), 17–18.
11. Nicholas V. Montalto, *A History of the Intercultural Education Movement, 1924–1941* (New York: Garland Publishing, 1982).
12. Warner Olivier, "Cops Don't Have to Be Brutal," *The Saturday Evening Post*, December 28, 1946, p. 20.
13. See, for instance, Thomas J. Sugrue, "Crabgrass-Roots Politics: Race, Rights, and the Reaction Against Liberalism in the Urban North, 1940–1964," *The Journal of American History* 82, no. 2 (1995): 551–78.
14. Perlstein, "American Dilemmas," 370–75.
15. Shirley Ann Wilson Moore, *To Place Our Deeds: The African American Community in Richmond, California, 1910–1963* (Berkeley: University of California Press, 2000), 7.
16. Lee D. Fridell, *The Story of Richmond: El Cerrito-San Pablo-Pinole-Hercules* (Richmond: Board of Trustees, Richmond Union High School District, 1954), 34–35.
17. Joseph C. Whitnah, *The City That Grew from a Rancho: A History of Richmond, California* (Richmond: Chamber of Commerce of Richmond, CA, 1944), 34; George Emanuels, *California's Contra Costa County: An Illustrated History* (Walnut Creek, CA: Diablo Books, 1990), 130–39.
18. Whitnah, *The City That Grew from a Rancho*, 37.
19. Wenkert, *An Historical Digest*, 2.
20. Moore, *To Place Our Deeds*, 9; *Richmond: The Early Years* (Richmond: Independent Printing, 1960), document in the Richmond Collection of the Richmond Public Library.
21. Wenkert, *An Historical Digest*, 3; Fridell, *The Story of Richmond*, 84–85; "History of the Richmond Library," August 14, 1940, manuscript in the Richmond Collection of the Richmond Public Library.
22. Fridell, *The Story of Richmond*, 59–61; "The Story of Richmond Schools" by Dr. Walter T. Helms, City Superintendent Emeritus, Richmond Public

Schools, manuscript in the Richmond Collection of the Richmond Public Library.
23. Ibid., 61.
24. Whitnah, *The City That Grew from a Rancho*, 102–3.
25. Ibid., 105–7.
26. Ibid., 113.
27. Brown, "The Impact of War Worker Migration on the Public School System of Richmond, California, from 1940 to 1945," 22.
28. Whitnah, *The City That Grew from a Rancho*, 111; Sixteenth Census of the United States: 1940, Population, Volume II, Part I, 610.
29. Fridell, *The Story of Richmond*, 61.
30. McVittie, "An Avalanche Hits Richmond," 73.
31. Brown, "The Impact of War Worker Migration on the Public School System of Richmond, California, from 1940 to 1945," 50; McVittie, "An Avalanche Hits Richmond," 80; "The Story of Richmond Schools."
32. Brown, "The Impact of War Worker Migration on the Public School System of Richmond, California, from 1940 to 1945," 50–51.
33. In 1941, when poor visibility led a high school board member's child to be sent home from Richmond High, Helms agreed to install lights, but only on the second floor of the high school. See ibid., 62.
34. "Richmond Took a Beating," *Fortune*, February 1945, p. 262.
35. "U.S. Pours Millions in the East Bay," *Richmond Independent*, July 27, 1940.
36. "Richmond Has Zero in Defense Funds," *Richmond Independent*, August 3, 1940.
37. Wenkert, *An Historical Digest*, 18.
38. Arthur Verge, "Daily Life in Wartime California," in *The Way We Really Were: The Golden State in the Second Great War*, ed. Roger W. Lotchin (Urbana: University of Illinois Press, 2000), 13–29.
39. In November 1942, Kaiser stunned the world by launching the *Robert E. Peary* from the Richmond yards in four days, fifteen hours, and twenty-six minutes. Although not a sustainable rate (the launching was a publicity stunt), the record indicates the revolutionary transformation shipbuilding underwent during World War II. See Kennedy, *Freedom from Fear*, 650–52; Marilyn S. Johnson, *The Second Gold Rush: Oakland and the East Bay in World War II* (Berkeley: University of California Press, 1993), 66. On Kaiser's role in building "Liberty" and "Victory" ships, particularly in the Richmond shipyards, see Mark S. Foster, *Henry J. Kaiser: Builder in the Modern American West* (Austin: University of Texas Press, 1989); Stephen B. Adams, *Mr. Kaiser Goes to Washington: The Rise of a Government Entrepreneur* (Chapel Hill: University of North Carolina Press, 1997).
40. For a description of the "assembly-line methods" adopted by Kaiser, see Frederic C. Lane, *Ships for Victory: A History of Shipbuilding under the U.S. Maritime Commission in World War II, Historical Reports on War Administration, United States Maritime Commission, No. 1* (Baltimore: Johns Hopkins Press, 1951), 202–35.
41. Johnson, *The Second Gold Rush*, 32–34; Moore, *To Place Our Deeds*, 43.
42. "Richmond C of C Opens Drive to Mobilize for Expansion of Business," *Richmond Independent*, September 16, 1941, p. 1.

43. "City Asked to Keep Step with Kaiser Company," *Richmond Independent*, December 5, 1941, pp. 1–2.
44. Gerald D. Nash, *The American West Transformed: The Impact of the Second World War* (Lincoln: University of Nebraska Press, 1985), 69.
45. U.S. Department of Commerce, Bureau of the Census, Population, ser. CA-3, Characteristics of the Population, Labor Force, Families, and Housing, no. 3, "San Francisco Bay Congested Production Area, April 1944," 14.
46. Population, ser. CA-3, Characteristics of the Population, Labor Force, Families, and Housing, no. 3, "San Francisco Bay Congested Production Area, April 1944," 14.
47. Two changes in 1940 census data reporting make it difficult to precisely identify the racial and ethnic characteristics of Richmond's residents at this time: the Bureau of the Census ceased to report data disaggregating the white population into native of native-born, native of foreign-born, and foreign born, and it returned to the practice (discontinued in the 1930 census) of counting people of Mexican descent as white. In comparing data from the 1930 and 1940 census, however, it is clear that a large majority of Richmond's residents were of European ancestry. See U.S. Department of Commerce, Bureau of the Census, Fifteenth Census of the United States: 1930, Population, Volume III, Part I, 261 and Sixteenth Census of the United States: 1940, Population, Volume II, Part I, 610.
48. Sixteenth Census of the United States: 1940, Population, Volume II, Part I, 610. Also, see Wenkert, *An Historical Digest*, 18.
49. "Richmond Took a Beating," 264.
50. McVittie, "An Avalanche Hits Richmond," 5.
51. Nash, *The American West Transformed*, 70.
52. Lawrence P. Crouchett, Lonnie G. Bunch, and Martha Kendall Winnacker, *Visions toward Tomorrow: The History of the East Bay Afro-American Community, 1852–1977* (Oakland: Northern California Center for Afro-American History and Life, 1989), 49.
53. "Richmond Took a Beating," 264.
54. University of California, Berkeley. Bancroft Library. Henry J. Kaiser Papers, Carton 159, Folder 25, "Education Report," 2.
55. A steady increase in student enrollment began early as January 1941, when over the course of one week secondary school enrollments increased from 3,149 students to 3,204 students. See Richmond Union High School District School Board Minutes, 1108 Bissell Ave., Richmond, CA, (January 14, 1941).
56. McVittie, "An Avalanche Hits Richmond," 20; Brown, "The Impact of War Worker Migration on the Public School System of Richmond, California, from 1940 to 1945," 2.
57. I. L. Kandel, *The Impact of the War Upon American Education* (Chapel Hill: University of North Carolina Press, 1948), 41–76.
58. McVittie, "An Avalanche Hits Richmond," 73.
59. "More Than a Headache," *Richmond Independent*, September 4, 1941, p. 20.
60. "School Enrollment Shows Big Increase," *Richmond Independent*, September 10, 1941, p. 1.
61. "Helms to Ask Federal Funds for Schools," *Richmond Independent*, July 9 1941, p. 2.

62. Brown, "The Impact of War Worker Migration on the Public School System of Richmond, California, from 1940 to 1945," 129–30.
63. Ibid., 207–8.
64. "Housing Authority to Be Set Up by City to Meet Labor Influx," *Richmond Independent*, January 14, 1941, pp. 1, 6; Woodington, "Federal Public War Housing in Relation to Certain Needs and the Financial Ability of the Richmond School District," 37–38; Moore, *To Place Our Deeds*, 84–85.
65. Prior to the war, most of Richmond's black residents lived in North Richmond. City boundaries ran approximately through the area, leaving the unincorporated half of North Richmond without garbage collection, utilities, paved streets, and sewage disposal. Segregation practices on the part of the RHA are well documented. Moore, *To Place Our Deeds*, 84–89; Gretchen Lemke-Santangelo, *Abiding Courage: African-American Migrant Women and the East Bay Community* (Raleigh: University of North Carolina Press, 1996), 78–88; Johnson, *The Second Gold Rush*, 105–8; Crouchett, Bunch, and Winnacker, *Visions Toward Tomorrow*, 49.
66. By the end of the war, the Lanham Act funded the construction of over 700,000 housing units in more than 1,000 communities for approximately 4 million workers and their families. U.S. Housing Agency, Federal Public Housing Authority, *Public Housing*. Washington: U.S. Government Printing Office, March 1946, p. 7.
67. Woodington, "Federal Public War Housing in Relation to Certain Needs and the Financial Ability of the Richmond School District," 38.
68. "Testimony of Harry A. Barbour, Executive Director of the Housing Authority of the City of Richmond, Calif." Subcommittee of the House Committee on Naval Affairs Investigating Congested Areas, *Hearings before the United States House Committee on Naval Affairs*, 78th Congress, 1st Session, April 12–17, 1943, p. 852.
69. Richmond Union High School District School Board Minutes (August 12, 1941).
70. McVittie, "An Avalanche Hits Richmond," 2.
71. Ibid., 9.
72. "Testimony of J. A. McVittie, City Manager of the City of Richmond," Subcommittee of the House Committee on Naval Affairs Investigating Congested Areas, *Hearings before the United States House Committee on Naval Affairs*, 78th Congress, 1st Session, April 12–17, 1943, p. 836.
73. Woodington, "Federal Public War Housing in Relation to Certain Needs and the Financial Ability of the Richmond School District," 38–82. For a federal listing of Richmond's wartime housing developments, including construction and management agencies, type of housing, development costs, and occupancy rates, see National Archives and Record Administration, Pacific Region (San Francisco), Record Group 12 "Records of the Office of Education," Subgroup "Office Files of Region XII, 1941–45, Box 2, Folder "U.S. Office Memorandum," "National Housing Agency, Directory of Active Public Housing," 18.
74. Ibid., 88–93.
75. "Richmond Builds Ships," *Western City*, February 1943, p. 16.
76. Ibid., 16–17.
77. "Testimony of Harry A. Barbour," 852–53.

78. "Testimony of Thomas M. Carlson, City Attorney for Richmond," Subcommittee of the House Committee on Naval Affairs Investigating Congested Areas, *Hearings before the United States House Committee on Naval Affairs*, 78th Congress, 1st Session, April 12–17, 1943, p. 835.
79. "Testimony of J. A. McVittie," 836.
80. "Vacation to End for 8,000 Local Children," *Richmond Independent*, January 3 1942, p. 1.
81. "More Room Needed, School Board Told," *Richmond Independent*, January 8 1942, pp. 1–2.
82. Henry J. Kaiser Papers, Carton 159, Folder 25, "Education Report," 1; Woodington, "Federal Public War Housing in Relation to Certain Needs and the Financial Ability of the Richmond School District," 96.
83. Henry J. Kaiser Papers, Carton 159, Folder 25, "Education Report," 1.
84. "Enrollment in Schools Here Exceeds 18,000," *Richmond War Homes Weekly*, October 2, 1943, p. 1.
85. McVittie, "An Avalanche Hits Richmond," 73–77; "Testimony of Walter T. Helms, City Superintendent of Schools, Richmond, Calif.," Subcommittee of the House Committee on Naval Affairs Investigating Congested Areas, *Hearings before the United States House Committee on Naval Affairs*, 78th Congress, 1st Session, April 12–17, 1943, p. 885.
86. Woodington, "Federal Public War Housing in Relation to Certain Needs and the Financial Ability of the Richmond School District," 120.
87. Interview with Marian Sauer.
88. Brimhall, Alice. An oral history conducted by Jon Plutte for the Rosie the Riveter/World War II Home Front National Historical Park on May 14, 2001, at the Richmond Museum of History, Richmond, CA. National Park Service, Golden Gate National Recreation Area.
89. Haag, Evelyn. Interview by author. Walnut Creek, CA. July 12, 2000.
90. In direct response to Richmond's crisis, California's state-level "Citizens Committee on Youth in Wartime" passed a resolution "condemning the double session practice" as deleterious to the education of Richmond's students. The committee also noted, however, that because the primary cause of the double session policy was a limited availability of "critical materials" with which to construct new classrooms, it did not believe "anything more than a slight deviation from the policy could be obtained, regardless of the amount of effort expended." California State Archives, D4173, California State War Council, Citizens Committee on Youth in Wartime, Box 2, Folder 1, "Minutes of the Meeting of Citizens Committee on Youth in Wartime, November 1, 1943," 13.
91. Helms sought federal assistance throughout 1942, but was only minimally successful. In November of that year, for instance, Helms received a grant from the Federal Works Agency for $10,000 to construct three classrooms at Longfellow Junior High School and two at El Cerrito Junior-Senior High School. However, the grant was contingent upon the district providing an additional $30,000 for the project. See Richmond Union High School District School Board Minutes (November 10, 1942).
92. "Testimony of Walter T. Helms," 885.
93. Henry J. Kaiser Papers, Carton 159, Folder 25, "Education Report," 2.

94. Brown, "The Impact of War Worker Migration on the Public School System of Richmond, California, from 1940 to 1945," 210.
95. "Testimony of Walter T. Helms," 885.
96. "Helms Delivers Ultimatum to Government Men," *Richmond Independent*, March 10, 1943, p. 1.
97. McVittie, "An Avalanche Hits Richmond," 75–76. Still, recommendations made in August 1944 by the War Production Board to the U.S. Office of Education for school construction in Richmond were pending in May of the following year. See National Archives and Record Administration, Pacific Region (San Francisco), Record Group 12 "Records of the Office of Education," Subgroup "Office Files of Region XII, 1941–45, Box 1, Folder "Consumer Activities," "Letter from J. Walter Blair, Regional Coordinator for Community Facilities Program, War Production Board, to Miss Florence Beardsley, Consultant on School Service, U.S. Office of Education, dated May 18, 1945."
98. Quoted in "Testimony of Walter T. Helms," 888.
99. McVittie, "An Avalanche Hits Richmond," 77.
100. Kenneth Paul O'Brien and Lynn Hudson Parsons, eds., *The Home-Front War: World War II and American Society* (London: Greenwood Press, 1995), 3.
101. William O'Neill, *A Democracy at War: America's Fight at Home and Abroad in World War II* (New York: Free Press, 1993), 241–46; O'Brien and Parsons, eds., *The Home-Front War: World War II and American Society*, 107; Susan M. Hartmann, *The Home Front and Beyond: American Women in the 1940s* (Boston: Twayne Publishers, 1982), 102–3.
102. Thomas James, *Exile Within: The Schooling of Japanese Americans, 1942–1945* (Cambridge, MA: Harvard University Press, 1987), 47.
103. Throughout the war years, *The American School Board Journal* published a variety of articles addressing the teacher shortage and suggesting a variety of strategies to resolve it. These included a campaign to recruit teachers with slogans such as "You Are Needed To Teach" and intensive training courses to quickly prepare new recruits. See, for instance, "For Next Fall–Wanted 250,000 School Teachers," *The American School Board Journal* 104, no. 5 (1942): 18, 68; Harold J. Bowers, "Teacher Recruitment in Wartime," *The American School Board Journal* 104, no. 3 (1942): 45–46; Everett H. Fixley, "Meeting the Teacher Shortage," *The American School Board Journal* 106, no. 5 (1943): 16; Benjamin W. Frazier, "How Teacher Shortages Are Being Met," *The American School Board Journal* 108, no. 2 (1944): 39–41.
104. James, *Exile Within*, 47.
105. "Private Problems," *Time*, July 12, 1943, p. 74.
106. Hartmann, *The Home Front and Beyond*, 103–4; Kandel, *The Impact of the War Upon American Education*, 165.
107. Weiler, *Country Schoolwomen*, 227–29.
108. "Class I" indicated a new teacher still in the process of obtaining a bachelor's degree. A "Class II" teacher, having obtained a bachelor's degree, received a starting salary of $1,740. Richmond Union High School District School Board Minutes (May 21, 1942).
109. An unskilled laborer earned 95 cents per hour and typically worked a 50-hour week for 50 weeks of the year. Moore, *To Place Our Deeds*, 43.

110. See Richmond Union High School District School Board Minutes (May 20, 1941); Moore, *To Place Our Deeds*, 43–44.
111. Richmond Union High School District School Board Minutes (May 20, 1941).
112. Richmond Union High School District School Board Minutes (May 21, 1942).
113. Richmond Union High School District School Board Minutes (May 30, 1943). By taking advantage of the tight labor market during World War II, Richmond's teachers received substantial pay increases. Nevertheless, by 1946 the average industrial worker's pay in the United States was estimated to have increased 80 percent in real dollars, while nationally the average teacher's income declined by 20 percent. See David M. Donahue, "Rhode Island's Last Holdout: Tenure and Married Women Teachers at the Brink of the Women's Movement," *History of Education Quarterly* 42, no. 1 (2002): 64.
114. "Teacher Lack Feared Here," *Richmond Independent*, May 14, 1943, pp. 1–2.
115. Brown, "The Impact of War Worker Migration on the Public School System of Richmond, California, from 1940 to 1945," 280.
116. Ibid., 281.
117. J. Paul Leonard, "Survey of the Richmond Public Schools," (Richmond: Boards of Education of the Richmond School District and the Richmond Union High School District, 1947), 731–732. In Richmond, there was no "marriage bar," legal or otherwise, that required women to resign their positions upon marriage. Historians debate the prewar prevalence of such a marriage bar nationally. Geraldine Clifford's research suggests the marriage bar was "far from a universal phenomenon, even in city school systems, and that its presence varied widely both within and across states, and was often circumvented by teachers and school officials for their own purposes." Jackie Blount and Kathleen Weiler, on the other hand, suggest the dropping of the marriage bar explains the dramatic decline in the number of single women comprising the teaching profession between 1940, when single women accounted for 69 percent of female teachers, and 1960, when only 30 percent of women teachers were single. Conversation with Geraldine Clifford. August 24, 2000. Berkeley, CA; Blount, *Destined to Rule the Schools*, 102; Weiler, *Country Schoolwomen*, 227. For an informative case study addressing the issue of tenure in relation to the marriage bar, see Donahue, "Rhode Island's Last Holdout," 50–74.
118. Interview with Evelyn Haag.
119. Leonard, "Survey of the Richmond Public Schools," 731–32.
120. Woodington, "Federal Public War Housing in Relation to Certain Needs and the Financial Ability of the Richmond School District," 119.
121. Ibid., 121–22.
122. Kandel, *The Impact of the War Upon American Education*, 65.
123. Moore, *To Place Our Deeds*, 74.
124. Kandel, *The Impact of the War Upon American Education*, 64–65.
125. Lange's son and brother both worked in the city's shipyards during the war years. Charles Wollenberg, *Photographing the Second Gold Rush: Dorothea Lange and the East Bay at War, 1941–1945* (Berkeley: Heyday Books, 1995), 16–20.

126. Prior to 1930, California law permitted the segregation of Chinese, Japanese, "Mongolians," and "Indian" students. A ruling by State Attorney General U. S. Webb in that year modified the education code to permit the legal segregation of Mexican-American students. "It is well known," wrote Webb, "that the greater portion of the population of Mexico are Indians, and when such Indians migrate to the United States they are subject to the laws applicable generally to other Indians." In 1935, the code was further modified to exempt Native-Americans, but in such a way as to permit the continued segregation of Mexican-Americans. Quoted in Meyer Weinberg, *A Chance to Learn: The History of Race and Education in the United States* (Cambridge: Cambridge University Press, 1977), 166. Also, see Charles Wollenberg, *All Deliberate Speed: Segregation and Exclusion in California Schools, 1855–1975* (Berkeley: University of California Press, 1976), 118; Gilbert G. Gonzalez, *Chicano Education in the Era of Segregation* (Philadelphia: Balch Institute Press, 1990), 136–47; Rubén Donato, *The Other Struggle for Equal Schools: Mexican Americans During the Civil Rights Era* (Albany: State University of New York Press, 1997), 14–17; Thomas P. Carter, *Mexican Americans in School: A History of Educational Neglect* (New York: College Entrance Examination Board, 1970), 67–70.

127. Although it was a significant ruling in the legal history of school segregation, few historians have explored the ramifications of the *Mendez* decision. Neither James T. Patterson nor Peter Irons, for instance, thoroughly examine the case in their recent studies of *Brown v. Board of Education*. See James T. Patterson, *Brown V. Board of Education: A Civil Rights Milestone and Its Troubled Legacy* (Oxford: Oxford University Press, 2001); Peter Irons, *Jim Crow's Children: The Broken Promise of the Brown Decision* (New York: Viking, 2002).

128. One scholar has called this decision "prophetic" in relation to the *Brown* ruling, especially in regard to McCormick's claim that "[t]he 'equal protection of the laws' pertaining to the public school system in California is not provided by furnishing in separate schools the same technical facilities, textbooks, and courses of instruction to children of Mexican ancestry that are available to the other public school children regardless of their ancestry. A paramount requisite in the American system of public education is social equality. It must be open to all children by unified school association regardless of lineage." See Irving G. Hendrick, *The Education of Non-Whites in California, 1849–1970* (San Francisco: R&E Research Associates, 1977), 102–3.

129. A legal technicality prevented the *Mendez* decision from being cited as direct precedent in the *Brown* opinion because California law never technically sanctioned the segregation of Mexican-Americans. The case was cited, however, in a number of state-level school segregation cases. Moreover, interpretations of this ruling vary in relation to the "separate but equal" doctrine established by *Plessey v. Ferguson*. See Wollenberg, *All Deliberate Speed*, 108–31; Weinberg, *A Chance to Learn*, 166–70; Gonzalez, *Chicano Education in the Era of Segregation*, 147–56; Hendrick, *The Education of Non-Whites in California, 1849–1970*, 102–3.

130. Wollenberg, *All Deliberate Speed*, 108–9, 132.

131. Ibid., 120.

132. The literature on these movements is extensive. Given space constraints, I only briefly summarize them here.

133. Richard Weiss, "Ethnicity and Reform: Minorities and the Ambience of the Depression Years," *The Journal of American History* 66, no. 3 (1979): 566.
134. Ibid., 566, 575.
135. Kennedy, *Freedom from Fear*, 760–63.
136. Quoted in Ibid., 760.
137. Ibid., 760–61.
138. Ronald Takaki, *Double Victory: A Multicultural History of America in World War II* (Boston: Little, Brown, 2000), 5.
139. Ibid., 41–42.
140. R. Fred Wacker, "Assimilation and Cultural Pluralism in American Social Thought," *Phylon* 40, no. 4 (1979): 332.
141. See R. Fred Wacker, "An American Dilemma: The Racial Theories of Robert E. Park and Gunnar Myrdal," *Phylon* 37, no. 2 (1976): 117–18; Lee D. Baker, *From Savage to Negro: Anthropology and the Construction of Race, 1896–1954* (Berkeley: University of California Press, 1998); Elazar Barkan, *The Retreat of Scientific Racism: Changing Concepts of Race in Britain and the United States between the World Wars* (Cambridge: Cambridge University Press, 1992), 279–340.
142. Interpretations of this development in U.S. history vary. See, for instance, David A. Hollinger, "Ethnic Diversity, Cosmopolitanism and the Emergence of the American Liberal Intelligentsia," *American Quarterly* 27, no. 2 (1975): 133–51; Gary Gerstle, "Liberty, Coercion, and the Making of Americans," *The Journal of American History* 84, no. 2 (1997): 524–58; Weiss, "Ethnicity and Reform: Minorities and the Ambience of the Depression Years," 566–85; Peggy Pascoe, "Miscegenation Law, Court Cases, and Ideologies of 'Race' in Twentieth-Century America," *The Journal of American History* 83, no. 1 (1996): 44–69.
143. Walter A. Jackson, "The 'American Creed' from a Swedish Perspective: The Wartime Context of Gunnar Myrdal's an American Dilemma," in *The Estate of Social Knowledge*, ed. JoAnne Brown and David K. van Keuren (Baltimore: Johns Hopkins University Press, 1991), 209. Also, see Jackson's definitive work on Myrdal, Walter A. Jackson, *Gunnar Myrdal and America's Conscience: Social Engineering and Racial Liberalism, 1938–1987* (Chapel Hill: University of North Carolina Press, 1990).
144. Perlstein, "American Dilemmas: Education, Social Science, and the Limits of Liberalism," 369.
145. David Tyack, Robert Lowe, and Elisabeth Hansot, *Public Schools in Hard Times: The Great Depression and Recent Years* (Cambridge, MA: Harvard University Press, 1984), 171.
146. Tyack, "Constructing Difference: Historical Reflections on Schooling and Social Diversity," 17–18.
147. Perlstein, "American Dilemmas: Education, Social Science, and the Limits of Liberalism," 366–368. On the influence of intercultural education during World War II in the cities of New York and Seattle, respectively, see Robert Shaffer, "Multicultural Education in New York City During World War II," *New York History* 77, no. 3 (1996): 301–32; Yoon K. Pak, *Wherever I Go, I Will Always Be a Loyal American: Schooling Seattle's Japanese Americans During World War II* (New York: RoutledgeFalmer, 2002).

148. Helen Heffernan and Corinne Seeds, "Intercultural Education in the Elementary School," in *Education for Cultural Unity: Seventeenth Yearbook of the California Elementary School Principals' Association* (California Elementary School Principals' Association, 1945), 76–85.
149. Ibid., 78.
150. Ibid., 84.
151. Brown, "The Impact of War Worker Migration on the Public School System of Richmond, California, from 1940 to 1945," 303.
152. Ibid., 300.
153. Ibid., 299.
154. Black students, for instance, are depicted as members of the Roosevelt Junior High School Traffic Squad and Choral Group and the Richmond High School track and football teams. School yearbooks and newspapers are located in the Richmond collection of the Richmond Public Library and the Richmond Museum of History.
155. "Parents Protest Lack of Action by School Dept.," *Richmond Independent*, October 3, 1945, pp. 1–2.
156. "Disputes Arise in School Meet over Knifings," *Contra Costa Gazette*, October 4, 1945.
157. "Parents Protest Lack of Action by School Dept.," 1.
158. Ibid., 1–2.
159. "Faculties Get Order to Assert Their Authority," *Richmond Independent*, October 4 1945, p. 1.
160. Ibid., 1.
161. On historiographical issues surrounding the use of oral history in investigations into World War II specifically, see Roger Horowitz, "Oral History and the Story of America and World War II," *The Journal of American History* 82, no. 2 (1995): 617–24.
162. Okie and Arkie were labels applied to primarily white emigrants from Oklahoma and Arkansas. Quoted in Brown, "The Impact of War Worker Migration on the Public School System of Richmond, California, from 1940 to 1945," 293.
163. Interview with Alice Brimhall.
164. Interview with Evelyn Haag.
165. Quoted in Brown, "The Impact of War Worker Migration on the Public School System of Richmond, California, from 1940 to 1945," 229.
166. Quoted in ibid., 228.
167. On the education of Japanese and Japanese-American students in the United States during World War II, see James, *Exile Within*; Pak, *Wherever I Go, I Will Always Be a Loyal American*, among others.
168. Melgoza, Chris. Interview by author. Newark, CA, January 30, 2003.
169. Quoted in Brown, "The Impact of War Worker Migration on the Public School System of Richmond, California, from 1940 to 1945," 40.
170. Johnson, *The Second Gold Rush*, 83–112.
171. U.S. Department of Commerce, Bureau of the Census, Seventeenth Census of the United States: 1950, General Characteristics of the Population, Volume II, Part 5, pp. 5–102.

172. "Richmond—War-Born Boom That Didn't Bust," by Richard Reinhardt, 1953, manuscript in the Richmond Collection of the Richmond Public Library.
173. Cy W. Record, "Willie Stokes at the Golden Gate," *The Crisis* 56, no. 6 (1949): 187.
174. Ibid., 187.
175. "Richmond—War-Born Boom That Didn't Bust," by Richard Reinhardt, 1953, manuscript in the Richmond Collection of the Richmond Public Library.
176. "From 'Workingman's Town' to 'All-America City 1954': The Socio-Political Economy of Richmond, California during World War II," by William Sokol, June 1971, manuscript in the Richmond Collection of the Richmond Public Library.
177. "Community Progress Report for 1950: Richmond, California," (Richmond: Richmond Chamber of Commerce, 1950).
178. "Schools and Recreation: The Master Plan of Richmond, California. A Report on Schools, Parks, and Playgrounds." Prepared by the Richmond City Planning Commission, Richmond, CA. January 1948. Document located in the Richmond Collection of the Richmond Public Library. As of November 1948, there were still 7,318 elementary school pupils attending 204 classes on double session in Richmond. Two surveys of Richmond's school districts were completed within three years of the end of World War II. See F. W. Hart and L. H. Peterson, "A Schoolhousing Survey of the Richmond City Elementary School District and the Richmond Union High School District," (Richmond: Richmond City Elementary School Board of Education and the Richmond Union High School Board of Trustees, 1947); Leonard, "Survey of the Richmond Public Schools."
179. McVittie, "An Avalanche Hits Richmond," 77.
180. "Community Progress Report for 1950: Richmond, California."
181. Wenkert, *An Historical Digest*, 50–52.

Chapter 5

1. Grace Thorne Allen, Maxone Davis, and Warner Olivier, "Eight-Hour Orphans," *The Saturday Evening Post*, October 10, 1942, p. 20.
2. Robert B. Westbrook, "Fighting for the American Family: Private Interests and Political Obligation in World War II," in *The Power of Culture: Critical Essays in American History*, ed. Richard Wightman Fox and T. J. Jackson Lears (Chicago: University of Chicago Press, 1993), 200–202.
3. D'Ann Campbell, *Women at War with America: Private Lives in a Patriotic Era* (Cambridge, MA: Harvard University Press, 1984), 103.
4. See, for instance, Barbara Beatty, *Preschool Education in America: The Culture of Young Children from the Colonial Era to the Present* (New Haven, CT: Yale University Press, 1995); Sonya Michel, *Children's Interests/Mothers' Rights: The Shaping of America's Child Care Policy* (New Haven, CT: Yale University Press, 1999); Elizabeth Rose, *A Mother's Job: The History of Day Care, 1890–1960* (New York: Oxford University Press, 1999).
5. Rose, *A Mother's Job*, 153.

6. Gertrude M. Hengerer, "Study of Youth Services in Contra Costa County," (Contra Costa County: Division of Field Services of the California Youth Authority, 1945), 112–113.
7. Because the Kaiser shipyards produced cargo and transport ships for the U.S. Maritime Commission, the Commission played a role in Richmond similar to that of the U.S. military in other boomtowns.
8. "Nursery School Observes Birth Date Tomorrow," *The Richmond Independent*, May 31, 1944, p. 9.
9. My use of the term "Progressive" in this chapter refers to the child-centered pedagogical theories and practices espoused by John Dewey and labeled "curricular progressivism" by many scholars. On the historiography of "Progressive Education," see Herbert M. Kliebard, *The Struggle for the American Curriculum, 1893–1958*, 2nd ed. (New York: Routledge, 1995), 231–52.
10. "150 Women Do a Big Job," *Richmond War Homes Weekly*, December 31, 1943, p. 1.
11. Emilie Stoltzfus, *Citizen, Mother, Worker: Debating Public Responsibility for Child Care after the Second World War* (Chapel Hill: University of North Carolina Press, 2003), 151.
12. Lois Meek Stolz, "Look to the Bulwarks of Democracy," *Childhood Education* 18, nos. 1/9 (1941/1942): 196.
13. The second conference was called by Woodrow Wilson in 1919 and the third by Franklin Roosevelt in 1930.
14. "White House Conference on Children in a Democracy," (Washington, DC: 1941). For a detailed analysis of the report, see Kriste Lindenmeyer, *"A Right to Childhood": The U.S. Children's Bureau and Child Welfare, 1912–46* (Urbana: University of Illinois Press, 1997), 203–10.
15. "White House Conference on Children in a Democracy," 4
16. Sonya Michel, "American Women and the Discourse of the Democratic Family in World War II," in *Behind the Lines: Gender and the Two World Wars*, ed. Margaret Randolph Higonnet, et al. (New Haven, CT: Yale University Press, 1987), 154–55.
17. Westbrook, "Fighting for the American Family," 202
18. Maureen Honey, *Creating Rosie the Riveter: Class, Gender, and Propaganda During World War II* (Amherst: University of Massachusetts Press, 1984), 130–37.
19. "Proceedings of Conference on Day Care of Children of Working Mothers with Special Reference to Defense Areas Held in Washington, DC July 31 and August 1, 1941" (paper presented at the Conference on Day Care of Children of Working Mothers With Special Reference to Defense Areas, Washington, DC, July 31 and August 1, 1941). For a history of the role of the U.S. Children's Bureau during World War II, see Lindenmeyer, *A Right to Childhood*, especially Chapter 8.
20. Ibid., 12.
21. Ibid.
22. On women's employment during the Great Depression, see Susan Ware, *Holding Their Own: American Women in the 1930s* (Boston: Twayne Publishers, 1982).
23. David M. Kennedy, *Freedom from Fear: The American People in Depression and War, 1929–1945* (New York: Oxford University Press, 1999), 162–63.

24. Steven Mintz and Susan Kellogg, *Domestic Revolutions: A Social History of American Family Life* (New York: Free Press, 1988), 134–35.
25. Kennedy, *Freedom from Fear*, 163.
26. Mintz and Kellogg, *Domestic Revolutions*, 136.
27. Alice Kessler-Harris, *Out to Work: A History of Wage-Earning Women in the United States* (New York: Oxford University Press, 1982), 259–61; Kennedy, *Freedom from Fear*, 164.
28. Kessler-Harris, *Out to Work*, 251.
29. Ibid., 259.
30. Mintz and Kellogg, *Domestic Revolutions*, 139.
31. As Elizabeth Rose notes, unemployed fathers who were available to provide full-time care for their children rarely did so. Rose, *A Mother's Job*, 136.
32. Ibid., 137–38.
33. On child care during the Great Depression, see Margaret O'Brien Steinfels, *Who's Minding the Children? The History and Politics of Day Care in America* (New York: Simon and Schuster, 1973), 34–68; Bernard Greenblatt, *Responsibility for Child Care: The Changing Role of Family and State in Child Development*, The Jossey-Bass Behavioral Science Series (San Francisco: Jossey-Bass, 1977), 15–78; Geraldine Youcha, *Minding the Children: Child Care in America from Colonial Times to the Present* (New York: Scribner, 1995), 309–311; Rose, *A Mother's Job*, 125–52; Michel, *Children's Interests/Mothers' Rights*, 118–141; Beatty, *Preschool Education in America*, 177–85; among others.
34. However, because many of these educators were elementary and secondary school teachers who had not previously taught two- to five-year-olds, they frequently lacked knowledge of developmentally appropriate pedagogy. Michel, *Children's Interests/Mothers' Rights*, 122–23.
35. Quoted in ibid., 121.
36. Ibid., 119.
37. Beatty, *Preschool Education in America*, 184.
38. Amy Kesselman, *Fleeting Opportunities: Women Shipyard Workers in Portland and Vancouver During World War II and Reconversion* (Albany: State University of New York Press, 1990). For studies of women's work in shipyards and other defense industries during World War II, also see Susan M. Hartmann, *The Home Front and Beyond: American Women in the 1940s* (Boston: Twayne Publishers, 1982); Honey, *Creating Rosie the Riveter: Class, Gender, and Propaganda During World War II*; Doris Weatherford, *American Women and World War II* (New York: Facts on File, 1990); Chester W. Gregory, *Women in Defense Work During World War II: An Analysis of the Labor Problem and Women's Rights* (New York: Exposition Press, 1974); Campbell, *Women at War with America*; Karen Beck Skold, "The Job He Left Behind: American Women in the Shipyards During World War II," in *Women, War, and Revolution*, ed. Carol R. Berkin and Clara M. Lovett (New York: Holmes & Meier, 1980), 55–75. For oral histories of working women during World War II, see Sherna Berger Gluck, *Rosie the Riveter Revisited: Women, the War, and Social Change* (Boston: Twayne Publishers, 1987); Studs Terkel, *"The Good War:" An Oral History of World War II* (New York: Pantheon Books, 1984). For a firsthand memoir of shipyard life, see Katherine Archibald, *Wartime Shipyard: A Study in Social Disunity* (Berkeley: University of California Press, 1947).
39. Kesselman, *Fleeting Opportunities*, 67–74.

40. On the "maternalist" response to the employment of working mothers, see Gwendolyn Mink, *The Wages of Motherhood: Inequality in the Welfare State, 1917–1942* (Ithaca, NY: Cornell University Press, 1995), 162–73.
41. "Proceedings of Conference on Day Care of Children of Working Mothers with Special Reference to Defense Areas Held in Washington, DC July 31 and August 1, 1941," 14; "Policies Regarding the Employment of Mothers of Young Children in Occupations Essential to National Defense," *The Child* 6, no. 8 (1942): 213.
42. "Policies Regarding the Employment of Mothers of Young Children in Occupations Essential to National Defense," 213.
43. See "Children's Bureau Commission on Children in Wartime: First Meeting, March 16–18, 1942" (Washington, DC: U.S. Department of Labor and U.S. Children's Bureau, 1942); "Policy of the War Manpower Commission on Employment in Industry of Women with Young Children," *The Child* 7, no. 4 (1942): 49–50.
44. "Five O'clock Mothers," *Journal of Home Economics* 34, no. 2 (1942): 107.
45. Kesselman, *Fleeting Opportunities*, 72.
46. Allen, Davis, and Olivier, "Eight-Hour Orphans"; Dorothy Thompson, "Children of Working Mothers," *The Ladies' Home Journal*, July 1942, p. 6; "Women Seek U.S. Aid for Day Nurseries," *The Christian Science Monitor*, July 15, 1942, p. 8; "Mothers Scorned for Child Neglect," *New York Times*, May 21, 1943, p. 14.
47. Allen, Davis, and Olivier, "Eight-Hour Orphans," 21, p. 105.
48. Agnes Meyer, *Journey through Chaos* (New York: Harcourt, Brace, 1944), 152–53.
49. William M. Tuttle, "America's Home Front Children in World War II," in *Children in Time and Place: Developmental and Historical Insights*, ed. Glen H. Elder, John Modell, and Ross D. Parke (New York: Cambridge University Press, 1993), 69–78.
50. Karen Anderson, *Wartime Women: Sex Roles, Family Relations, and the Status of Women During World War II* (Westport, CT: Greenwood Press, 1981), 97–111.
51. Gladys Denny Shultz, "Who's Going to Take Care of Me, Mother, If You Take a War-Plant Job?" *Better Homes and Gardens*, May 1943, p. 61.
52. "Plan Is Laid to Curb Delinquency; Mothers in War Jobs Creat Problem," *New York Times*, September 25, 1942, p. 23.
53. I. L. Kandel, *The Impact of the War Upon American Education* (Chapel Hill, NC: University of North Carolina Press, 1948), 55.
54. Anderson, *Wartime Women*, 96; "Richmond Took a Beating," *Fortune*, February 1945, p. 267.
55. "Child Delinquency Is Deemed Serious," *New York Times*, November 20, 1942, p. 19.
56. Allen, Davis, and Olivier, "Eight-Hour Orphans," 106.
57. Kandel, *The Impact of the War Upon American Education*, 55–56; Lindenmeyer, "A Right to Childhood," 224–230; Anderson, *Wartime Women*, 95–102.
58. Richard Polenberg, *War and Society: The United States, 1941–1945* (Philadelphia: J. B. Lippincott, 1972), 149.
59. "Extended School Services: For Children of Working Mothers," *Education for Victory* 1, no. 14 (1942): 10.

60. Honey, *Creating Rosie the Riveter*, 31–59.
61. Ibid., 30–41
62. Ibid., 63.
63. On various agencies' and organizations' political maneuvering resulting from this acquiescence, see Howard Dratch, "The Politics of Child Care in the 1940s," *Science and Society* 38, no. 2 (1974): 167–204. On the politics of early childhood education advocacy prior to the war, see Barbara Beatty, "The Politics of Preschool Advocacy: Lessons from Three Pioneering Organizations," in *Who Speaks for America's Children? The Role of Child Advocates in Public Policy*, ed. Carol J. De Vita and Rachel Mosher-Williams (Washington, DC: Urban Institute Press, 2001), 165–90.
64. Leonard W. Mayo, "Legislation for the Protection of Children in Wartime," (Washington, DC: U.S. Department of Labor, Children's Bureau, 1943), 8–9.
65. *Nursery Schools Vital to America's War Effort*, ed. U.S. Office of Education, Federal Security Agency, vol. 3, *School Children and the War Series* (Washington, DC: U.S. Government Printing Office, 1943), 1.
66. Ibid., 1.
67. Ibid., 12.
68. Susan E. Riley, "Caring for Rosie's Children: Federal Child Care Policies in the World War II Era," *Polity* 26, no. 4 (1994): 660–61.
69. Congressional debate over child care policy did take place in relation to the War Area Child Care Act (also known as the "Thomas Bill"). This piece of legislation, however, which passed the Senate but died in the House of Representatives in 1943, did not threaten the existence or promote the expansion of the wartime nursery schools. Instead, it sought to remove the child care program from under the authority of the Federal Works Administration and turn it over to the U.S. Office of Education and Children's Bureau. See Michel, *Children's Interests/Mothers' Rights*, 134–35; Natalie Marie Fousekis, "Fighting for Our Children: Women's Activism and the Battle for Child Care in California, 1940–1965" (Ph.D. diss., University of North Carolina, Chapel Hill, 2000), 28–30.
70. Riley, "Caring for Rosie's Children: Federal Child Care Policies in the World War II Era," 663.
71. Dratch, "The Politics of Child Care in the 1940s," 175–76. Natalie Marie Fousekis notes that much city and state support for the expansion of nursery schools was the result of "grassroots activism" by women who were members of a diverse group of organizations, including local CIO auxiliaries, heads of private non-profit day nurseries, and traditional women's groups, as well as working mothers and early childhood educators. See Fousekis, "Fighting for Our Children."
72. Michel, *Children's Interests/Mothers' Rights*, 132–33.
73. Department of Social Welfare/War Services Bureau Records/F3729: 46–48/Folder 1. National Archives-Pacific Region, San Bruno, California.
74. Dratch, "The Politics of Child Care in the 1940s," 176.
75. Anderson, *Wartime Women*, 125.
76. Ibid., 125–26.
77. Fousekis, "Fighting for Our Children," 54.
78. California State Archives, D4173, California State War Council, Citizens Committee on Youth in Wartime, Box 2, Folder 5, "Minutes of the Meeting of

Citizens Committee on Youth in Wartime, January 1, 1944," "State Department of Social Welfare, Office Memorandum, From Lucile Kennedy to Margaret S. Watkins, dated November 1, 1943, Regarding Child Care Conference, October 28–29, 1943," 2.
79. Quoted in William M. Tuttle, *Daddy's Gone to War: The Second World War in the Lives of America's Children* (New York: Oxford University Press, 1993), 81.
80. University of California, Berkeley. Bancroft Library. Henry J. Kaiser Papers, Carton 287, Folder 24, "Proposal."
81. Henry J. Kaiser Papers, Carton 289, Folder 20, "A Graphic Portrayal of the First Six Months Experience of Women Employed in the Kaiser Shipyards, July to December 1942."
82. Hubert O. Brown, "The Impact of War Worker Migration on the Public School System of Richmond, California, from 1940 to 1945" (Ph.D. diss., Stanford University, 1973), 265. During World War II, defense industry leaders throughout the United States claimed that high absenteeism on the part of working mothers was detrimental to productivity. See, for instance, "Women Drop Out," *Business Week*, August 21, 1943, p. 88–90; "More Child Care," *Business Week*, August 26, 1944, p. 41–42. In his study of American working women, historian William Chafe cited a 1943 survey of female defense employees indicating that 40 percent of all women who left their paid positions in factories and shipyards cited "marital, household, and allied difficulties" as the reason for their resignation, in contrast with only 9 percent who cited "poor wages or working conditions." William Henry Chafe, *The American Woman: Her Changing Social, Economic, and Political Roles, 1920–1970* (London: Oxford University Press, 1972), 159–160.
83. Brown, "The Impact of War Worker Migration on the Public School System of Richmond, California, from 1940 to 1945," 265.
84. Ibid., 69.
85. Alicia Barber, "Maritime Child Development Center," (Richmond, CA: Historic American Buildings Survey, 2001), 8.
86. Helms's position was accurate. In February 1943, California Governor Earl Warren signed into law legislation permitting public school districts in the state to administer nursery schools using funds provided by both the federal government and parent fees. See Division of Public School Administration Child Care Center Staff, "Report of Child Care Centers Administered and Operated by California School Districts," (Sacramento: California State Department of Education, 1949), 2.
87. "Fund Allotted for Nursery School Here," *Richmond Independent*, October 19, 1942, p. 1.
88. "Organization to Be Set up for Nursery School," *Richmond Independent*, November 3 1942; "City Moves to Ask U.S. Aid for 10 Day Nurseries Here," *Richmond Independent*, January 6, 1943, p. 9.
89. "School Department Files Application to Operate Child Care Centers Here," *Richmond Independent*, February 10, 1943.
90. "First Nursery School Opens Today: Working Mothers See Tots Safely in Modern School," *Richmond War Homes Weekly*, April 9, 1943, p. 1.
91. Ibid., 1.
92. "For Mothers Only," *Fore 'n' Aft*, April 23, 1943, p. 4.

93. Richmond Museum of History, Richmond, CA, Monica Haley Papers, Folder–"Financial Records," "Richmond Child Care Centers–Richmond Schools–Richmond, California, Financial Report, May 1945;" "Child Care Centers Open," *Richmond War Homes Weekly*, November 27, 1943, p. 1. Parents with more than four children were discouraged from using the schools. See California State Archives, D4173, California State War Council, Citizens Committee on Youth in Wartime, Box 2, Folder 5, "Minutes of the Meeting of Citizens Committee on Youth in Wartime, January 1, 1944," "State Department of Social Welfare, Office Memorandum, From Lucile Kennedy to Margaret S. Watkins, dated November 1, 1943, Regarding Child Care Conference, October 28–29, 1943," 5.
94. "First Nursery School Opens Today: Working Mothers See Tots Safely in Modern School," 1; "For Mothers Only," 4; "Mothers by the Day," *Fore 'n' Aft*, September 3 1943, p. 3.
95. Richmond Museum of History, Richmond, CA, Monica Haley Papers, Folder–"Menus."
96. Richmond Museum of History, Richmond, CA, Monica Haley Papers, Folder–"Maritime Nursery," "Maritime Extended Day Care Activity Program." "Extended Day Care" was the title given to Richmond's five- through sixteen-year-old before and after school program. In the Monica Haley Papers, sources addressing the city's nursery school programs are frequently filed with the extended day care programs.
97. Monica Haley Papers, Folder–"Menus."
98. Monica Haley Papers, Folder–"Maritime Nursery," "Maritime Extended Day Care Activity Program."
99. "Eight Hour Orphans," *Fore 'n' Aft*, May 7, 1943, p. 6.
100. Ibid., 6–7.
101. Ibid., 6–7.
102. Powers, Ruth. An oral history conducted in 2001 by Jon Plutte for the Rosie the Riveter/World War II Home Front National Historical Park. National Park Service, Golden Gate National Recreation Area.
103. Prout, Mary Hall. An oral history conducted in 2002 by Ben Bicais, Regional Oral History Office, Bancroft Library, University of California, Berkeley. Courtesy, Bancroft Library.
104. Ibid.
105. Ibid.
106. Ibid.
107. This was a frequently stated aim of many of the wartime nursery schools in the United States as well as the intent of federal policy makers. See Beatty, *Preschool Education in America*, 187–188. For the success of nursery schools, nationally, in achieving this aim, see Tuttle, *Daddy's Gone to War*, 86–88.
108. Interview with Mary Hall Prout.
109. Richmond Museum of History, Richmond, CA, Monica Haley Papers, Folder–"Schedules," "Specific Objectives for Richmond Child Care Centers" dated 1945.
110. Richmond Museum of History, Richmond, CA, Monica Haley Papers, Folder–"Schedules," "Submitted by Monica Haley, Weekly Schedule, January 1945." Haley eventually published the curriculum for this program. See Richmond Museum of History, Richmond, CA, Monica Haley Papers, "Art and

Craft Manual by Monica Haley, Richmond Children's Centers, October 1965." Following the war, Haley was again promoted and assigned responsibility for the supervision of the art program for all of Richmond's public schools, a position she held until her retirement in 1966. See "Creative Beginnings: Richmond Child Care Centers, Art and History from the Early Years – July 24–December 12, 1993," manuscript located in the Richmond Museum of History, Richmond, CA.
111. Richmond Museum of History, Richmond, CA, Monica Haley Papers, "Child Care Centers, Richmond Schools, Richmond, CA, Parents' Bulletin No. 2," 3.
112. "Child Art Principles Based Upon the Spontaneous Easel Paintings of Children Ages Two to Twelve," by Monica Haley, manuscript located in the Richmond Museum of History, Richmond, CA, Monica Haley Papers, 23–26.
113. Ibid.
114. Ibid.
115. Richmond Museum of History, Richmond, CA, Monica Haley Papers, "Photograph Collection."
116. "Child Art Principles Based Upon the Spontaneous Easel Paintings of Children Ages Two to Twelve," 24.
117. Monica Haley Papers, "Photograph Collection."
118. Richmond Museum of History, Richmond, CA, Monica Haley Papers, Folder–"Quotes from the Children."
119. Ibid.
120. Ibid.
121. Ibid.
122. "Child Art Exhibit in Richmond," *Oakland Post-Enquirer*, October 3, 1944, p. 15.
123. Ibid., 15.
124. "Children's Art Display Lauded," *Richmond Independent*, November 22, 1946, p. 3.
125. On the similarities and distinctions between these educational theories and practices, see Beatty, *Preschool Education in America*.
126. Guy Montrose Whipple, ed., *The Twenty-Eighth Yearbook of the National Society for the Study of Education: Preschool and Parental Education* (Bloomington, IL: Public School Publishing Company, 1929).
127. Rose H. Alschuler, *Two to Six: Suggestions for Parents of Young Children* (New York: W. Morrow, 1933); Rose H. Alschuler, ed., *Children's Centers: A Guide for Those Who Care for and About Young Children* (New York: W. Morrow, 1942).
128. Alschuler, ed., *Children's Centers: A Guide for Those Who Care for and About Young Children*, 25–26.
129. "Child Art Principles Based Upon the Spontaneous Easel Paintings of Children Ages Two to Twelve," 13.
130. Richmond Museum of History, Richmond, CA, Monica Haley Papers, Folder–"School Arts."
131. "Child Art Principles Based Upon the Spontaneous Easel Paintings of Children Ages Two to Twelve," 13.
132. Henry J. Kaiser Papers, Carton 289, Folder 20, "A Graphic Portrayal of the First Six Months Experience of Women Employed in the Kaiser Shipyards,

July to December 1942"; "Kaiser's Children," *Business Week*, May 22, 1943, p. 40.
133. The first, consisting of 6,005 units, was built near the site of Nystrom Elementary School, not far from Kaiser Shipyard Number Two, while the second, also constructed relatively close to Shipyard Number Two, was a 3,990-unit project. University of California, Berkeley. Bancroft Library. Henry J. Kaiser Papers, Carton 287, Folder 23, "United States Maritime Commission 6,000 Unit Housing Project, Richmond, California," dated October 13, 1942, and Folder 24, "Proposal: Proposed USMC Housing Project Nursery, 9 December 1942."
134. University of California, Berkeley. Bancroft Library. Henry J. Kaiser Papers, Carton 159, Folder 25, "Education Report," 2; Barber, "Maritime Child Development Center," 20.
135. "Kaiser's Children," 40; Catherine Landreth, "The Nursery School of the Institute of Child Welfare of the University of California, Berkeley." An oral history conducted in 1981 by Dan Burke, Regional Oral History Office, Bancroft Library, University of California, Berkeley.
136. Catherine Landreth, *Education of the Young Child: A Nursery School Manual* (New York: John Wiley, 1942). In 1943, Landreth was called on by the California State Department of Education to contribute to developing a statewide program for the care of children of working mothers. See "California Program for the Care of Children of Working Parents," *Bulletin of the California State Department of Education*, August 1943. Landreth's reputation also led to her active participation in a Department of Education survey of preschools operating throughout the state at the end of the war. See Division of Public School Administration Child Care Center Staff, "Report of Child Care Centers Administered and Operated by California School Districts," (Sacramento: California State Department of Education, 1949).
137. Haley studied under Landreth at UC Berkeley, was familiar with Landreth's work, and drew inspiration from it. See Richmond Museum of History, Richmond, CA, Monica Haley Papers, Folder–"Education: Discipline and Teacher Training," "Landreth Quotes."
138. Landreth, *Education of the Young Child*; Catherine Landreth, "The Nursery School of the Institute of Child Welfare of the University of California, Berkeley." An oral history conducted in 1981 by Dan Burke. Also, see Catherine Landreth, "Practices in Childhood Education," in *The Forty-Sixth Yearbook of the National Society for the Study of Education*, ed. Nelson B. Henry (Chicago: University of Chicago Press, 1948), 129–41; Catherine Landreth and Howard Moise, "Unit Plan for Nursery Schools," *Progressive Architecture* 30, no. 3 (1949): 79–83; Barber, "Maritime Child Development Center," 18–25.
139. Interview with Ruth Powers.
140. Catherine Landreth, "The Nursery School of the Institute of Child Welfare of the University of California, Berkeley." An oral history conducted in 1981 by Dan Burke.
141. Ibid.
142. "Kaiser's Children," 40.
143. Interview with Mary Hall Prout.

144. "Kaiser's Children," 40–42; "60 Enrolled as First Nursery Unit Is Opened," *The Richmond Independent*, June 2, 1943, p. 4; "24-Hour Nursery School Opens," *Richmond War Homes Weekly*, November 6, 1943, p. 1.
145. On the Swan Island and Oregonship Kaiser Child Service Centers, see Kesselman, *Fleeting Opportunities*, 77–89; Sally C. Hurwitz, "War Nurseries-Lessons in Quality," *Young Children* 53, no. 5 (1998): 37–39; Carol Slobodin, "When the U.S. Paid for Day Care," *Day Care and Early Education* 3, no. 1 (1975): 23–25, 49; James L. Hymes, "The Kaiser Child Service Centers," in *Care of the Children of Working Mothers, Early Childhood Education: Living History Interviews* (Carmel: Hacienda Press, 1978), 26–56; James L. Hymes, "The Emergency Nursery Schools and the Wartime Child Care Centers: 1933–1946," in *Reaching Large Numbers of Children, Early Childhood Education: Living History Interviews* (Carmel: Hacienda Press, 1979), 5–27; James L. Hymes, "The Kaiser Child Service Centers–50 Years Later: Some Memories and Lessons," *Journal of Education* 177, no. 3 (1995): 23–38.
146. "150 Women Do a Big Job," 1.
147. "Burner" was the term applied to the worker who cut materials using a welding torch. "From 'Workingman's Town' to 'All-America City 1954': The Socio-Political Economy of Richmond, California during World War II," by William Sokol, June 1971, manuscript in the Richmond Collection of the Richmond Public Library.
148. "24-Hour Nursery School Opens," 1; "Time to Retire," *Fore 'n' Aft*, December 10, 1943, p. 4.
149. Hengerer, "Study of Youth Services in Contra Costa County," 113. In 1944, *Business Week* reported that first-year operating costs for the Richmond Nursery Schools were $190,801, with $122,480 provided through the Lanham Act and $68,321 coming from parent fees and state and local support. "More Child Care," 42.
150. Hartmann, *The Home Front and Beyond*, 59; Riley, "Caring for Rosie's Children: Federal Child Care Policies in the World War II Era," 655–75; Anderson, *Wartime Women*, 146; Tuttle, *Daddy's Gone to War*, 82.
151. Stoltzfus, *Citizen, Mother, Worker*, 138, 145.
152. Exact numbers of children enrolled in the nursery schools between 1943 and 1945 are unavailable. However, combined enrollment in the city's "child care" programs, including before and after school "extended day care" centers and nursery schools, peaked at approximately 1,230. By May 1945, the city's child care programs reportedly served an estimated 848 working mothers, with well over half of these women employed by the Kaiser shipyards. See Hengerer, "Study of Youth Services in Contra Costa County," 112–13; Richmond Museum of History, Richmond, CA, Monica Haley Papers, Folder–"Occupational Classification of Mothers of Children Enrolled in the Richmond Child Care Centers, May 18, 1945."
153. "Nursery School Observes Birth Date Tomorrow," 9.
154. See California State Archives, D4173, California State War Council, Citizens Committee on Youth in Wartime, Box 2, Folder 5, "Minutes of the Meeting of Citizens Committee on Youth in Wartime, January 1, 1944," "State Department of Social Welfare, Office Memorandum, From Lucile Kennedy to Margaret S. Watkins, dated November 1, 1943, Regarding Child Care Conference,

October 28–29, 1943," 7; Rose, *A Mother's Job*, 166; Youcha, *Minding the Children*, 313–14.
155. "Always Room for One More Tot: Some Openings Continue in All Nursery Schools," *Richmond War Homes Weekly*, July 31, 1943, p. 4.
156. "Nursery Care Is Available," *Richmond War Homes Weekly*, April 8 1944, p. 1.
157. "Mothers by the Day," 2.
158. Quoted in Polenberg, *War and Society*, 149.
159. Kesselman, *Fleeting Opportunities*, 84.
160. Hengerer, "Study of Youth Services in Contra Costa County," 113.
161. Shirley Ann Wilson Moore, *To Place Our Deeds: The African American Community in Richmond, California, 1910–1963* (Berkeley: University of California Press, 2000), 68.
162. Marilyn S. Johnson, *The Second Gold Rush: Oakland and the East Bay in World War II* (Berkeley: University of California Press, 1993), 116.
163. Cited in Chafe, *The American Woman*, 164.
164. Campbell, *Women at War with America*, 82.
165. On the many expressions of this ambivalence during the war years, see Kessler-Harris, *Out to Work*, 299.
166. Rose, *A Mother's Job*, 153.
167. Division of Public School Administration Child Care Center Staff, "Report of Child Care Centers Administered and Operated by California School Districts," (Sacramento: California State Department of Education, 1949), i.
168. James L. Hymes, "More Quantity, More Quality," *Frontiers of Democracy* 9, no. 73 (1942): 71.
169. Stoltzfus, *Citizen, Mother, Worker*, 160.
170. Division of Public School Administration Child Care Center Staff, "Report of Child Care Centers Administered and Operated by California School Districts," (Sacramento: California State Department of Education, 1949), 2.
171. Riley, "Caring for Rosie's Children," 663.
172. "Report of Child Care Centers Administered and Operated by California School Districts," 2; Youcha, *Minding the Children*, 332.
173. Stoltzfus, *Citizen, Mother, Worker*, 140–41.
174. Quoted in ibid., 150, 162.
175. Ibid., 150.
176. In 1990, due to Richmond school district budgetary problems, Contra Costa County and the West Contra Costa County YMCA took over administration of the centers. Barber, "Maritime Child Development Center," 31–33.
177. "Report of Child Care Centers Administered and Operated by California School Districts," 2–3.
178. Ibid., 3; Stoltzfus, *Citizen, Mother, Worker*, 165–76.

Chapter 6

1. "Report of the United States Education Mission to Germany," (Washington, DC: Department of State, 1946).
2. Ibid., xii.
3. *Germany, 1947–1949: The Story in Documents* (Washington, DC: Department of State, Office of Public Affairs, Publication 3556, European and British Commonwealth Series 9, 1950), 49.

4. Lucius D. Clay, *Decision in Germany* (New York: Doubleday, 1950).
5. "Report of the United States Education Mission to Germany," 19.
6. Ibid., 23.
7. Ibid., 30.
8. Ibid., 50.
9. Roger L. Geiger, *To Advance Knowledge: The Growth of America's Research Universities, 1900–1940* (New York: Oxford University Press, 1986).
10. Harvey Kantor, *Learning to Earn: School, Work and Vocational Reform in California, 1880–1930* (Madison: University of Wisconsin Press, 1988).
11. Herbert M. Kliebard, *The Struggle for the American Curriculum, 1893–1958*, 2nd ed. (New York: Routledge, 1995), 210.
12. Ibid., 212.
13. I. L. Kandel, *The Impact of the War Upon American Education* (Chapel Hill: University of North Carolina Press, 1948), 188.
14. Ibid., 188.
15. Division of Public School Administration Child Care Center Staff, "Report of Child Care Centers Administered and Operated by California School Districts," (Sacramento: California State Department of Education, 1949), i.
16. H. M. Kallen, "The War and Education in the United States," *The American Journal of Sociology* 48, no. 3 (1942): 331.
17. Ibid., 336.
18. Kallen qualified his claim by noting that although public schools in the United States refused to cultivate "warlike virtues," they also tended "to repress and pervert" democracy in their "administrative hierarchies" and authoritarian qualities. Ibid., 335–36.
19. Ibid., 342.
20. Ibid., 333.
21. Bernard Bailyn, *Education in the Forming of American Society* (New York: Vintage Books, 1960), 48.

Selected Bibliography

Interviews

Berka (Minard), Paula. 2000. Interview by author. Palo Alto, CA. September 25, 2000.

Brimhall, Alice. An oral history conducted by Jon Plutte for the Rosie the Riveter/World War II Home Front National Historical Park at the Richmond Museum of History, Richmond, CA. National Park Service, Golden Gate National Recreation Area, 2001.

Edmondson, Peter. Interview by author. Palo Alto, CA. September 23, 2000.

Edmondson (Allen), Sally. Interview by author. Palo Alto, CA. September 23, 2000.

Haag, Evelyn. Interview by author. Walnut Creek, CA. July 12, 2000.

Marshall, Clyde. Interview by author. Palo Alto, CA. June 11, 2002.

Martin, Henry. Interview by author. Palo Alto, CA. August 7, 2000.

Melgoza, Chris. Interview by author. Newark, CA. January 30, 2003.

Paulin (Manning), Joan. Interview by author. Palo Alto, CA. September 15, 2000.

Philips, Charles. Interview by author. Palo Alto, CA. July 21, 2002.

Powers, Ruth. An oral history conducted by Jon Plutte for the Rosie the Riveter/World War II Home Front National Historical Park. National Park Service, Golden Gate National Recreation Area, 2001.

Prout, Mary Hall. An oral history conducted by Ben Bicais, Regional Oral History Office, Bancroft Library, University of California, Berkeley, 2002.

Sauer, Marian. An oral history conducted by Jon Plutte for the Rosie the Riveter/World War II Home Front National Historical Park. National Park Service, Golden Gate National Recreation Area, 2000.

Published Sources

Newspapers

"Faculties Get Order to Assert Their Authority." *Richmond Independent*, October 4, 1945.
"Housing Authority to Be Set Up by City to Meet Labor Influx." *Richmond Independent*, January 14, 1941.
"More Room Needed, School Board Told." *Richmond Independent*, January 8, 1942.
"Pursuit Plane: First Day of School Drive Nets $14,750." *Daily Palo Alto Times*, April 8, 1943.
"Vocational College May Be Set Up to Use War Shop Equipment." *Daily Palo Alto Times*, January 14, 1944.
"Women Seek U.S. Aid for Day Nurseries." *The Christian Science Monitor*, July 15, 1942.
"60 Enrolled as First Nursery Unit Is Opened." *The Richmond Independent*, June 2, 1943.
"Aviation Club Formed; International Writes Letters." *The Campanile*, December 10, 1943.
"Board Asked Not to Set School Program 'Til Harvest Situation Crystalizes." *Daily Palo Alto Times*, May 31, 1943.
"C. W. Lockwood Assumes Control." *Daily Palo Alto Times*, January 3, 1942.
"Cadet Corps to Be Part of P.A. High School Life." *Daily Palo Alto Times*, September 6, 1944.
"Cadet Corps to Be Part of Paly Life." *The Campanile*, September 28, 1944.
"California Geared to Demands of War." *New York Times*, June 28, 1942.
"Child Art Exhibit in Richmond." *Oakland Post-Enquirer*, October 3, 1944.
"Child Delinquency Is Deemed Serious." *New York Times*, November 20, 1942.
"Children's Art Display Lauded." *Richmond Independent*, November 22, 1946.
"City Asked to Keep Step with Kaiser Company." *Richmond Independent*, December 5, 1941.
"City Moves to Ask U.S. Aid for 10 Day Nurseries Here." *Richmond Independent*, January 6, 1943.
"Curriculum Changes Disclosed to Seniors; Four Classifications Offered to Students." *The Campanile*, January 15, 1943.

"Discussion of Junior College Project Is Lively." *Daily Palo Alto Times*, February 2, 1945.
"Disputes Arise in School Meet over Knifings." *Contra Costa Gazette*, October 4, 1945.
"Education Board Suggests Course to 'Harden' Boys." *Daily Palo Alto Times*, October 11, 1940.
"Farm to Run Full Blast This Summer; 2000 Expected in Expanded Courses." *Stanford Daily*, May 14, 1942.
"Forum: Alternative Advised to Junior College." *Daily Palo Alto Times*, March 9, 1945.
"Forum: Writer Doesn't Favor Junior College Here." *Daily Palo Alto Times*, February 6, 1945.
"Fund Allotted for Nursery School Here." *Richmond Independent*, October 19, 1942.
"Girls' League War Projects Successful." *The Campanile*, October 29, 1943.
"Helms Delivers Ultimatum to Government Men." *Richmond Independent*, March 10, 1943.
"Helms to Ask Federal Funds for Schools." *Richmond Independent*, July 9, 1941.
"High School Girls Make Dressings for Red Cross." *Daily Palo Alto Times*, January 15, 1943.
"High School Harvesters Earn $26,540." *Daily Palo Alto Times*, January 26, 1943.
"Jr. College Expansion Held Unjustified." *Daily Palo Alto Times*, March 8, 1945.
"Junior College Straw Poll Is Heavily Against Project." *Daily Palo Alto Times*, March 21, 1945.
"Local Farmers Hit by Labor Shortage; Depend on Students." *The Campanile*, September 24, 1942.
"Many Students Aid Labor Trouble by Working in Local Business." *The Campanile*, April 2, 1943.
"Martin Teaches Morse Code." *The Campanile*, April 2, 1943.
"More Than a Headache." *Richmond Independent*, September 4, 1941.
"Mothers Scorned for Child Neglect." *New York Times*, May 21, 1943.
"New Semester Courses Prepare for War." *The Campanile*, January 22, 1943.
"No High School Cadet Corps." *Daily Palo Alto Times*, September 13, 1940.
"Nursery School Observes Birth Date Tomorrow." *The Richmond Independent*, May 31, 1944.
"Organization to Be Set Up for Nursery School." *Richmond Independent*, November 3, 1942.

"Palo Alto High School to Continue Student Work Experience Program." *Daily Palo Alto Times*, September 2, 1943.
"Parents Protest Lack of Action by School Dept." *Richmond Independent*, October 3, 1945.
"Picture of Paly's B-25 Bomber Here." *The Campanile*, October 15, 1943.
"Plan Is Laid to Curb Delinquency; Mothers in War Jobs Creat Problem." *New York Times*, September 25, 1942.
"Red Cross Collections Go Over the Top." *The Campanile*, November 19, 1943.
"Richmond C of C Opens Drive to Mobilize for Expansion of Business." *Richmond Independent*, September 16, 1941.
"Richmond Has Zero in Defense Funds." *Richmond Independent*, August 3, 1940.
"School Board Defers Junior College Project." *Daily Palo Alto Times*, March 23, 1945.
"School Can Buy Medium Bomber." *Daily Palo Alto Times*, May 13, 1943.
"School Department Files Application to Operate Child Care Centers Here." *Richmond Independent*, February 10, 1943.
"School Enrollment Shows Big Increase." *Richmond Independent*, September 10, 1941.
"School Head to Emphasize Fundamentals." *Daily Palo Alto Times*, December 2, 1941.
"Sequoia High Accepts Paly's Challenge; War Stamp Purchasing Duel Underway." *The Campanile*, October 29, 1942.
"Students Take Math Courses as Aid to War." *The Campanile*, April 2, 1943.
"Superintendent Lockwood Explains." *Daily Palo Alto Times*, April 13, 1943.
"Teacher Lack Feared Here." *Richmond Independent*, May 14, 1943.
"To Define Hold of Democracy." *New York Times*, August 13, 1939.
"Toughen Up: Ray to Enlarge, Improve Program of Physical Fitness at High School." *Daily Palo Alto Times*, July 10, 1942.
"Trooper Reeves: 'It's Rugged'; Field Enlists in Nurse Corps." *The Campanile*, October 15, 1943.
"U.S. Pours Millions in the East Bay." *Richmond Independent*, July 27, 1940.
"Vacation to End for 8,000 Local Children." *Richmond Independent*, January 3, 1942.
"War Industry Courses Are Thrown Open." *Stanford Daily*, January 29, 1942.
"Western Educators Plan Commission for Co-Operation in National Defense." *Stanford Daily*, June 26, 1941.

SELECTED BIBLIOGRAPHY   231

"Wilbur Hits 18-Year-Old Draft Bill." *Stanford Daily*, November 4, 1942.
"Work Program and Tutoring on Curriculum." *The Campanile*, March 31, 1944.
"World Affairs: Students to Study Peace Plans." *The Campanile*, March 12, 1943.
Allen, B. "No Gym for War-Working Students?" *The Campanile*, April 9, 1943.
Blitzer, Carol. "The 1940s: On the Home Front." *Palo Alto Weekly*, April 15, 1994.
Fine, Benjamin. "Army's College Program Is Reported Bogged Down." *New York Times*, May 22, 1943.
———. "Liberal Arts Eclipsed by Vocational Courses." *New York Times*, January 24, 1943.
———. "War Status Held Vital at Schools." *New York Times*, February 13, 1942.
Hays, Mary Katherine, and Frank Greenfield. "Uniforms Appear in Paly Halls as Cadet Corps Gets Started." *Daily Palo Alto Times*, October 5, 1944.
Hutton, Jean. "Many of the Seniors at Palo Alto High School Already Have College or Career Plans Made." *Daily Palo Alto Times*, March 14, 1942.
———. "Palo Alto High School Students Are Busy Harvesting Valley Crops." *Daily Palo Alto Times*, October 7, 1942.
———. "War Reflected in Classrooms and Activities." *Daily Palo Alto Times*, March 2, 1942.
Kresge, Mike. "Stanford Revises Curriculum to Meet Demands of War." *Stanford Daily*, January 12, 1942.
Loomis, Fred. "All Out for Victory." *The Campanile*, January 15, 1943.
Maycock, Betty. "Students Swamp War-Important Classes." *Daily Palo Alto Times*, September 22, 1943.
Maycock, Sally. "Join the Junior Red Cross." *The Campanile*, November 10, 1942.
Mead, Bill. "Senior Classes Making Tours of Defense Center." *The Campanile*, October 1, 1942.
Ray, Howard C. "School Adapts 'Physical Ed' to Wartime." *Daily Palo Alto Times*, October 1, 1942.
Shalett, Sidney M. "New Plan Suspends Liberal Education." *New York Times*, December 18, 1942.
Stever, B. "Man Behind the Man Behind the Gun." *The Campanile*, April 2, 1943.
Zubal, Kay. "Senior High School Slants Curriculum Towards War." *Daily Palo Alto Times*, January 27, 1943.

Bulletins/Newsletters/Yearbooks

"150 Women Do a Big Job." *Richmond War Homes Weekly*, December 31, 1943.
"24-Hour Nursery School Opens." *Richmond War Homes Weekly*, November 6, 1943.
"Always Room for One More Tot: Some Openings Continue in All Nursery Schools." *Richmond War Homes Weekly*, July 31, 1943.
"Army Instead of Navy to Train Men Here." *Stanford Today*, January 18, 1943.
"Berkeley High Students Go to Work." *Berkeley Jacket*, May 15, 1942.
"Child Care Centers Open." *Richmond War Homes Weekly*, November 27, 1943.
"Eight Hour Orphans." *Fore 'n' Aft* (May 7, 1943): 6–7.
"Enrollment in Schools Here Exceeds 18,000." *Richmond War Homes Weekly*, October 2, 1943.
"Extended School Services: For Children of Working Mothers." *Education for Victory* 1, no. 14 (1942): 10.
"First Nursery School Opens Today: Working Mothers See Tots Safely in Modern School." *Richmond War Homes Weekly*, April 9, 1943.
"For Mothers Only." *Fore 'n' Aft* (April 23, 1943): 4.
"Full-Time Japanese Class Now Being Given." *Stanford Today*, January 18, 1943.
"Mothers by the Day." *Fore 'n' Aft* (September 3, 1943): 2–3.
"Nursery Care Is Available." *Richmond War Homes Weekly*, April 8, 1944.
"Stanford Steps Ahead." *Stanford Today*, January 18, 1943.
"Time to Retire." *Fore 'n' Aft* (December 10, 1943): 4.
"Vocational and Technical Wartime Training." *Education for Victory* 1, no. 2 (1942): 7–8.
"War Production Workers Training Program." *Education for Victory* 1, no. 14 (1942): 15–18.
"War Work Conference Sets Vocational Education Goals." *Education for Victory* 1, no. 21 (1943): 1, 20.
Stanford University Bulletin. Annual Register, 1929. Stanford, CA: Stanford University Press, 1929.
Stanford University Bulletin. Annual Register, 1933. Stanford, CA: Stanford University Press, 1933.
Stanford University Bulletin. Annual Register, 1941. Stanford, CA: Stanford University Press, 1941.
Stanford University Bulletin. Annual Register, 1942. Stanford, CA: Stanford University Press, 1942.

SELECTED BIBLIOGRAPHY   233

Stanford University Bulletin. Annual Register, 1943. Stanford, CA: Stanford University Press, 1943.
Stanford University Bulletin. Annual Register, 1944. Stanford, CA: Stanford University Press, 1944.
Stanford University Bulletin. Annual Register, 1945. Stanford, CA: Stanford University Press, 1945.
Stanford University Bulletin. Annual Register, 1946. Stanford, CA: Stanford University Press, 1946.
Stanford University Bulletin. Announcement of Courses: 1942–43. Stanford, CA: Stanford University, 1942.
Stanford University Bulletin. Announcement of Courses: 1943–44. Stanford, CA: Stanford University, 1943.
Stanford University Bulletin. Announcement of Courses: 1945–46. Stanford, CA: Stanford University, 1945.
U.S. Office of Education Federal Security Agency, ed. *Nursery Schools Vital to America's War Effort.* Vol. 3, *School Children and the War Series.* Washington, DC: U.S. Government Printing Office, 1943.

Reports/Handbooks/Conference Proceedings

"Annual Report of the President of Stanford University, 1941." Stanford: Stanford University, 1941.
"Annual Report of the President of Stanford University, 1942." Stanford: Stanford University, 1942.
"Annual Report of the President of Stanford University, 1943." Stanford: Stanford University, 1943.
"Annual Report of the President of Stanford University, 1944." Stanford: Stanford University, 1944.
"Annual Report of the President of Stanford University, 1945." Stanford: Stanford University, 1945.
"Children's Bureau Commission on Children in Wartime: First Meeting, March 16–18, 1942." Washington, DC: U.S. Department of Labor and U.S. Children's Bureau, 1942.
"Community Progress Report for 1950: Richmond, California." Richmond, CA: Richmond Chamber of Commerce, 1950.
"Education and the Defense of American Democracy." Washington, DC: Educational Policies Commission of the National Education Association and the American Association of School Administrators, 1940.
"Handbook on Education and the War." The National Institute on Education and the War: Sponsored by the U.S. Office of Education Wartime Commission, Washington, DC, August 28–31, 1942.

"Proceedings of Conference on Day Care of Children of Working Mothers with Special Reference to Defense Areas Held in Washington, DC July 31 and August 1, 1941." Paper presented at the Conference on Day Care of Children of Working Mothers With Special Reference to Defense Areas, Washington, DC, July 31 and August 1, 1941.

"Report of the United States Education Mission to Germany." Washington, DC: Department of State, 1946.

"Stanford University: The Founding Grant with Amendments, Legislation and Court Decrees." Stanford, CA: Stanford University Press, 1971.

"A War Policy for American Schools." Washington, DC: Educational Policies Commission of the National Education Association and the American Association of School Administrators, 1942.

"What the Schools Should Teach in Wartime." Washington, DC: Educational Policies Commission of the National Education Association and the American Association of School Administrators, 1943.

"White House Conference on Children in a Democracy." Washington, DC, 1941.

Barber, Alicia. "Maritime Child Development Center." Richmond, CA: Historic American Buildings Survey, 2001.

Briggs, Thomas H., and Will French, eds. "Education for Democracy." Proceedings of the Congress on Education on Democracy, Teachers College, Columbia University, 1939.

California Cadet Corps: The Cadet Manual. Sacramento: California State Printing Office, 1953.

California High School Cadets: A Manual for Period Instruction. Sacramento: Adjutant General, State of California, 1944.

Davis, Albert M. "Proposal for the Reorganization of the Secondary Schools and the Establishment of a Four-Year Junior College within the Palo Alto Unified School District." Palo Alto, CA: Palo Alto Unified School District, 1944.

Fifty Questions and Answers on Army Specialized Training Program. Washington, DC: War Department, 1943.

Hart, F. W., and L. H. Peterson. "A Schoolhousing Survey of the Richmond City Elementary School District and the Richmond Union High School District." Richmond, CA: Richmond City Elementary School Board of Education and the Richmond Union High School Board of Trustees, 1947.

Hengerer, Gertrude M. "Study of Youth Services in Contra Costa County." Contra Costa County, CA: Division of Field Services of the California Youth Authority, 1945.

Higher Education and the War: The Report of a National Conference of College and University Presidents, Held in Baltimore, Md., January 3–4,

1942, edited by Clarence Stephen Marsh. Vol. 6, *Reports of Committees of the Council*. Washington, DC: American Council on Education, 1942.

Higher Education Cooperates in National Defense: The Report of a Conference of Government Representatives and College and University Administrators, Held in Washington, DC, July 30–31, 1941, edited by Clarence Stephen Marsh. Vol. 5, *Reports of Committees of the Council*. Washington, DC: American Council on Education, 1941.

Holbrook, C. R. "Palo Alto Unified School District Financial Report for 1943–1944." Palo Alto, CA: Palo Alto Unified School District, 1944.

———. "Palo Alto Unified School District Financial Report for 1944–1945." Palo Alto, CA: Palo Alto Unified School District, 1945.

Horsby, Henry H. *Engineering, Science, and Management War Training: Final Report*. Washington, DC: U.S. Office of Education, 1946.

Landreth, Catherine. *Education of the Young Child: A Nursery School Manual*. New York: John Wiley, 1942.

Leonard, J. Paul. "Survey of the Richmond Public Schools." Richmond, CA: Boards of Education of the Richmond School District and the Richmond Union High School District, 1947.

Marsh, Clarence Stephen, ed. *Organizing Higher Education for National Defense: The Report of a Conference Called by the National Committee on Education and Defense Held in Washington, DC, February 6, 1941*. Vol. 4, *Reports of Committees of the Council*. Washington, DC: American Council on Education, 1941.

Mayo, Leonard W. "Legislation for the Protection of Children in Wartime." Washington, DC: United States Department of Labor, Children's Bureau, 1943.

McVittie, J. A. "An Avalanche Hits Richmond." Richmond: City of Richmond, CA, 1944.

Overturf, J. R. "Report of the Superintendent of Schools of the Palo Alto Unified School District." Palo Alto, CA: Palo Alto Unified School District, 1941.

Studebaker, John W. "Annual Report of the United States Commissioner of Education: For the Fiscal Year Ended June 30, 1940." Washington, DC: U.S. Office of Education, 1940.

———. "Annual Report of the United States Commissioner of Education: For the Fiscal Year Ended June 30, 1941." Washington, DC: U.S. Office of Education, 1941.

The Humanities Look Ahead. Stanford, CA: Stanford University Press, 1943.

Journals/Magazines

"Class of '45." *Time* (September 29, 1941): 37–38.
"Committee on Humanities Education in the South." *Higher Education* 1, no. 6 (1945): 7.
"Cover Art." *The American School Board Journal* 105, no. 3 (1942).
"Cover Art." *The American School Board Journal* 106, no. 5 (1943).
"Cover Art." *The American School Board Journal* 109, no. 3 (1944).
"Five O'clock Mothers." *Journal of Home Economics* 34, no. 2 (1942): 107.
"For Next Fall—Wanted 250,000 School Teachers." *The American School Board Journal* 104, no. 5 (1942): 18, 68.
"Freedom Must Be Learned." *Time* (January 25, 1943): 43.
"High Schools, Air-Conditioned." *Time* (October 12, 1942): 74.
"Humanities Head." *Time* (June 8, 1942): 61–62.
"Kaiser's Children." *Business Week* (May 22, 1943): 40–42.
"More Child Care." *Business Week* (August 26, 1944): 41–42.
"Policies Regarding the Employment of Mothers of Young Children in Occupations Essential to National Defense." *The Child* 6, no. 8 (1942): 213.
"Policy of the War Manpower Commission on Employment in Industry of Women with Young Children." *The Child* 7, no. 4 (1942): 49–50.
"Private Problems." *Time* (July 12, 1943): 74–75.
"Professors at Work." *Time* (June 14, 1943): 56.
"Richmond Builds Ships." *Western City* (February 1943): 14–19.
"Richmond Took a Beating." *Fortune* (February 1945): 262, 264–65, 267–69.
"School's Open—for War." *Time* (September 14, 1942): 86.
"Stanford Goes Humanist." *Time* (March 23, 1942): 60.
"Women Drop Out." *Business Week* (August 21, 1943): 88–90.
Allardyce, Gilbert. "The Rise and Fall of the Western Civilization Course." *The American Historical Review* 87, no. 3 (1982): 695–725.
Allen, Grace Thorne, Maxone Davis, and Warner Olivier. "Eight-Hour Orphans." *The Saturday Evening Post* (October 10, 1942): 20–21, 105–6.
Baldwin, Robert D. "The Impact of War on American Education." *Educational Administration and Supervision* 31, no. 4 (1945): 403–20.
Benedict, Ruth. "Transmitting Our Democratic Heritage in the Schools." *The American Journal of Sociology* 48, no. 6 (1943): 722–27.
Bowers, Harold J. "Teacher Recruitment in Wartime." *The American School Board Journal* 104, no. 3 (1942): 45–46.

Bradley, Omar N. "What You Owe Your Country." *Collier's* (February 26, 1949): 38.
Bruce, William G. "Schools- but Not as Usual." *The American School Board Journal* 105, no. 4 (1942): 11.
Conant, James Bryant. "No Retreat for the Liberal Arts." *New York Times Magazine* (February 21, 1943): 5, 37.
Davis, O. L. "The American School Curriculum Goes to War, 1941–1945: Oversight, Neglect, and Discovery." *Journal of Curriculum and Supervision* 8, no. 2 (1993): 112–27.
Donahue, David M. "Rhode Island's Last Holdout: Tenure and Married Women Teachers at the Brink of the Women's Movement." *History of Education Quarterly* 42, no. 1 (2002): 50–74.
Doyle, Henry Grattan. "Americans, Awake to Language Needs." *The American School Board Journal* 102, no. 3 (1941): 19–21, 98.
Dratch, Howard. "The Politics of Child Care in the 1940s." *Science and Society* 38, no. 2 (1974): 167–204.
Elmott, Charlotte D. "Survey of High School Wartime Practices." *California Journal of Secondary Education* 17, no. 7 (1942): 395–409.
Fixley, Everett H. "Meeting the Teacher Shortage." *The American School Board Journal* 106, no. 5 (1943): 16.
Frazier, Benjamin W. "How Teacher Shortages Are Being Met." *The American School Board Journal* 108, no. 2 (1944): 39–41.
Garrett, Alan W. "Planning for Peace: Visions of Postwar American Education During World War II." *Journal of Curriculum & Supervision* 11, no. 1 (1995): 6–38.
Gerstle, Gary. "Liberty, Coercion, and the Making of Americans." *Journal of American History* 84, no. 2 (1997): 524–58.
Gloss, G. M. "Aviation and Physical Education." *The American School Board Journal* 105, no. 1 (1942): 23–25.
Grattan, C. Hartley. "The Historians Cut Loose." *The American Mercury* 11, no. 44 (1927): 413–30.
Hanson, David E. "Home-Front Casualties of War Mobilization: Portland Public Schools, 1941–1945." *Oregon Historical Quarterly* 96, no. 2–3 (1996): 192–225.
Harap, Henry. "Front Lines in Education." *Educational Leadership* 1, no. 1 (1943): 42–43.
Hollinger, David A. "Ethnic Diversity, Cosmopolitanism and the Emergence of the American Liberal Intelligentsia." *American Quarterly* 27, no. 2 (1975): 133–51.
Horowitz, Roger. "Oral History and the Story of America and World War II." *Journal of American History* 82, no. 2 (1995): 617–24.

Hurwitz, Sally C. "War Nurseries-Lessons in Quality." *Young Children* 53, no. 5 (1998): 37–39.
Hymes, James L. "The Kaiser Child Service Centers- 50 Years Later: Some Memories and Lessons." *Journal of Education* 177, no. 3 (1995): 23–38.
———. "More Quantity, More Quality." *Frontiers of Democracy* 9, no. 73 (1942): 71.
Kallen, H. M. "The War and Education in the United States." *The American Journal of Sociology* 48, no. 3 (1942): 331–42.
Labaree, David. "Public Goods, Private Goods: The American Struggle over Educational Goals." *American Educational Research Journal* 34, no. 1 (1997): 39–81.
Landreth, Catherine, and Howard Moise. "Unit Plan for Nursery Schools." *Progressive Architecture* 30, no. 3 (1949): 79–83.
Lee, Edwin A. "Vocational Education and the War Offensive." *The American School Board Journal* 104, no. 4 (1942): 25–26.
Lee, Gordon C. "Government Pressures on the Schools During World War II." *History of Education Journal* 2, no. 3 (1951): 65–74.
Linder, Ivan. "Strengthening Palo Alto's Nonacademic Work." *California Journal of Secondary Education* 17, no. 4 (1942): 215–17.
Lindsay, Frank B. "Preflight Aeronautics in California Schools." *California Journal of Secondary Education* 18, no. 1 (1943): 9–12.
Lockwood, Charles W. "Palo Alto's Students Work in the Harvests." *California Journal of Secondary Education* 18, no. 4 (1943): 236–37.
Loss, Christopher P. "'The Most Wonderful Thing Has Happened to Me in the Army': Psychology, Citizenship, and American Higher Education in World War II." *The Journal of American History* 92, no. 3 (2005): 864–91.
Meyer, Agnes E. "From Buffalo to Wichita." *Educational Leadership* 1, no. 5 (1943): 67–70.
Mitrany, David. "The Humanities Look Ahead." *Nature* 154, no. 3917 (1944): 654–55.
Olivier, Warner. "Cops Don't Have to Be Brutal." *The Saturday Evening Post* (December 28, 1946): 20, 81–82.
Pascoe, Peggy. "Miscegenation Law, Court Cases, and Ideologies of 'Race' in Twentieth-Century America." *The Journal of American History* 83, no. 1 (1996): 44–69.
Perdew, Phillip W. "The Secondary School Program in World War II." *History of Education Journal* 3, no. 2 (1952): 33–48.
Record, Cy W. "Willie Stokes at the Golden Gate." *The Crisis* 56, no. 6 (1949): 175–79, 87–88.
Riley, Susan E. "Caring for Rosie's Children: Federal Child Care Policies in the World War II Era." *Polity* 26, no. 4 (1994): 655–75.

Rogers, Frederick Rand. "The Amazing Failure of Physical Education." *The American School Board Journal* 109, no. 6 (1944): 17–19.
Shaffer, Robert. "Multicultural Education in New York City During World War II." *New York History* 77, no. 3 (1996): 301–32.
Shultz, Gladys Denny. "Who's Going to Take Care of Me, Mother, If You Take a War-Plant Job?" *Better Homes and Gardens* (May 1943): 9, 61–62, 78–79.
Slobodin, Carol. "When the U.S. Paid for Day Care." *Day Care and Early Education* 3, no. 1 (1975): 23–25, 49.
Stallones, Jared. "Hanna and Stanford: Saving the University by Throwing It to the Wolves." *Midwest History of Education Journal* 26, no. 1 (1999): 151–56.
Stolz, Lois Meek. "Look to the Bulwarks of Democracy." *Childhood Education* 18, no. 1/9 (1941/1942): 196.
Studebaker, John W. "The American Schools and Colleges in the War." *The American School Board Journal* 105, no. 2 (1942): 35–36.
Sugrue, Thomas J. "Crabgrass-Roots Politics: Race, Rights, and the Reaction against Liberalism in the Urban North, 1940–1964." *The Journal of American History* 82, no. 2 (1995): 551–78.
Thompson, Dorothy. "Children of Working Mothers." *The Ladies' Home Journal* (July 1942): 6.
Tyack, David B. "Constructing Difference: Historical Reflections on Schooling and Social Diversity." *Teachers College Record* 95, no. 1 (1993): 8–34.
Ugland, Richard M. "'Education for Victory': The High School Victory Corps and Curricular Adaptation During World War II." *History of Education Quarterly* 19, no. 4 (1979): 435–51.
Uhler, William P. "Military Training in Secondary Schools." *The American School Board Journal* 102, no. 2 (1941): 28–29.
Wacker, R. Fred. "An American Dilemma: The Racial Theories of Robert E. Park and Gunnar Myrdal." *Phylon* 37, no. 2 (1976): 117–25.
———. "Assimilation and Cultural Pluralism in American Social Thought." *Phylon* 40, no. 4 (1979): 325–33.
Weiss, Richard. "Ethnicity and Reform: Minorities and the Ambience of the Depression Years." *The Journal of American History* 66, no. 3 (1979): 566–85.

Books/Theses

Adams, Stephen B. *Mr. Kaiser Goes to Washington: The Rise of a Government Entrepreneur.* Chapel Hill, NC: University of North Carolina Press, 1997.

Alschuler, Rose H. *Two to Six: Suggestions for Parents of Young Children.* New York: W. Morrow, 1933.

Alschuler, Rose H., ed. *Children's Centers: A Guide for Those Who Care for and About Young Children.* New York: W. Morrow, 1942.

Anderson, Karen. *Wartime Women: Sex Roles, Family Relations, and the Status of Women During World War II.* Westport, CT: Greenwood, 1981.

Archibald, Katherine. *Wartime Shipyard: A Study in Social Disunity.* Berkeley: University of California Press, 1947.

Bailyn, Bernard. *Education in the Forming of American Society.* New York: Vintage Books, 1960.

Baker, Lee D. *From Savage to Negro: Anthropology and the Construction of Race, 1896–1954.* Berkeley: University of California Press, 1998.

Barkan, Elazar. *The Retreat of Scientific Racism: Changing Concepts of Race in Britain and the United States between the World Wars.* Cambridge: Cambridge University Press, 1992.

Barnes, Harry Elmer. *A History of Historical Writing.* 2nd ed. New York: Dover, 1963.

Beatty, Barbara. "The Politics of Preschool Advocacy: Lessons from Three Pioneering Organizations." In *Who Speaks for America's Children? The Role of Child Advocates in Public Policy*, edited by Carol J. De Vita and Rachel Mosher-Williams. Washington, DC: Urban Institute Press, 2001.

———. *Preschool Education in America: The Culture of Young Children from the Colonial Era to the Present.* New Haven, CT: Yale University Press, 1995.

Beesley, Patricia. *The Revival of the Humanities in American Education.* New York: Columbia University Press, 1940.

Blakey, George T. *Historians on the Homefront: American Propagandists for the Great War.* Lexington, KY: University of Kentucky Press, 1970.

Blount, Jackie. *Destined to Rule the Schools: Women and the Superintendency, 1873–1995.* New York: State University of New York Press, 1998.

Blum, John Morton. *V Was for Victory: Politics and American Culture During World War II.* New York: Harcourt Brace Jovanovich, 1976.

Brown, Hubert O. "The Impact of War Worker Migration on the Public School System of Richmond, California, from 1940 to 1945." Ph.D. diss., Stanford University, 1973.

Campbell, D'Ann. *Women at War with America: Private Lives in a Patriotic Era*. Cambridge, MA: Harvard University Press, 1984.

Cardozier, V. R. *Colleges and Universities in World War II*. Westport, CT: Praeger, 1993.

Carter, Thomas P. *Mexican Americans in School: A History of Educational Neglect*. New York: College Entrance Examination Board, 1970.

Chafe, William Henry. *The American Woman: Her Changing Social, Economic, and Political Roles, 1920–1970*. London: Oxford University Press, 1972.

Clay, Lucius D. *Decision in Germany*. New York: Doubleday, 1950.

Cohen, Ronald D. "World War II and the Travail of Progressive Schooling: Gary, Indiana, 1940–1946." In *Schools in Cities: Consensus and Conflict in American Educational History*, edited by Ronald K. Goodenow and Diane Ravitch, 263–86. New York: Holmes & Meier, 1983.

Cremin, Lawrence. *American Education: The Metropolitan Experience, 1876–1980*. New York: Harper & Row, 1988.

Crouchett, Lawrence P., Lonnie G. Bunch, and Martha Kendall Winnacker. *Visions toward Tomorrow: The History of the East Bay Afro-American Community, 1852–1977*. Oakland: Northern California Center for Afro-American History and Life, 1989.

Donato, Rubén. *The Other Struggle for Equal Schools: Mexican Americans During the Civil Rights Era*. Albany: State University of New York Press, 1997.

Douglass, John Aubrey. *The California Idea and American Higher Education*. Stanford, CA: Stanford University Press, 2000.

Elliott, Orrin Leslie. *Stanford University: The First Twenty-Five Years*. Stanford, CA: Stanford University Press, 1937.

Emanuels, George. *California's Contra Costa County, CA: An Illustrated History*. Walnut Creek: Diablo Books, 1990.

Escobar, Edward J. "Zoot-Suiters and Cops: Chicano Youth and the Los Angeles Police Department During World War II." In *The War in American Culture: Society and Consciousness During World War II*, edited by Lewis A. Erenberg and Susan E. Hirsch, 284–309. Chicago: University of Chicago Press, 1996.

Foster, Mark S. *Henry J. Kaiser: Builder in the Modern American West*. Austin: University of Texas Press, 1989.

Fousekis, Natalie Marie. "Fighting for Our Children: Women's Activism and the Battle for Child Care in California, 1940–1965." Ph.D. diss., University of North Carolina at Chapel Hill, 2000.

Fridell, Lee D. *The Story of Richmond: El Cerrito-San Pablo-Pinole-Hercules*. Richmond, CA: Board of Trustees, Richmond Union High School District, 1954.

Furney, Oakley, and C. Kenneth Beach. "Vocational Education for National Defense." In *The Forty-Second Yearbook of the National Society for the Study of Education: Part I- Vocational Education*, edited by Nelson B. Henry, 184–96. Chicago: Department of Education, University of Chicago, 1943.

Geiger, Roger L. *Research and Relevant Knowledge: American Research Universities since World War II*. New York: Oxford University Press, 1993.

———. *To Advance Knowledge: The Growth of America's Research Universities, 1900–1940*. New York: Oxford University Press, 1986.

General Education in a Free Society. Cambridge, MA: Harvard University Press, 1945.

Germany, 1947–1949: The Story in Documents. Washington, DC: Department of State, Office of Public Affairs, Publication 3556, European and British Commonwealth Series 9, 1950.

Giordano, Gerard. *Wartime Schools: How World War II Changed American Education*, edited by Alan R. Sadovnik and Susan F. Semel. Vol. 34, *History of Schools & Schooling*. New York: Peter Lang, 2004.

Gluck, Sherna Berger. *Rosie the Riveter Revisited: Women, the War, and Social Change*. Boston: Twayne Publishers, 1987.

Gonzalez, Gilbert G. *Chicano Education in the Era of Segregation*. Philadelphia: Balch Institute Press, 1990.

Goodwin, Doris Kearns. *No Ordinary Time: Franklin and Eleanor Roosevelt, the Homefront in World War II*. New York: Simon and Schuster, 1994.

Greenblatt, Bernard. *Responsibility for Child Care: The Changing Role of Family and State in Child Development, The Jossey-Bass Behavioral Science Series*. San Francisco: Jossey-Bass, 1977.

Greene, Theodore M., Charles C. Fries, Henry M. Wriston, and William Dighton. *Liberal Education Re-Examined: Its Role in a Democracy*. New York: Harper and Brothers, 1943.

Gregory, Chester W. *Women in Defense Work During World War II: An Analysis of the Labor Problem and Women's Rights*. New York: Exposition Press, 1974.

Gruber, Carol S. *Mars and Minerva: World War I and the Uses of Higher Learning in America*. Baton Rouge: Louisiana State University Press, 1975.

Hampel, Robert L. *The Last Little Citadel: American High Schools since 1940*. Boston: Houghton Mifflin, 1986.

Harris, Mark J., Franklin D. Mitchell, and Steven J. Schechter. *The Homefront: America During World War II*. New York: G. P. Putnam, 1984.

Hartmann, Susan M. *The Home Front and Beyond: American Women in the 1940s*. Boston: Twayne Publishers, 1982.

Hawkins, Layton S., Charles A. Prosser, and John C. Wright. *Development of Vocational Education*. Chicago: American Technical Society, 1951.

Heffernan, Helen, and Corinne Seeds. "Intercultural Education in the Elementary School." In *Education for Cultural Unity: Seventeenth Yearbook of the California Elementary School Principals' Association*, 76–85: California Elementary School Principals' Association, 1945.

Hendrick, Irving G. *The Education of Non-Whites in California, 1849–1970*. San Francisco: R&E Research Associates, 1977.

Hirsch, Susan E. "No Victory at the Workplace: Women and Minorities at Pullman During World War II." In *The War in American Culture: Society and Consciousness During World War II*, edited by Lewis A. Erenberg and Susan E. Hirsch, 241–62. Chicago: University of Chicago Press, 1996.

Honey, Maureen. *Creating Rosie the Riveter: Class, Gender, and Propaganda During World War II*. Amherst, MA: University of Massachusetts Press, 1984.

Hutchins, Robert Maynard. *The Higher Learning in America*. New Haven, CT: Yale University Press, 1936.

Hymes, James L. "The Emergency Nursery Schools and the Wartime Child Care Centers: 1933–1946." In *Reaching Large Numbers of Children*, 5–27. Carmel: Hacienda Press, 1979.

———. "The Kaiser Child Service Centers." In *Care of the Children of Working Mothers*, 26–56. Carmel: Hacienda Press, 1978.

Irons, Peter. *Jim Crow's Children: The Broken Promise of the Brown Decision*. New York: Viking, 2002.

Jackson, Walter A. "The 'American Creed' from a Swedish Perspective: The Wartime Context of Gunnar Myrdal's *An American Dilemma*." In *The Estate of Social Knowledge*, edited by JoAnne Brown and David K. van Keuren. Baltimore: Johns Hopkins University Press, 1991.

———. *Gunnar Myrdal and America's Conscience: Social Engineering and Racial Liberalism, 1938–1987*. Chapel Hill: University of North Carolina Press, 1990.

James, Thomas. *Exile Within: The Schooling of Japanese Americans, 1942–1945*. Cambridge, MA: Harvard University Press, 1987.

Johnson, Marilyn S. *The Second Gold Rush: Oakland and the East Bay in World War II*. Berkeley: University of California Press, 1993.

Jordan, David Starr. *The Days of a Man*. 2 vols. Vol. 1. New York: World Book, 1922.

Kaestle, Carl F. *Pillars of the Republic: Common Schools and American Society, 1780–1860*. New York: Hill and Wang, 1983.

Kandel, I. L. *The Impact of the War Upon American Education*. Chapel Hill: University of North Carolina Press, 1948.

Kantor, Harvey, and David B. Tyack, eds. *Work, Youth, and Schooling: Historical Perspectives on Vocationalism in American Education*. Stanford, CA: Stanford University Press, 1982.

Kantor, Harvey. *Learning to Earn: School, Work and Vocational Reform in California, 1880–1930*. Madison: University of Wisconsin Press, 1988.

Keefer, Louis E. *Scholars in Foxholes: The Story of the Army Specialized Training Program in World War II*. Jefferson, NC: McFarland, 1988.

Kefauver, Grayson N. "Relation of Vocational Education to National Defense." In *The Forty-Second Yearbook of the National Society for the Study of Education: Part I- Vocational Education*, edited by Nelson B. Henry, 33–52. Chicago: Department of Education, University of Chicago, 1943.

Kennedy, David M. *Freedom from Fear: The American People in Depression and War, 1929–1945*. New York: Oxford University Press, 1999.

Kesselman, Amy. *Fleeting Opportunities: Women Shipyard Workers in Portland and Vancouver During World War II and Reconversion*. Albany: State University of New York Press, 1990.

Kessler-Harris, Alice. *Out to Work: A History of Wage-Earning Women in the United States*. New York: Oxford University Press, 1982.

Kiester, Edwin. *Donald B. Tresidder: Stanford's Overlooked Treasure*. Stanford, CA: Stanford Historical Society, 1992.

Kimball, Alice Windsor. *The First Year at Stanford: Sketches of Pioneer Days at Leland Stanford Junior University*. San Francisco: Stanley-Taylor, 1905.

Kirk, Robert W. *Earning Their Stripes: The Mobilization of American Children in the Second World War*. New York: Peter Lang, 1994.

Kliebard, Herbert M. *The Struggle for the American Curriculum, 1893–1958*. 2nd ed. New York: Routledge, 1995.

———. *Schooled to Work: Vocationalism and the American Curriculum, 1876–1946*. New York: Teachers College Press, 1999.

Landreth, Catherine. "Practices in Childhood Education." In *The Forty-Sixth Yearbook of the National Society for the Study of Education*, edited by Nelson B. Henry, 129–41. Chicago: University of Chicago Press, 1948.

Lane, Frederic C. *Ships for Victory: A History of Shipbuilding under the U.S. Maritime Commission in World War II, Historical Reports on War Administration, United States Maritime Commission, No. 1*. Baltimore: Johns Hopkins Press, 1951.

Lazerson, Marvin, and W. Norton Grubb, eds. *American Education and Vocationalism: A Documentary History, 1870–1970*. New York: Teachers College Press, 1974.
Lemke-Santangelo, Gretchen. *Abiding Courage: African-American Migrant Women and the East Bay Community*. Raleigh: University of North Carolina Press, 1996.
Leslie, Stuart W. *The Cold War and American Science: The Military-Industrial-Academic Complex at MIT and Stanford*. New York: Columbia University Press, 1993.
Lewis, C. S. *The Weight of Glory and Other Addresses*. New York: Macmillan, 1949.
Lindenmeyer, Kriste. *"A Right to Childhood": The U.S. Children's Bureau and Child Welfare, 1912–46*. Urbana: University of Illinois Press, 1997.
Lingeman, Richard. *Don't You Know There's a War On? The American Home Front, 1941–1945*. New York: G. P. Putnam, 1970.
Lotchin, Roger W. *Fortress California: 1910–1961*. New York: Oxford University Press, 1992.
Lowen, Rebecca S. *Creating the Cold War University: The Transformation of Stanford*. Berkeley: University of California Press, 1997.
McClure, Arthur F., James Riley Chrisman, and Perry Mock. *Education for Work: The Historical Evolution of Vocational and Distributive Education in America*. London: Associated University Press, 1985.
McParland, Lucille Lyon. "Vocations and the Vocational Training Program." Master's thesis, Stanford University, 1944.
Michel, Sonya. "American Women and the Discourse of the Democratic Family in World War II." In *Behind the Lines: Gender and the Two World Wars*, edited by Margaret Randolph Higonnet, Jane Jenson, Sonya Michel and Margaret Collins Weitz, 154–67. New Haven, CT: Yale University Press, 1987.
———. *Children's Interests/Mothers' Rights: The Shaping of America's Child Care Policy*. New Haven, CT: Yale University Press, 1999.
Miller, Guy C., ed. *Palo Alto Community Book*. Palo Alto, CA: Arthur H. Cawston Publisher, 1952.
Millett, Fred B. *The Rebirth of Liberal Education*. New York: Harcourt, Brace, 1945.
Mink, Gwendolyn. *The Wages of Motherhood: Inequality in the Welfare State, 1917–1942*. Ithaca, NY: Cornell University Press, 1995.
Mintz, Steven, and Susan Kellogg. *Domestic Revolutions: A Social History of American Family Life*. New York: Free Press, 1988.
Mitchell, J. Pearce. *Stanford University, 1916–1941*. Stanford, CA: Board of Trustees of the Leland Stanford Junior University, 1958.

Montalto, Nicholas V. *A History of the Intercultural Education Movement, 1924–1941*. New York: Garland, 1982.

Moore, Shirley Ann Wilson. *To Place Our Deeds: The African American Community in Richmond, California, 1910–1963*. Berkeley: University of California Press, 2000.

Murphy, Marjorie. *Blackboard Unions: The AFT and the NEA, 1900–1980*. Ithaca, NY: Cornell University Press, 1990.

Myrdal, Gunnar. *An American Dilemma: The Negro Problem and Modern Democracy*. New York: Harper and Brothers, 1944.

Nash, Gerald D. *The American West Transformed: The Impact of the Second World War*. Lincoln: University of Nebraska Press, 1985.

O'Brien, Kenneth Paul, and Lynn Hudson Parsons, eds. *The Home-Front War: World War II and American Society*. London: Greenwood Press, 1995.

O'Coin, Andre Roger. "Vocational Education During the Great Depression and World War II: Challenge, Innovation and Continuity." Ph.D. diss., University of Maryland, College Park, 1988.

O'Neill, William. *A Democracy at War: America's Fight at Home and Abroad in World War II*. New York: Free Press, 1993.

Pak, Yoon K. *Wherever I Go, I Will Always Be a Loyal American: Schooling Seattle's Japanese Americans During World War II*. New York: Routledge Falmer, 2002.

Pangle, Lorraine Smith, and Thomas L. Pangle. *The Learning of Liberty: The Educational Ideas of the American Founders*. Lawrence: University of Kansas Press, 1993.

Patterson, James T. *Brown V. Board of Education: A Civil Rights Milestone and Its Troubled Legacy*. Oxford: Oxford University Press, 2001.

Perkinson, Henry J. *The Imperfect Panacea: American Faith in Education, 1865–1976*. 2nd ed. New York: Random House, 1977.

Perlstein, Daniel. "American Dilemmas: Education, Social Science, and the Limits of Liberalism." In *The Global Color Line: Racial and Ethnic Inequality and Struggle from a Global Perspective*, edited by Pinar Batur-VaderLippe and Joe Feagin, 357–79. Stamford, CT: JAI Press, 1999.

Perrett, Geoffrey. *Days of Sadness, Years of Triumph: The American People, 1939–1945*. New York: Coward, McCann and Geoghegan, 1973.

Polenberg, Richard. *War and Society: The United States, 1941–1945*. Philadelphia: J. B. Lippincott, 1972.

Ravitch, Diane. "Education and Democracy." In *Making Good Citizens: Education and Civil Society*, edited by Diane Ravitch and Joseph P. Viteritti, 15–29. New Haven, CT: Yale University Press, 2001.

———. *The Troubled Crusade: American Education, 1945–1980*. New York: Basic Books, 1983.
Reese, William J. *America's Public Schools: From the Common School to No Child Left Behind*. Baltimore: Johns Hopkins University Press, 2005.
———. "Public Schools and the Elusive Search for the Common Good." In *Reconstructing the Common Good in Education*, edited by Larry Cuban and Dorothy Shipps, 13–31. Stanford, CA: Stanford University Press, 2000.
Reich, Robert B., ed. *The Power of Public Ideas*. Cambridge, MA: Ballinger, 1988.
Reuben, Julie. "Patriotic Purposes: Public Schools and the Education of Citizens." In *The Public Schools*, edited by Susan Fuhrman and Marvin Lazerson, 1–24. Oxford: Oxford University Press, 2005.
Robinson, Edgar Eugene, and Paul Carroll Edwards, eds. *The Memoirs of Ray Lyman Wilbur*. Stanford, CA: Stanford University Press, 1960.
Rose, Elizabeth. *A Mother's Job: The History of Day Care, 1890–1960*. New York: Oxford University Press, 1999.
Snyder, Thomas D. "120 Years of American Education: A Statistical Portrait." 1–107. Washington, DC: U.S. Department of Education National Center for Education Statistics, 1993.
Spaull, Andrew. "World War II and the Secondary School Curriculum: A Comparative Study of the USA and Australia." In *Education and the Second World War: Studies in Schooling and Social Change*, edited by Roy Lowe, 159–76. Bristol: Falmer Press, 1992.
Spring, Joel. *The American School, 1642–1985*. New York: Longman, 1986.
Steinfels, Margaret O'Brien. *Who's Minding the Children? The History and Politics of Day Care in America*. New York: Simon and Schuster, 1973.
Stoltzfus, Emilie. *Citizen, Mother, Worker: Debating Public Responsibility for Child Care after the Second World War*. Chapel Hill: University of North Carolina Press, 2003.
Swett, John. *Public Education in California: Its Origin and Development, with Personal Reminiscences of Half a Century*. New York: American Book, 1911.
Takaki, Ronald. *Double Victory: A Multicultural History of America in World War II*. Boston: Little, Brown, 2000.
Terkel, Studs. *"The Good War:" An Oral History of World War II*. New York: Pantheon Books, 1984.
Thelin, John R. *A History of American Higher Education*. Baltimore: Johns Hopkins University Press, 2004.
Tuttle, William M. "America's Home Front Children in World War II." In *Children in Time and Place: Developmental and Historical Insights*,

edited by Glen H. Elder Jr., John Modell and Ross D. Parke, 27–46. New York: Cambridge University Press, 1993.

———. *Daddy's Gone to War: The Second World War in the Lives of America's Children*. New York: Oxford University Press, 1993.

Tyack, David B. *Seeking Common Ground: Public Schools in a Diverse Society*. Cambridge, MA: Harvard University Press, 2003.

Tyack, David, Robert Lowe, and Elisabeth Hansot. *Public Schools in Hard Times: The Great Depression and Recent Years*. Cambridge, MA: Harvard University Press, 1984.

VanDoren, Mark. *Liberal Education*. New York: Henry Holt, 1943.

Verge, Arthur. "Daily Life in Wartime California." In *The Way We Really Were: The Golden State in the Second Great War*, edited by Roger W. Lotchin, 13–29. Urbana: University of Illinois Press, 2000.

Veysey, Laurence R. *The Emergence of the American University*. Chicago: University of Chicago Press, 1965.

Ware, Susan. *Holding Their Own: American Women in the 1930s*. Boston: Twayne, 1982.

Weatherford, Doris. *American Women and World War II*. New York: Facts on File, 1990.

Weiler, Kathleen. *Country Schoolwomen: Teaching in Rural California, 1850–1950*. Stanford, CA Stanford University Press, 1998.

Weinberg, Meyer. *A Chance to Learn: The History of Race and Education in the United States*. Cambridge: Cambridge University Press, 1977.

Wenkert, Robert. *An Historical Digest of Negro-White Relations in Richmond, California*. Berkeley: Survey Research Center, University of California, Berkeley, 1967.

Westbrook, Robert B. "Fighting for the American Family: Private Interests and Political Obligation in World War II." In *The Power of Culture: Critical Essays in American History*, edited by Richard Wightman Fox and T. J. Jackson Lears. Chicago: University of Chicago Press, 1993.

Whipple, Guy Montrose, ed. *The Twenty-Eighth Yearbook of the National Society for the Study of Education: Preschool and Parental Education*. Bloomington, IL: Public School Publishing, 1929.

Whitnah, Joseph C. *The City That Grew from a Rancho: A History of Richmond, California*. Richmond: Chamber of Commerce of Richmond, CA, 1944.

Willkie, Wendell L. "Freedom and the Liberal Arts." In *The Humanities after the War*, edited by Norman Foerster, 1–9. Princeton, NJ: Princeton University Press, 1944.

Winegar, B. C. "The Aeronautics Curriculum Gains Momentum." In *Integration of the War Effort and of the Long-Term Program in California Secondary Schools*, edited by Aubrey A. Douglass, 27–30. Berkeley: California Society of Secondary Education, 1942.

Winslow, Ward. *Palo Alto, CA: A Centennial History.* Palo Alto, CA: Palo Alto Historical Association, 1993.

Wollenberg, Charles. *All Deliberate Speed: Segregation and Exclusion in California Schools, 1855–1975.* Berkeley: University of California Press, 1976.

———. *Photographing the Second Gold Rush: Dorothea Lange and the East Bay at War, 1941–1945.* Berkeley: Heyday Books, 1995.

Woodington, Donald DeVine. "Federal Public War Housing in Relation to Certain Needs and the Financial Ability of the Richmond School District." Ph.D. diss., University of California, Berkeley, 1954.

Youcha, Geraldine. *Minding the Children: Child Care in America from Colonial Times to the Present.* New York: Scribner, 1995.

Index

Adams, John, 4
Allardyce, Gilbert, 47
Alschuler, Rose, 152
American Association of School Administrators, 2
American Council of Learned Societies, 48–49
American Council on Education, 29–30
American Dilemma, An (Myrdal), 97, 117
Anderson, Mary, 131–32, 133, 135
Army Specialized Training Program (ASTP): curriculum, 39–40; ESMWT and, 43–44; establishment of, 37–38; financial benefits of, 27, 43, 167; influence on collegiate life, 40–43, 167; training areas, 38; Tresidder and, 44–45; Wilbur and, 38–39
ASTP. *See* Army Specialized Training Program
Attlee, Clement, 164
Aufbauschule, 164
average daily attendance, 79–81

Bailyn, Bernard, 176
Baldwin, Stanley, 1
Baltimore Conference on Higher Education, 29–30
Bates, George, 110–11

Beard, Charles A., 1
Bedford, Clay, 102–3
Beesley, Patricia, 49
Benedict, Ruth, 97, 116
Benton, William, 163–64
Berka, Paula, 65, 89, 91
Berkeley, CA. *See* University of California, Berkeley
Berufsschule, 165
Bestor, Arthur, 53
Beswick, John C., 78–79
Beukema, Herman, 38–39
Boas, Franz, 116
bonds. *See* war bonds
Boucher, Erla, 174
Bradley, Omar, 51
Brimhall, Alice, 108–9, 121
Brown, Harold Chapman, 47–48
Brown v. Board of Education, 99, 114

Cadet Corps, 75
Carlson, Thomas, 107
Carnegie Foundation, 100
Children's Bureau. *See* U.S. Children's Bureau
Children's Centers (Alschuler), 152
Citizen, Mother, Worker (Stoltzfus), 17–18
citizenship training: American Council of Learned Societies and, 48–49; Congress on

Education for Democracy and, 1–2; education and, 4–7, 15, 16, 17–18, 21, 22; Loss on, 15; Palo Alto schools and, 64; Roosevelt on, 3, 4; Stanford University and, 52, 55; Stoltzfus on, 17–18
civic-professionalism, 113–23; color-blind ideology and, 118–19; conceptions of professions, 117–18; conceptions of race, 116–17; reaction to rise of fascism, 115–16
Civil Aeronautics Administration, 30
Civilian Conservation Corps, 167–68
Clay, Lucius, 164
Cold War, 175
Colombat, Frank, 72
color-blind ideology (racial), 97–99, 117–18, 120. *See also* integration, racial; racism
Commission on Children in Wartime, 140
Conant, James Bryant, 3, 51, 52
Congress on Education for Democracy, 1, 2, 3, 6
conservationism, 170–71, 172, 173–74, 176; backlash against, 98–99
Counts, George, 3
Creating the Cold War University (Lowen), 31

Davis, Elmer, 48
Davis, O. L., 14, 16–17
Davis, Paul, 31, 32, 39
denazification, 164, 165
Dewey, John, 152
Dexter, Walter F., 83
Dodds, John W., 55–56, 57
draft: age requirements, 7, 27, 86, 171; agriculture and, 89; ESMWT and, 35, 167; impact on children, 127, 135; impact on defense industry, 111; impact on higher education, 28–29, 31; impact on women, 127, 135, 169; male student enrollment and, 12, 28–29, 166; physical education programs and, 74
DuBois, Rachel Davis, 118

Edmondson, Peter, 10, 11, 76, 89, 91
Edmondson, Sally, 65, 76
EDT program. *See* Engineering Defense Training program
education: civic function of, 4–7
"Education and the Defense of American Democracy," 61
Education for ALL American Youth, 168
Education of the Young Child (Landreth), 154
Educational Policies Commission, 2, 7, 61, 66, 170
Emergency Nursery Schools, 128, 133–34, 141, 143. *See also* nursery schools
Engineering, Science, and Management War Training (ESMWT), 33–37, 167
Engineering Defense Training program (EDT), 33
ESMWT. *See* Engineering, Science, and Management War Training
Evening High School, 78–79, 81, 93
Executive Order 9066, 123
extracurricular activities, 84–91, 172, 176; harvesting jobs, 88–90; Junior Red Cross, 85; Morse Code Club, 88; sale of war stamps and bonds, 90–91; Victory Corps, 86–88

Fachschule, 165
farmers, 88–90
fascism, reaction to, 115–16
Federal Works Agency (FWA), 106
Fine, Benjamin, 46
Fletcher, R. E., 75
Ford Motor Company, 100, 102
Fred D. Paar Terminal Company, 100
Froebel, Friedrich, 152

General Education in a Free Society, 52, 168
George-Deen Act, 78, 79
G.I. Bill, 62, 175
Giodano, Gerard, 16–17
Goodykoontz, Bess, 163
Grant, Eugene L., 36–37
Great Depression, 26, 169
Gruber, Carol, 47
Grundschule, 164

Haag, Evelyn, 11, 109, 112, 121–22
Haley, Monica, 148–52, 153–54, 163; development of nursery school curriculum, 148; focus on easel painting, 148–52; influences, 153
Hall, Arthur, 142
Hanna, Paul, 31–32, 39, 44
Hansot, Elizabeth, 117
Heffernan, Helen, 97, 118
Heinig, Christine, 134
Helms, Walter: civic-professionalism and, 98, 113–14, 172–73; financial decisions, 101; hiring, 100–101; homefront mobilization and, 125; institutional racism and, 98, 119–20, 124; migrant students and, 113–14; overcrowding and teacher shortage, 104–6, 107–13
Hill, Henry H., 163

Honey, Maureen, 139
Hoover, Herbert, 26
housing shortages, 103
Howell, C. V., 120

immigration, 5, 8
integration, racial, 9, 99. *See also* color-blind ideology (racial); racism
IQ testing, 119

Jackson, J. Hugh, 36–37
Jefferson, Thomas, 4
Jim Crow, 9
Johnson, Marietta, 152
Johnson, Marilyn, 124
Junior Red Cross, 10, 63, 85, 88
juvenile delinquency, 127, 129, 137–38, 160

Kaestle, Carl, 5
Kaiser, Henry J., 102–3
Kaiser Corporation: federalization of shipyards, 102–3, 107; Landreth and, 154; wages, 112, 122; war-worker migration and, 104, 105
Kallen, Horace M., 174
Kandel, I. L., 52, 172
Kantor, Harvey, 167
Kefauver, Grayson N., 80
Kennedy, David, 3, 13, 77, 116
Kerr, Florence, 141
Kesselman, Amy, 135, 157
Kindergarten, 164
Kliebard, Herbert, 76–77, 168

Labaree, David, 5–6

labor shortage, 7, 10, 17, 33, 111, 134, 139; Palo Alto schools and, 63, 88, 89
Landreth, Catherine, 154–55
Lange, Dorothea, 114, 123
Lanham Act, 105–7, 109, 173
Lee, Robert D., 96
Lemke-Santangelo, Gretchen, 9
Lenroot, Katharine, 130
Lewis, C. S., 45–46
Liberal Education Re-examined, 48–49
Liberty Ships, 96, 103, 145, 153, 157
Life Adjustment Education, 168–69
Linder, Ivan, 72–73, 82
Lingeman, Richard R., 9, 13
Lockwood, Charles W., 65, 66, 83, 90
Lovett, Robert A., 86
Lowe, Robert, 117
Lowen, Rebecca, 31, 175

Macdonald, Augustion S., 99
Mann, Horace, 5
Maritime Commission. *See* U.S. Maritime Commission
Marshall, Clyde, 42–43
Martin, Henry, 10, 11, 74, 88
McCormick, Paul J., 114–15
McNutt, Paul V., 92
McSherry, Frank J., 80
Melgoza, Chris, 123
Mendez et al. v. Westminster School District, 114–15
Michel, Sonya, 131
migration, wartime workers and, 19, 103, 104–5, 170
military draft. *See* draft
Millett, Fred B., 52
Morris, George, 84
Morris, Samuel B., 34
Morse Code Club, 88
Mumford, Lewis, 53–54, 171

Myrdal, Gunnar, 97, 117

NAACP, 1, 99, 124–25
Nash, Gerald, 103
National Committee on Education and Defense, 29–30
national defense: higher education and, 28–33
National Education Association: Educational Policies Commission and, 2–3; national defense and, 30; report on wartime education, 66; Studebaker and, 84; teacher shortages and, 111
National Youth Authority, 167
New Deal, 26
Niebuhr, Reinhold, 163
Nolte, Richard, 88
nursery schools, 127–61; creation of, 127–28; importance of, 129–30; Kaiser Corporation and, 129, 142, 154; Landreth and, 154–55; Lanham Act and, 141–43; "Nursery Schools Vital to America's War Effort," 140–41. Powers on, 145–46; private, 152; Prout on, 146–47; Terrace Nursery School, 143–45; under-utilization of, 157–59; U.S. Office of Education and, 140–41; women's employment and, 130–39. *See also* Emergency Nursery Schools; Haley, Monica

Oberrealschule, 164
October Reports, 67–68, 72
Office of Civil Defense, 30
Office of Education. *See* U.S. Office of Education
Office of War Information (OWI), 47–48

INDEX 255

O'Neill, William, 2, 13
Organizing Higher Educaton for National Defense conference, 30
Oriental Studies, 55–56, 57
Overturf, J. R., 65, 78
OWI. *See* Office of War Information

Palo Alto schools, 61–94; aeronautics classes, 74; attempts to create a junior college, 82–84; Cadet Corps and, 74–75; community and, 64; consistency and change in the wartime curriculum, 64–76; extracurricular activities, 84–91; fine arts courses, 72–73; foreign language courses, 68; Junior Red Cross and, 85, 88; Lockwood and, 65–67; math courses, 68; number of class periods per week, 69–72; October Reports and, 67–68; Pearl Harbor's impact on, 65–66; Peninsula Defense Training Center and, 76–84; physical education, 73–74; science courses, 68; students' wartime employment and, 88–90; U.S. History courses, 68, 72; VEND program and, 77–79, 80; Victory Corps and, 86–88; war stamps and, 90–91; wartime curriculum, 66–76
Patterns of Culture (Benedict), 116
Paulin, Joan, 65, 91
Peninsula Defense Training Center: establishment of, 62, 93, 172; overview, 76–84; Palo Alto schools and, 73, 168
Perlstein, Daniel, 117
Pestalozzi, Johann, 152
Philips, Charles, 10, 11, 41–42
physical education: Cadet Corps and, 75; draft deferments and, 74–75; farm work and, 90; increased emphasis on, 62, 66, 73–74; militarization of, 21, 93; Stanford University and, 172
Pierce, John, 120
Polenberg, Richard, 138
Post, Millie, 85
Powers, Ruth, 145–46, 154, 160
Pratt, Caroline, 152
Progressive Education movement, 129, 134, 153, 156
Prosser, Charles A., 168
Prosser Resolution, 168
Prout, Mary Hall, 11

racism: civic-professionalism and, 96–97, 98, 126; color-blind ideology and, 117, 118–19; education and, 118–19; nursery schools and, 158; rise of fascism and, 115–17. *See also* color-blind ideology (racial); integration, racial
Realschule, 164
Red Cross. *See* Junior Red Cross
Reese, William, 23
Richmond, CA, 95–126; civic-professionalism, 113–23; overcrowding and teacher shortage, 104–13; Richmond Housing Authority (RHA), 105–6, 109
Riley, Susan, 141
Rockefeller Foundation, 52, 55–56
Rockwell, Norman, 139
Roosevelt, Franklin D.: bonds and, 90, 92; Congress on Education for Democracy and, 2, 3; Defense Training Act and, 77; on education's civic function, 4; OWI and, 48; race and, 9, 97, 116; vocational training and, 77
Roosevelt Junior High School, 110, 120

256 INDEX

Rosie the Riveter, 139
Rush, Benjamin, 4
Russell, William F., 2

Salsman, Byrl R., 90
Santa Fe Railroad, 99
Sauer, Marian, 95, 97, 98, 108, 109
Seeds, Corinne, 97, 118
Selective Service, 7. *See also* draft
Sharing America program, 91
Smith, Jeffery, 53
Smith-Hughes Act, 77–79
Stalin, Josef, 164
Standard Oil, 99–100
Stanford University, 25–59; admission criteria, 26; ASTP and, 37–45; course offerings, 34–35; Engineering, Science, and Management War Training, 33–37; enrollment, 29; higher education and national defense, 28–33; School of Humanities, 45–55; Statement of Principle, 29; tuition, 26
Stimson, Henry, 46
Stokes, Willie, 124–25
Stoltzfus, Emily, 17–18
Studebaker, John, 1, 65, 77, 84–86, 90

Takaki, Ronald, 9, 116
teacher shortages, 22, 96, 104–13, 125
Todd-California Shipbuilding Corporation, 102
Tresidder, Donald B.: contract research and, 25–26, 27, 59; ESMWT and, 37, 44; national defense and, 31; private industry and, 26; School of Humanities and, 56–57

Truman, Harry S., 164
Tuttle, William, 137
Two to Six (Alschuler), 152
Tyack, David, 117

Ugland, Richard, 86
unemployment, 7, 77, 111, 132–34, 169
University of California, Berkeley, 11, 32, 43, 152, 154–55, 167
U.S. Children's Bureau, 130, 131, 136, 138, 140
U.S. Maritime Commission, 102, 107, 110
U.S. Office of Education, 27, 29, 33–34, 37
U.S. Women's Bureau, 131, 133, 135

Van Doren, Mark, 46
VEND. *See* Vocational Education for National Defense
Victory Corps, 86–88
Victory Ships, 96
vocational education, 165, 167–68
Vocational Education for National Defense (VEND): creation of, 77–78; dissolution of, 176; distinct features of, 78; Palo Alto schools and, 78, 80–82; suburban school districts and, 168
Volksschule, 164

Wacker, R. Fred, 116
Walker, Frank F., 43
war bonds, 10, 21, 63, 85, 88, 90–91, 92
War Manpower Commission, 7, 136, 142
War Production Board, 106, 110
War Public Services Bureau, 141

Warren, Earl, 51, 114–15
war stamps, 10, 21, 63, 85, 90–91, 92
Webster, Noah, 4
Weiss, Richard, 115
Westbrook, Robert, 131
White House Conference on Children in a Democracy, 130–31
Wilbur, Ray Lyman: ASTP and, 38–39, 45; contract research and, 27, 166; draft and enrollment, 28–29; Hanna and, 32; liberal arts program and, 28, 48; national defense and, 30–32; Organizing Higher Educaton for National Defense conference, 30; School of Humanities and, 50–51, 54–55, 56, 171; World War II and, 25
Willkie, Wendel, 25, 28, 51
Wollenberg, Charles, 115
Women's Bureau. *See* U.S. Women's Bureau
women's employment, 130–43
Woodrow Wilson Elementary School, 95, 108
Works Projects Administration, 105, 141, 169, 173
Wright, J. C., 81

Zook, George, 163

GPSR Compliance

The European Union's (EU) General Product Safety Regulation (GPSR) is a set of rules that requires consumer products to be safe and our obligations to ensure this.

If you have any concerns about our products, you can contact us on

ProductSafety@springernature.com

In case Publisher is established outside the EU, the EU authorized representative is:

Springer Nature Customer Service Center GmbH
Europaplatz 3
69115 Heidelberg, Germany

www.ingramcontent.com/pod-product-compliance
Lightning Source LLC
LaVergne TN
LVHW011810060526
838200LV00053B/3722